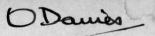

Macmillan Professional Masters

Marketing

Macmillan Professional Masters

Marketing

Robert G. I. Maxwell

Former Director of the Diploma in Management Studies at Croydon College

MACMILLAN

First published by Pan Books Ltd in 1983 as *Marketing: A Fresh Approach*
in the Breakthrough series.

Fully updated and revised edition published by
MACMILLAN EDUCATION LTD
Houndmills, Basingstoke, Hampshire RG21 2XS
and London
Companies and representatives
throughout the world

Typeset by TecSet Ltd, Wallington, Surrey

Printed in the People's Republic of China

British Library Cataloguing in Publication Data
Maxwell, Robert G. I.
Marketing—Rev ed.
1. Marketing
I. Title
658.8
ISBN 0–333–48789–3
ISBN 0–333–48790–7 Pbk
ISBN 0–333–48791–5 Pbk export

Contents

Part III MARKETING STRATEGY AND BUSINESS POLICY

x *Contents*

Part I

Behaviour and the Environment – People, Products and Marketing

1 The Way We Buy

1.1 Let's Go Shopping

In my imagination I can see you in a bookshop; there is a bustle of other people around you, a hum of conversation and the occasional 'ping' of a cash register in the background. For some reason you have picked up this book and are reading these first few lines.

You know that the book is about marketing so I am going to assume that you have some reason for wanting to know a bit more than you already do about the subject. Don't be surprised at my assumption, because all of us, whenever we go shopping are at the receiving end of marketing. Of course we do not think of it like that. Generally we have not got the time, nor for that matter the inclination, unless . . . and that's what this book is all about.

What we are now going to do together in this first chapter is to examine what we do before, during and after a purchase. We'll look at some common experiences that most people have when shopping for different kinds of goods. Is there any kind of pattern, or process, through which we go when we buy something? If there is, and we can identify it, would it not then be reasonable to assume that other people go through broadly similar processes; not necessarily identical, of course, because each of us is different?

1.2 What is a Purchase?

The bookshop we started off in also sells newspapers and magazines, sweets and tobacco, ice-cream and some children's toys; it is a typical 'CTN' – the abbreviation used for 'confectioner, tobacconist and news-agent'. You really came in to pay for the week's deliveries of papers and to buy some cigarettes (or sweets if you are a non-smoker). These two items represent different kinds of purchase.

The newspapers you bought on credit. That means that they were probably put through your letter box early in the morning by a schoolboy earning some pocket money. You did not pay for them then; so the owner of the shop has to trust you to pay within a reasonable time. Until you do you have had all the benefits of the newspapers for nothing! But, because you have no intention of doing a moonlight flit, and in any case you want to continue getting the news, you exchange the papers you have already had for money. That money represents value both to you and the shopkeeper. But you prefer the newspapers to the money, he prefers the money to the newspapers; so you exchange.

In the case of sweets you would pay cash on the spot, making an immediate exchange. So the major difference between these two inexpensive transactions is that in the former the shopkeeper lent you the 'value' of the papers. Now that, if we pause to reflect on it, is an additional benefit nothing to do with the newspapers themselves; the shopkeeper is giving us something extra! Does he also offer anything extra apart from the sweets you buy? Yes, he does; he offers you choice – chocolate or mints, wine gums or chewing gum, toffees or barley sugar and so on. It does not matter too much to him which you choose so long as you get what you believe, or *perceive*, to be value in exchange for cash.

I have just used the words 'perceive to be value'. Because they are so important in answering the question 'What is a purchase?' at the beginning of this section, we need to dwell on them a little.

As each of us is different it is going to be likely that we will buy things, the same things, for different reasons: take newspapers. Why do you buy them? For the news? What news – sport, politics, crime? For the crossword? Perhaps for the job advertisements, or the Saturday shopping pages; maybe the entertainment on offer in the district particularly attracts your attention. It's unlikely, but nevertheless possible, that you need newspaper to pack around a valuable piece of china that you are sending overseas as a wedding present for a friend (unlikely because there are so many equally practical alternatives that would cost you nothing). But somewhere you have your own reason and it's in that reason, or those reasons, that you 'perceive value' to such an extent that you are ready to part with some of your money!

But whenever 'perceived values' are negative the reverse is true; you would then prefer to use your money, or save it, for something else. What is important is that you recognize that perceived values can be positive or negative; they can encourage you to buy or they can stop you. They therefore play a very important part in our purchasing behaviour.

1.3 More Differences in Purchasing

There are a large number of other places where we buy that most people visit regularly too. Of course there is such a wide variety that you will certainly have some I have not included: supermarkets for groceries, canteens or pubs for lunch and a drink, chemists, petrol stations, greengrocers, bakers, cinemas or discos, street markets, hairdressers, post offices.

All of the examples that I have given carry kinds of products that we can put into a certain category. But my list included some 'shops' which mainly offer a service rather than a product. Have you got them? And what made you choose them? A product is something tangible; you can handle it. But I'm sure you picked the services for precisely the opposite reasons: cinema, disco, hairdresser, post office.

In marketing we have to be very careful about how we use these words: product and service. Very often 'product' is used to mean both, and that is how it will be used in this book unless there is a special reason for making the differences very clear in a particular discussion or context.

But what did I mean earlier when I suggested that we could put the products (and services) into a certain category? Remember we were talking about kinds of shop that we visited regularly; we go there often, say once a week. Most of the purchases we make so often are relatively low-cost, frequently consumed items that we have to replace often. Taken individually these products may not really be that important to us, although the full supermarket basket which we push to the check-out may carry up to £50 worth of goods or even more.

Let us put all such items into a category and call them

- *fast-moving consumer goods* (FMCG for short).

But it is not always true to say that a certain type of shop will always carry a certain category of product. One of the problems of classifying things in the way we have just done is that there are always exceptions.

Let's take an organization like Woolworth. Most of us probably cannot remember the days when sixpence was the highest price charged; that was before the Second World War.

To keep prices down that low Woolworth dealt in FMCGs. Look at one now! There are still FMCGs but also a lot of other things including electrical goods, furniture, kitchen and other household equipment. Because stores like Woolworth are large, wealthy and powerful, they are able to widen out their product ranges to cover lots of different things and therefore also attract more customers like you and me.

But there are many other shops which will specialize. Some of them will belong to chains or multiples, that is to say they have ten or more branches; others will be just the one shop owned and managed by a local person. This latter kind of business is usually known as an 'independent'. There are also of course the department stores, each department specializing in a certain kind of product, but all under the same roof.

When I asked you earlier to think of a number of kinds of shop that you regularly visited, I was, if you remember, a little cautious about suggesting that all of those you listed would turn out to be FMCG shops. By now you will appreciate that many shops which you may have quite rightly put down, because you visit them often, also carry other goods which, under no stretch of the imagination, could be called 'fast moving'. Think of another shop which almost all of us are likely to know. How about Boots the Chemist?

There is one section of most Boots branches which illustrates quite well what I am trying to get at. Think of the film and camera counter. Would *you* think of a film as something fast moving? Well of course it depends on how enthusiastic a photographer you are! But I'm sure you would agree that we could certainly think of it as being disposable – we use it up. The same would apply to the batteries, flash bulbs and so on, all of which would be on that counter. Although so far I have been calling such products as these fast moving, let me now introduce another word, which we will meet again later when we are looking at industrial products. The word is 'consumables'.

But on this counter there are many other products which are neither fast moving nor consumable. They are the cameras, flash guns, photograph albums, slide projectors and many others which you could think of or look at next time you are in Boots. They have a degree of permanence, don't they? This puts them into a totally different category, that of

- *consumer durable* (CD for short).

They are called 'durable' simply because they last; we use them rather than consume them.

Many of us are more familiar with thinking of 'consumer durables' as washing machines, television sets, or cookers; these are important and relatively expensive household appliances. Motorcars must also fall into this category. I deliberately chose some less commonly used examples. The distinction between these types of consumer product is important. When we begin to look in detail at different marketing approaches we will find that the product category can make a great deal of difference in what we do.

1.4 Is there a Purchasing Pattern or Process?

Right at the beginning of this chapter I suggested that there might be a pattern or 'process' through which most of us go when buying something. Over the last twenty or thirty years a great deal of work and research has been done to see if such a process does exist.

If we can try to understand what happens when somebody buys something, if we can also assume that the experience is going to be shared by most people, what better place to start looking than to our own feelings and behaviour? Do you think we could build up a model, a sort of diagram, which would illustrate in outline at least the steps we go through? Well, if you are agreeable, let's try.

What better way to start than by thinking of two types of purchase that I have recently made and describing them to you; they are of the kind which you could just as easily have made yourself. One is a fluorescent tube for lighting the kitchen, the other a Christmas pudding to send to a friend in Germany.

1.5 The Story of the Fluorescent Tube

Soon after I bought my house about twenty years ago, I fitted a strip (or fluorescent) light in the kitchen. My third replacement tube has just packed up – I think that qualifies them as being consumer durables, don't you? (You can't say the same for the average light bulb!)

Now this left the kitchen in darkness! What I, or rather more importantly my wife, needed was light.

Step 1 Perceived need – caused by dissatisfaction or lack of something.

What happened next you can surely guess: yes, that's right, I was asked to go down to the shops and get a new tube. Nothing to it – or was there?

Because these tubes had been lasting for a long time, how much did they cost now after years of inflation? Did I have enough money on me? I don't know, so I took a fiver from my wife! Then, I wasn't too sure about the fitting; I had to search my memory. Even then, not being too sure, I decided to take the dead tube out; that puzzled me for about a minute until I remembered that the ends of the fitting hinged outwards releasing it. Now with the old tube I could go to the shops and get a replacement.

But which shop? I thought that I would most probably have to go to a specialist electrical shop, which narrowed my choice down to about six possibles within a mile's radius of where I live. Several considerations began to enter into my selection; particularly, did any one shop offer any advantages over all the others? For a start I was not going to 'shop around' for the purpose of comparing prices: I needed to be able to park the car easily and nearby; I knew some of the shops, I had previously bought from them. Of these there was one with a new owner who had previously helped me with a small electrical repair at no cost. I decided to give him my custom.

When I got to the shop I had more decisions to make. I did not know what make of tube I wanted or even if it mattered! But remembering that I had the old one in my hand surely the maker's name must have been on it somewhere. It was; but I could not decipher it, the print was too small and I did not have my reading glasses with me! The shopkeeper took one look at the fittings and took down a new tube from his shelves. He made the final decision for me – the make. I still remain in blissful ignorance as to whether the new one was the same make as the old, and frankly it does not matter one little bit to me.

Step 2 Internal and external search – recalling from our own past experience (internal), or with the help of others (external), information about potential alternatives.

Step 3 Evaluation of alternatives – making successive decisions to eliminate the choices.

The make of tube did not matter to me; if we assume that the shopkeeper had several makes in stock, whichever one he gave to me would not be of great importance to him either. Where does that leave the manufacturer?

Step 4 Purchase decision

In most shopping situations we make choices between products each of which could satisfy our perceived need (*step 1*). But as manufacturers and shopkeepers compete for our custom it is vital that they somehow give us cause to remember them.

Step 5 Experience recall – remembering how we used or consumed previously bought products, and the experience of shopping for them.

I think we are now in a position to turn this sequence of steps into our model. See Figure 1.1.

1.6 The Story of the Christmas Pudding

For a number of years I have known the headmaster of a German school. He stays with me and I stay with him when we are in each other's countries. Recently his daughter visited England for the first time and stayed with my family for the fortnight she was here.

English traditions inevitably cropped up in conversation, Christmas amongst them. The Germans do not have Christmas pudding the way we do, so I offered to send one when the time came; and in due course I did.

I knew exactly where I was going to buy a suitable pudding – it was going to be from Marks & Spencer. Although I have never had one of their puddings, they have such a good reputation for quality food that I felt sure I could not go far wrong.

Later I heard that the family had enjoyed the pudding, and even made some brandy butter to go with it.

1.7 Building on Experience

This chapter opened with the proposal that we would look for a pattern, or process, in purchasing and examine how we behaved before, during and after it. Figure 1.1 takes us only so far. But before we develop it any further, let us review one or two points to see how they link in.

Self-check

Step 1 of the model was 'perceived need'. We've used this word 'perceived' before in a slightly different connection. What was it?

When I was discussing 'What is a purchase?', back on page 3, the two illustrations were about newspapers and sweets. What did we exchange money for?

Value – that's right. But wait a minute: surely we don't get value until we use or consume the product! 'Use or consume' – where did those words come in during our description of the model? If you turn back to

---

Fig 1.1   *Steps in the buying process*

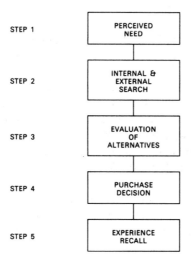

STEP 1	PERCEIVED NEED
STEP 2	INTERNAL & EXTERNAL SEARCH
STEP 3	EVALUATION OF ALTERNATIVES
STEP 4	PURCHASE DECISION
STEP 5	EXPERIENCE RECALL

page 8, you'll find them in *step 5*. Does this mean that we have now suddenly made a jump from *step 1* to *step 5*? Well no, it doesn't mean that; but it does bring into our model another set of links in our buying patterns. In this section we are going to examine these other links, and then put them together.

Because we perceive a need, it does not necessarily mean that we are going to do something about it. Suppose my fluorescent tube in the kitchen had not burned out but had failed because of a power cut! My need would still be the same – light. In these circumstances my wife and I would grope for matches and candles, try to remember where we had hidden the torch, knowing that before long we would get back our normal source of light from the mains power supply. How would we know? Because this has happened to us before, we would first go to the front door and look up and down the street. If everything was in total darkness, we would know that the cause was a power failure, not just our own fuse-box. No problem to solve any more! But the first time this happens to you, it's both a problem and a worry.

Therefore because of our previous experience we will, in various circumstances, perceive our needs differently; we have *learned* from the past or from what we have been told by other people.

Our model's *step 5*, then, can influence some future *step 1*:

• experience recall – perceived need.

If it can do that, does our ability to remember past experiences, both good ones and bad ones, also influence any of the other steps?

There cannot be any doubt that our past experiences, I am going to call them 'prior' experiences, have an effect on our future behaviour, including purchasing behaviour.

But supposing we are in a totally new situation, we may have a very extensive problem on our hands with no direct experience to draw on. Then *steps 2* and *3*, 'search' and 'evaluation', really come into their own. We have to relate what personal experience we do have to see how far that will take us towards a decision; and often in addition we ask advice from our friends or relatives. When these sources prove inadequate, as they frequently do, we then have to depend on information given us by the manufacturers or shops – commercial experience.

So we have three kinds of experience to draw on – *personal*, *social* and *commercial*.

Recently I've been having treatment for a bad back and my doctor suggested that my lounge chair may not be giving me the proper support for the lower, lumbar, region of the spine. From him I got the name of a firm which sells ergonomically designed chairs for just this purpose.

(Ergonomics is concerned with design in relation to the human body.) I started a typical search process by ringing up the firm and asking for literature and prices. I was invited to the showroom to try out a number of suitable chairs. To do this I would have had to drive for about an hour to get there, and apparently expect to pay between £250 and £300. So I looked up Yellow Pages for names and addresses of suppliers of 'orthopaedic furniture'. In the meantime my wife had also been looking in local furniture shops. From these investigations my expectations were developing; and by comparison of information my perceived values were not rising as high as £250 or £300. By visiting shops, trying out a number of chairs and taking advantage of New Year sales, I was able to buy an orthopaedic chair, named as such by its makers – Parker Knoll. The price was £166.00 after a 10 per cent discount reduction for the sales: £16.60 deposit with a further nine interest-free monthly instalments of the same amount. In addition to that, the department store concerned offered to lend me a similar chair, at no extra charge, until the one with the fabric I had chosen was delivered from the factory in six to eight weeks' time.

All I have used so far is 'prior' experience. At least 'prior' in relation to the product, but not in relation to the store. If this had been your experience, would you think, as I do, that you have had a very good deal? And would you not be more inclined to use that store again – and again – and again?

For at least as long as it continued to live up to your expectations!

When prior experiences are considered like this, we use them as a means of anticipating a similar future. In relation to the store I have just mentioned I would expect good, courteous, considerate treatment; and it is that expectation that would bring me back to it again and again.

Our expectations play another part, in addition to anticipation, when we have made a purchase. They act as a means by which we can judge whether or not the product bought delivers value; we compare the expected value with the value we actually get – or think we get! So now we have a standard of measurement.

The decorators have just been in to do up our main bedroom. My wife and I had problems choosing a wallpaper to match the colour of some built-in wardrobes; this might be described as a 'peach' colour. We collected a whole series of samples with varying shades and patterns, placed them carefully up against the cupboards, examined them critically and then tried to visualize the whole room. Eventually we settled on one paper which, while not perfect in our opinion, we thought would look very nice. And so it does – up to a point. The colour is not quite right, but now we are going to have to live with it. Our expectations did not quite live up to the reality; but in this case nobody is to blame but ourselves! What will happen is that we will get used to it – or, to put it another way, we will adjust our expectations in the light of 'post' experience.

'Post' experience, therefore, is that which follows an event, from which we draw conclusions, which we memorize or store for future use. This process of memorizing we can call 'feedback'. The next time we find ourselves in a similar situation we remember and use that knowledge as 'prior' experience, possibly altering our behaviour quite dramatically.

This continual conversion of 'post' to 'prior' experience is happening to us all the time in relation to what we buy, where we buy, how much we pay and so on. We do not think about it consciously, except on those occasions, as now, when we are really examining the subject.

So it is time to summarize those other links in addition to the five steps of the buying process (Figure 1.2).

Fig 1.2 *Steps in the buying process*

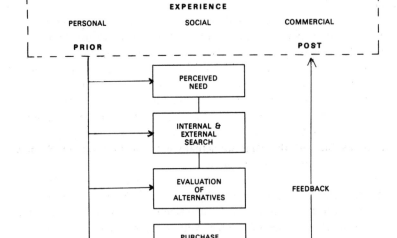

Exercises

1 Get a scrap of paper (an old envelope or something like that will do) and write down a few thoughts ('perceived values') on why you should *not* buy sweets or cigarettes.

2 In Section 1.2 the abbreviation CTN was used – what does it stand for?

3 From the following list of products classify them in the appropriate column:

Product	FMCG	CD
1 A disposable razor.		
2 A BiC ballpoint pen.		
3 A Parker ballpoint pen.		
4 A Parker ballpoint refill.		
5 A battery-operated electric toothbrush:		
(a) the batteries,		
(b) the motor,		
(c) the brush.		
6 A Dunhill gas cigarette lighter.		
7 The gas lighter refill.		

4 Using any example of a purchase you have made recently trace the sequence of the steps in the buying process, Figure 1.1.

5 There were three sources of experience that we, as purchasers, can draw on for information (search) which help us evaluate the alternatives. Can you remember what they were?

In addition to those three there were two types of experience preceding and following an event: what did we call them?

I also used a term for the process of memorizing: what was that?

2 The Way Business Buys

2.1 Introduction

Behind all the product examples that we examined in Chapter 1, and, indeed, behind every product example that you and I might experience as individual purchasers, there are masses of other transactions during the process of converting a raw material into a finished product. This is the world in which industrial marketing takes place, and the world we will be examining in this chapter. We will be taking the point of view of the business buyer and looking at the kinds of product and service that he purchases and the needs they have to satisfy.

Because none of us is likely to be experienced in all the various product types which are used in the industrial and business world, I am going to have to call on you to use not only your imagination but also your general knowledge, observant reading of newspapers and, I hope, a considerable degree of curiosity. There is in fact much in the world around us that we can draw on, and there are many parallels by which we can illustrate the workings of business quite regardless of the degree of our individual experience.

2.2 What Business Produces

As a starting point in looking at the whole area of 'what business buys' let us begin by thinking of that sequence of events which precedes the purchases which we make as individuals. For example, if you were to take a jar or tin of instant coffee from the shelf in your kitchen and trace what is now powder, or granules, right back to its source of origin, you would discover that there are 36 stages back to the original coffee bean somewhere in, say, Brazil. A high proportion of those stages represent changes of ownership, which I am going to call 'movement'; a further proportion involve 'processing'; and the third or final proportion will consist of periods of 'storage'.

So we can summarize so far by saying that there has been a great deal of 'movement', 'processing' and 'storage' behind most of the things we buy; activities, in fact, which change the form of an original raw material in a whole sequence of stages. We could say this in another way: conversion takes place.

Although you may never have looked at one particularly closely, what would you imagine a car headlamp is made of? Well, two things stand out clearly and quickly: they are glass and metal. However, there is also a bulb of some kind (it could for instance be a sealed halogen lamp), there is almost certainly a plastic or rubber seal around the rim and probably another watertight one at the bottom rear where the wires come out from the metal casing. You will surely know of one firm in the UK famous for its motorcar parts and accessories, particularly for lamps, and that is of course Lucas. Do Lucas make the metal casing of the headlamp themselves; or do they buy in metal sheet and form it into the shape required? Assume that sheet metal is supplied from the British Steel Corporation to Lucas, who then form the metal into the appropriate shapes. On the other hand now let us assume that Lucas do not make the glass but get it from Pilkingtons, another well-known British company. When that headlamp has been made it will probably end up with a major motor manufacturer as one of the many components in a vehicle.

So far in this section I have used two terms to describe types of product: the first was applied to the coffee and the second to the headlamp. For the coffee I used the expression 'raw material' on page 14 and just above I mentioned 'component'. There is an important distinction between these two:

- a raw material needs processing;
- a component has already been processed.

For example, there is not a single motor manufacturer that actually produces all the parts which are incorporated into, say, a car or a lorry. A very high proportion of them are supplied by other independent manufacturers and then they are assembled together to produce the 'finished product'; and it is that finished product which is eventually sold to its final user or consumer. Put another way, it then becomes a product which we are able to buy either direct from the manufacturer or from a shop distributing the goods on behalf of the manufacturer.

At the beginning of this section, on page 14, I used the words 'there has been a great deal of "movement", "processing" and "storage" behind most of the things we buy; activities, in fact, which change the form of an original raw material in a whole sequence of stages.'

The thought might have occurred to you that 'conversion' could be another way of saying, 'manufacturing' or 'production'; in a way you would be right, we could substitute those words. I have, however, very deliberately chosen to use the word 'conversion' because it applies better to many forms of industrial activity which are not the same as production or manufacturing.

Self-check

What do you know about motorcar manufacture? Possibly not much, so do not let that bother you. The question is – are all cars manufactured at the motorcar plant, say Longbridge in Birmingham, or are parts manufactured there and other parts, like the Lucas headlamps, 'assembled' there?

The answer is surely both, there is manufacture and assembly. Now switch the scene to a building site – also an industrial activity. But a house or office block is not manufactured, it is built. And I could make other distinctions of a similar kind. In order to find a word to cover all these possibilities I have adopted the term 'converting' for the subtitle of Figure 2.1.

Fig 2.1   *Industrial goods – 'converting' products*

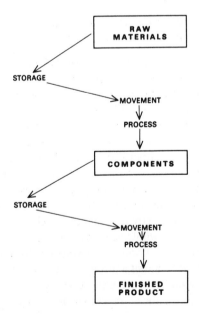

2.3 **More about 'Finished Products'**

We have to be rather careful of this term because what is a finished product to one firm may be the raw material for another. Let me explain. Back on a sheep farm, as soon as the wool had been sheared and baled it was, to the farmer, his finished product; but it would be of little use to us as consumers. Similarly when the wool manufacturer had washed it, spun it and dyed it, it was again ready for movement (remember 'change of ownership') to a clothing manufacturer.

Still keeping to product types that we have already mentioned, we can make the same point for the headlamp. Lucas supply components direct to manufacturers, but finished goods to motor accessory shops where you and I would buy a replacement. Then the headlamps become consumer durables!

2.4 **Summary**

What we have been discussing are those goods which are 'converted' in some way, in other words have some additional work done to them. We have used the terms, 'raw material', 'component' and 'finished product' to distinguish a kind of development, and as this takes place 'storage', 'movement' and 'processing' are involved. We also saw that a product can be classed as one thing by a seller, who has finished his work on it, and another by a buyer, who has yet to start.

The rather careful distinctions that I have made have a specific purpose: they will later on enable us to distinguish more easily the different types of people to whom we will be marketing, and the different methods which we may employ.

In total we have used three different terms for products so far, each of which has a distinct meaning:

Raw materials
Components
Finished products.

2.5 **'Enabling' Products**

The main thrust of our discussion so far was concerned with products as part of the manufacturing, or production, process. Now we are going to explore other kinds of goods without which the manufacturing processes could not take place.

Naturally it would be essential for these other kinds of products to have been produced; so earlier in their history, before they were bought to help the manufacturing processes, they in their turn had been converted from raw materials to components and finally to finished goods, at which stage they were bought for their individual uses.

Although there are three main subdivisions of these kinds of goods, I am going to give them a general title of 'enabling' goods.

So what is meant by the term 'enabling'? For the purposes of our initial illustration, accompany me on a walk through a big department store. While in the store I am reminded that my shoes need repairing because the heels are getting a little worn and I know that there is a 'repair bar' located in the store. When we reach the 'repair bar' we would see possibly two men working on some shoes on a bench, probably sitting on stools, using tools, having shelves or drawers behind them in which there are pieces of leather for the repairs, nails, glue and so on; there would be electric lights, probably a waste bin somewhere in a corner which may not be visible to the customers but which enables the floor to be kept reasonably tidy. There would also be some files, bills which the repair bar has received, the odd biro or pencil, paper, a till for the money with its till roll giving the customer a receipt. With a little imagination you can visualize the scene.

Now the vast majority of those products which I have just mentioned are not directly concerned with the activity of repairing shoes, but that activity could not take place in a business context without those additional products, 'enabling' the main activity or process, e.g. repairing shoes, to take place. Just to give you one particular example: the electric light is not a part of the shoe repairing process, but without it it would be almost impossible to carry on.

2.6 Capital Goods

The main characteristic of 'capital goods' is their length of life. For business purposes they would be expected to last, or remain in use, for several years. As we can also visualize, many items under this heading are very expensive.

2.7 Consumable Goods

These items must under no circumstances be confused, or mixed up, with raw materials. Remember we are talking about 'enabling' goods, e.g. those which help us, one might even say 'allow' us, to operate the conversion of the raw materials.

2.8 Services

Services are also an essential part of the 'enabling' process but do not, of course, exist in any physical sense; they are intangible.

Self-check

Without getting involved in any formal exercise can you list up to twenty 'enabling' products and services essential for the running of a café or canteen with which you were familiar. Good! Now add against each item its classification:

C – for capital.
Co – for consumable.
S – for service.

Now it is possible that you did not have all three kinds of enabling product/service on your original list. You might also have had an odd difficulty in classifying some products. For example did you have crockery? And where did you put it – under capital or consumable? Frankly you could use either, although I would tend to go for consumable because of constant breakages which in practice take place.

Catering, the example we have been using with the café, is generally regarded as a 'service industry'; strictly speaking it is certainly not manufacturing or production, but I think we can legitimately call it 'converting'; it converts food into meals! Increasingly the service sector of business is expanding – we have already mentioned insurance, banking and contract cleaning. All of these, and many others, are becoming an increasingly important part of the UK economy. We usually call these special types of business 'commercial', or talk generally of 'commerce' as distinct from (manufacturing) industry. The needs of commerce, therefore, will usually be confined to those three classifications which we are dealing with here. See figure 2.2.

However, you will recall that we began this section with the proposition that 'enabling' goods were needed to aid the manufacturing, or

---

Fig 2.2 *Commercial goods*

	'ENABLING'	
CAPITAL GOODS	SERVICES	CONSUMABLE GOODS

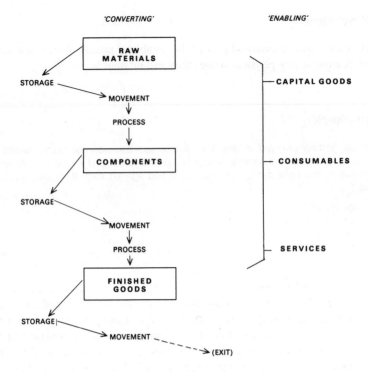

Fig 2.3 *Business goods classifications*

---

production, processes. This is so because every kind of business has its
'commercial' element, i.e. administration, personnel functions, money
and marketing. Therefore we can combine Figures 2.1 and 2.2.

2.9 Summary

During this Chapter we have drawn further distinctions between kinds of
product in the 'commercial' world of business. Because marketing
operates not alone but in concert with other business activities, we
created a link between what we have called here 'enabling' products and
'converting' ones. In particular we looked at 'capital goods', 'consumables' and 'services'.

2.10 Who Buys in Business?

In the summary, Section 2.4, I used the words 'The rather careful
(product) distinctions' will help us 'to distinguish more easily the

different types of people to whom we will be marketing'. It is now time to switch our attention to those people.

In order to do this I must assume that you have a sufficient knowledge of organizations in business to be able to identify with the different activities. It is certainly not my intention to make complicated illustrations; but as we have already discussed six different types of industrial and commercial product in the last two sections, the people involved in buying them must necessarily be diverse.

This diversity also gives rise to other complications. Some of the purchases will be quite simple, daily routine 'topping-up' activities carried out by fairly junior employees. After all one would not need to go too far up in the management structure to maintain the level of typewriter ribbons for the secretaries or the typing pool. Conversely, the installation of a new computer would have such a wide effect on the administrative systems of a business that senior management, right up to boards of directors, would have to be involved in any decision to buy.

2.11 Risk, Resources and Results

Later in this section, and for that matter also in subsequent chapters, I am going to refer to these words as the 'three *Rs*'. May I therefore ask you to make a mental note of them right now?

Risk Do you remember the story I told you on page 10 about my orthopaedic chair? Then you will also remember my discussion of 'expectations' on page 11 first, for a buyer, they are in anticipation of meeting a need, and second they provide a standard of measurement for value. In this personal example there is always a 'risk' that expectation of value and delivery of value will not match. Exactly the same principle applies in business, but risk is magnified enormously by the amounts of money that can be involved and the repercussions caused by a mistake! Compare the typewriter ribbons and the computer. In terms of risk, they are minor and major, and as a result the responsibility for making decisions about them will shift from junior to senior levels.

Resources So if 'risk' is one clue to 'Who buys in business?' the use of resources is another. They are in fact often linked. The person who can spend large sums of money, deploy large numbers of people, order huge quantities of materials and install advanced technological machinery will be no junior! Nor can we assume that any such commitment of resources is necessarily comparable between one business and another. £1000 may be a great deal of money for a small firm; it may be almost petty cash for a multinational!

Results The third factor that will affect business buying is the responsibility of management for results. So when somebody in a company places an order with a supplier, 'buys' in other words, it is done for a purpose in the 'expectation' of getting value. As these results assume greater importance for the future well-being of the business, we will find the decision-makers higher up in the seniority scale of management; we will also find more of them.

2.12 Decision-making Units

The purpose of understanding the significance of the three *R*s is to give marketers some indication of the complexity of purchasing decisions in business – what is it that is being bought, and who is buying? As, I think, most of us are sufficiently knowledgeable about what a computer can do, I'll stick to that as an example.

Self-check

What kind of product is a computer? Can you think of at least four departmental functions where one could be used? And finally can you imagine how many people would play some role, direct or indirect, in the decision to purchase one?

If we need to we can remind ourselves from Figure 2.3 on page 20 of the six different product classifications that we have developed; the computer is a capital good, one of the 'enabling' products. So what could we use it for? One of the most common uses is in an accounts department (remember how useful they are in doing all kinds of routine clerical work); production can also use them for scheduling of output, allocating raw materials and components to various parts of an assembly line; in a big company personnel records may be kept on computer files; many products are designed with the help of computers, so research and development could get involved with one; and, of course, marketing is increasingly using them for things like forecasting future sales.

If there are such extensive possibilities of using a computer, a great many people in the organization are going to get interested and involved with its purchase. Eventually, in a business, the buying procedures would be brought into operation and these will involve people. Now the marketers attempting to sell that computer will need to know exactly who these people are, and which amongst them are the key ones in making the purchase decision: they have got some digging to do – so what more appropriate to identifying these roles than to use the letters *SPADE*.

- *S* for 'starter' – the person who starts off the sequence of events that leads eventually to a purchase.
- *P* for 'purchaser' – the professional, the purchasing officer (or buyer), who controls the administrative procedure of placing the order.
- *A* for 'adviser' – those who have some say, or influence, such as technical knowledge and experience.
- *D* for 'decider' – the person who makes the choice of 'yes' or 'no' – 'go' or 'no go'.
- *E* for 'end user' – those who will actually make use of the product after purchase, and who can become 'advisers' on repeat purchases from their 'experience recall'.

It is surprising how few purchases are unaffected by interactions with other people. Naturally the extent of them will considerably change with the level of importance of the three *R*s.

By separating these kinds of product in the way we have it is much easier to focus our attention on to the membership of the decision-making units (DMUs) and their purchase motives. The office manager responsible for stationery is going to have a rather different outlook to the engineer using machine tools. We can surely see now how complicated some of these situations may become.

But in most cases in the 'real world' we deal with an individual product type, that is to say one of the six, not all of them. However, from a study point of view we are required to consider the side effects of any purchase we may undertake, and particularly later on, when we change our perspective, to recognize the significance for marketing. Broadly speaking, therefore, we can conclude that those which I have called 'converting' products will be bought because they directly concern, and affect, the end product being made and in turn affect the customers of that producer: major considerations will include quality, reliability, workability (within the manufacturing process), economy, price, performance and so on. The major considerations in the purchase of 'enabling' products will be their effect on the efficiency and effectiveness of operations by the producer. Indirectly, of course, these may also affect the relationships between that producer and his customers.

Another approach to buying is to think in terms of the type of purchase rather than the product.

- A 'straight re-buy', where you purchase the identical article or product that you have previously bought.
- A 'modified re-buy', where you purchase a similar article or product that you have previously bought, but with one or two modifications.
- A 'new buy', where you are purchasing a product for the first time.

The reason for considering these three categories is that the type of purchase can influence the buying process. A new buy may need a lot of research to find a suitable supplier; a modified re-buy may require some research, and certainly some discussion on the modifications; a straight re-buy, however, may simply involve picking up the telephone and asking your regular supplier for more!

2.13 Summary

Purchase decisions in business are taken by individuals but within the membership of decision-making units. As the importance of the three *R*s (risk, resources and results) grows the DMUs will become more senior in the levels of management and more complex. By dividing products into types within the two main headings of 'converting' and 'enabling' both the identities within the DMUs and the purchase motivations of the membership will become clearer.

Fig 2.4   Product Purchase Matrix

	'Converting' Raw material Component Finished product	'Enabling' Capital good Consumable Service
Straight re-buy		
Modified re-buy		
New buy		

Exercises

1 I doubt if there are many readers who do not own a sweater. Let us suppose that the sweater, whether you are wearing it or have it in a drawer somewhere, is made of wool. The 'raw material' of that sweater came from a living sheep somewhere in the world, possibly from the hills of Scotland or Wales, or perhaps from the mountains of Kashmir.

From your knowledge, or perhaps personal observation, fill in on the page your interpretation of each of the earliest stages in the journey of wool from sheep, to say, the garment manufacturer:

Process:
Storage:
Movement:
Storage:
Process:

2 Take a car as an example, allow yourself one minute and write down at least ten 'raw materials' and 'components' which make up part of that motorcar.

Now, as a second part, mark each item on your list as either RM (for raw material) or C (for component).

3 If you are a student and have not yet had the chance of visiting a factory, try to arrange such a visit and identify all the six product classifications covered in Section 2.13; seek them out; ask about them; discover, on site, their relationships.

If you are already in business and know a factory, do the same in your mind's eye.

Begin to explore!

4 From the following scenario, enter in the space provided on the right-hand side of the page the five roles, when they are shown to occur.

Role title

A member of the design staff, who had had previous experience of using plastics, suggests substitution of plastic for metal in making a product. 1 ___

His immediate superior mentions the idea, somewhat scathingly, over lunch one day to his friend the production manager, who surprises his colleague by seriously considering the possibility. 2 ___ ... 3 ___

'Could be something in it, you know. Might reduce costs and that might please the sales boys. We'd have to discuss it with them of course.' 4 ___

'But we'd have to bring in new plant and equipment, retrain labour and probably have to renegotiate piece rates.' 5 ___

'Of course. And get new costings.' 6 ___

(Some months later at a management meeting.)
Chief executive in the chair. 'Your opinions, please . . .
'Marketing, what's the verdict from our customers? . . . 7 ___
'Design, overcome all the snags? . . . 8 ___
'Production, are you satisfied with the spares position? . . . 9 ___
'Personnel, are the negotiations with the unions complete? . . . 10 ___
'Accounts, have you the cash flow projections?. . .' 11 ___
'Then let's go ahead,' says the chief executive. 12 ___
'Buyer, put the orders for the plant and equipment in hand. All of you, keep me informed of progress.' 13 ___

3 Where Marketing Begins

3.1 Introduction

The figure of 'Justice' on the rooftop of the Old Bailey in London holds a
sword in one hand and a pair of scales in the other – you must have seen
her, if not for real then at least on your television screen. These two
symbols, the sword and the balances, are not inappropriate for marketing.

Looking at products in the first two chapters, I have so far taken a
one-sided point of view, that of the buyer or purchaser. But when an
exchange takes place there must be at least two parties to the deal or
transaction. You will also recall that these transactions began with
'perceived need' and ended in an 'exchange for value'. Furthermore they
were the result of a decision taken by an individual, sometimes acting on
his own, at other times as part of a decision-making unit. Assuming that
you have been able to identify with some of the examples already given,
and have been able to elaborate upon them from your own experiences,
we are now in a position to begin to examine 'where marketing begins'.

3.2 Exchange and Choice

Marketing is the process which links producers and consumers by
enabling transactions of exchange to take place to the mutual and
continuing benefit of both parties. The permanence of such relationships
is relatively fleeting; there is a continuous and unremitting need to
maintain, care for or correct the balance of interest between the two
'sides'. Whenever this balance is sufficiently badly upset the sword of
retribution will descend.

Some 200 years ago Adam Smith, in a book entitled *The Wealth of
Nations*, stated that 'the purpose of production is consumption'. Today
the western developed economies, and increasingly other parts of the
world, are consumer societies.

If we cast our minds back over the earlier parts of this book and
reconsider very quickly the range of product types with which business as
a whole deals, and with which we as individual or business purchasers
may be involved, one thing should stand out clearly – the enormous

'assortment'. As we descended through the diagram, Figure 2.3, 'Business goods classifications', the final little word in brackets was 'exit'. In other words in the last chapter we continued no further than the end of this product categorization. But where does this 'exit' door lead? It leads directly to these exchanges for value. Figure 3.1 therefore leads us out through this 'exit' door to the exchanges, and during this chapter we will be developing the connecting links to exchanges from the customer, on the one hand, and from business on the other, balancing their mutual benefits of 'profit' and 'satisfaction'.

Self-check

Wherever you are, look around you and classify in their appropriate product types the articles you may see in your present surroundings.

Let me assume, for illustration, that you are (as indeed I am now) enjoying one of those rare sunny days in an English summer and sitting in a garden while you pursue this study of marketing. I see the grass for which we need a lawnmower; the flowers and flower beds and the tools that are associated with them; I look across to the extension of the garage and remember building it, mixing the cement for its base, building the walls of breeze-blocks and the piers at the corners of brick, glazing the window-frame and making the door; putting on the corrugated-sheet roof. I look above my head to the apple trees, whose blooms have now faded and on which the year's crop is beginning to show, and remind myself of the annual activity of pruning. I am reminded too that the chair I am sitting on is an old deckchair, the seat cover now sadly faded, the wooden frame badly warped but still capable at least of bearing my weight. And as I think of these products I can also visualize the processes by which their respective component parts or raw materials have been assembled together and have been distributed to many shops from which I bought them; and I realize that throughout the whole list of my possessions there is an enormous 'assortment' of goods which I use or consume. The comparable 'assortment' for a business enterprise would be many times greater.

Remind yourself of the 'assortment' that you use and possess and imagine all the things that have happened to those products on the long journey they made to reach your hands.

To help remind you make a quick reference to Figure 3.1 showing the two main categories of goods and services which we have already considered.

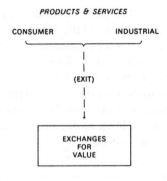

Fig 3.1   *Where marketing begins*

If both business and individual customers buy great assortments of products the main purpose of any business is to produce and finally exchange not an assortment, in the sense that we have been using it, but a fairly narrow specialized output.

I am not trying to imply here that a business does not make many products, indeed many products of different types, but that within its total activity there will be limits imposed upon it – technological capability, its expertise within a market, its managerial skill, its economic use of resources – which will contain its activities broadly within a particular field. You can very simply check on this statement by answering for yourself the question 'What business are the following companies in?'

Company name
Hertz
Vauxhall
Heinz
Bosch
Prudential
Xerox
Bowater
Smiths Instruments

You may feel that the responses which I have just asked you to give to a number of company names may conceal other activities in which these organizations take part, ones you either suspect or which you know about from your experience. This may well be true. But it does not alter the idea of some common theme running through a company's activities. Examine a company like ICI, or to give it its full name, Imperial Chemical Industries, which is one of the largest business organizations in the UK. You will know that it makes both consumer goods and industrial goods and because it is so famous we will have at least some superficial knowledge of its activities which we may draw upon. It produces, through a divisional structure, the following kinds of goods:

paints
pharmaceuticals (medicines);
fertilizers;
artificial fibres;
and others.

The coherence of these apparently diverse products, supplying very different markets and serving many different functions, rests in the underlying scientific and technological capability of the company – namely organic chemistry.

To identify the cohesive nature of some organizations is not always easy, nor readily apparent to an outside observer. There are cases, of course, when it need not be there at all; but these are exceptions to the rule.

We have then a distinct contrast – specialization in production, and assortment through consumption.

The assortments with which we as consumers deal are of two kinds:

• over the whole range of goods that we use or consume;
• within a particular kind of product.

We can illustrate this by displaying some simple choices in a form of matrix, shown below.

Let us suppose that we have just won £2000 on the pools and are wondering how to spend it. The choice in front of us is between a good holiday for two or the down-payment on a new car. We can see these choices displayed in the matrix below – Figure 3.2.

This simple description highlights the fact that consumers are faced with choices. These may be, as illustrated, between products of the same type or between products of a different kind one from another. In the second instance it is not always easy for the producers who specialize in a given area fully to comprehend and take into account that they are competing with many other demands upon consumers' money beyond their direct sphere of competition with other suppliers of their kind of goods.

Of fundamental importance, therefore, to the value of marketing is the fact that it is irrelevant in conditions where consumer choice does not exist.

In 1980 and 1981, during a period of social, economic and political trouble in Poland, a TV news item showed housewives queuing for meat

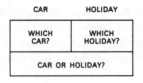

CAR   HOLIDAY

WHICH   WHICH
CAR?   HOLIDAY?

CAR OR HOLIDAY?

Fig 3.2   *Choice matrix*

which in normal circumstances would have been condemned as unfit for human consumption. In the prevailing circumstances of shortage these people had no choice, except one between poor-quality meat or none at all. This is hardly choice.

The sort of choice which is more relevant, at least to the introduction and operation of marketing, is that between products or between totally different kinds of product as illustrated in the matrix, Figure 3.2. Our choice is no longer between a car or a holiday, but of which car or which holiday.

The exercise of choice by the consumer balances the 'offering' of the product with his or her 'evaluation' of it. When the two match, and the consumer sees them as likely to satisfy the earlier 'perceived need', exchange will take place.

In opening this chapter, I made the suggestion that the symbol of the sword and the scales held by the figure of 'Justice' could be equally applicable to marketing. When a firm's 'offering' ceases to come up to the 'evaluations' of potential customers, exchanges will not happen. What does this mean in practice?

One nation which is often the subject of severe criticism is Japan. She is accused, particularly in Britain, of entering into very severe competition with other nations' industries to the point where they are finally destroyed. The motorcycle industry is a typical example.

Remaining, however, with the idea of consumer choice, it would be true to say that during the period when Japanese competition was destroying the British motorcyle industry the consumers were exercising a choice in favour of Japanese products. Why? For whatever reason, they saw better value in a Japanese motorbike than in its British equivalent. Tens of thousands of individuals exercised their separate choices in favour of the Japanese product; there was no collusion between them, no conspiracy to destroy famous names like BSA, Matchless, Ariel, Triumph. The Japanese offering was quite simply better.

3.3 **Summary**

Marketing is the process which links producers and consumers by enabling exchange transactions to take place in conditions of competitive choice to the mutual and continuing benefit of both parties. Consumers require a large 'assortment' of products and services and before exchanging go through an 'evaluation' process of the 'offering' put before them by suppliers. When these offerings and evaluations match, exchange will take place. On the other hand, producers have a tendency to specialize and become known for particular kinds of activity. Nevertheless the producer organizations have at their centre some integrating force which keeps, or should keep, their activities as a coherent whole.

If the balancing process, therefore, between a producer offering and a consumer evaluation ceases, for any reason, to synchronize, the accumulation of adverse consumer decisions in favour of other choices could destroy the effectiveness and indeed existence of an organization.

Find a friend, a colleague or a member of your family with whom you can discuss and compare notes about the offerings and your evaluation of them of the following companies, which have been paired together because they produce similar products.

Cadbury and Rowntree   Sainsbury and Tesco
Hoover and Electrolux   BP and Esso

In carrying out this activity with somebody else do not be surprised if your evaluations differ.

3.4 **Profit and Satisfaction**

At some time in your life you have made a deal with someone else and on its completion felt rather pleased with yourself. Whether this deal was of minor significance, like swapping a stamp to improve your own collection, or whether it involved completing a £ million contract, the principle is the same. Assume also that the other person associated with this deal felt reasonably pleased with him or herself, unless later there was cause for regret because you had tricked your victim! In Section 3.3, I used the words 'to the mutual and continuing benefit of both parties'. This is the particular area of exploration in this section.

Let us be clear at the outset that marketing is not concerned, never has been and hopefully never will be, with making a fast buck at other people's expense! Any person or business, and regrettably there are some, which acts in this way will sooner or later be found out. Only a few of them will achieve the gaudy notoriety of appearing on *That's Life* or *Nationwide's Watchdog* programmes on television.

You will also recognize the feeling of just having purchased a 'bargain'. Your self-satisfaction rises proportionately with the benefit you assume to have achieved for yourself at the expense of the person selling to you. These are human and natural emotions but far too impermanent to build a durable kind of business on them.

When considering the five steps in the buying process, I pointed out that a continuing relationship existed between supplier and consumer even after the purchase decision had been made and the exchange of ownership had taken place.

When our expectations of value have been achieved after an exchange has taken place the result is a level of satisfaction. I say 'level of satisfaction' deliberately because there are occasions, which you too will have shared, when our satisfactions are tempered by compromise. We have reduced our expectations of what we would have liked to something nearly as good because of a constraint imposed upon us. For example, our income level may be such that we have to watch prices carefully and buy of necessity what we know to be second best. Do you, for instance, always buy the 'best' instant coffee? Or do you buy that one which gives you a sufficient level of satisfaction for your immediate purpose?

Given this satisfaction level you are then in a position to make a similar purchase in the same set of circumstances sometime in the future. Given a level of dissatisfaction based on previous purchasing, the next time you find yourself in a position to buy, the act will be directed to another source, another product, possibly another shop.

Self-check

Think back over the previous week, consider the things you have bought during that time and identify at least one which represented a change in purchasing behaviour by you from previous practice. Then consider the cause of the dissatisfaction which made you change.

The cause of that change need not necessarily be in the product.

Businesses cannot afford to lose customers for long. For a time they may survive by cutting down on their costs and expenses, or living for a while on their reserves. This cannot last for long without money coming in from elsewhere. It may come from other businesses through mergers or takeovers, from government subsidies as in the case of Austin Rover (formerly British Leyland), from financial institutions such as the banks if they judge the longer-term prospects of turning that business round into a profitable future to be a viable commercial risk. Unless social need is deemed by government, at local or national level, to warrant relatively permanent subsidies, such as in many of our transport systems, the long-term requirement of business is one of profit.

'Profit' for our purpose may be described as the trading surplus of income less the expenses, which can be ploughed back into a business to maintain its health and vitality. Profit, therefore, and marketing are inextricably bound together; the former is a measure of the success of the latter.

Marketing is one of those terms which have acquired different meanings for different people. To some it has become a synonym for selling. Others think of it as the strident world of advertising and commercial persuasion. Both of these are functional activities within an organizational title of marketing. The way we are considering marketing here is rather as an attitude, a frame of mind, even a business philosophy, governing the whole behaviour of a commercial organization towards its consumer public. What has now come to be known as the 'marketing concept' is this all-embracing view.

If profit can be regarded as the operating surplus between revenue and all the expenses of a business, those expenses are incurred by all the activities throughout the business. The very process of production incurs expense; research and development, personnel selection and training, administration and financial charges all incur expenses. These then in the widest meaning of the term are as much a part of marketing as selling, distribution, advertising, market research, and those other functions we associate more closely with it.

We are now talking about whole organizations, not just parts of them; if this idea is real, the actions in all parts of an organization, insofar as directly or indirectly they affect the 'offering' made, will have a bearing on the exchange relationships between business and customer. When consumers turn away from your product, change that product. When your administration has become so top heavy and its costs disproportionately large compared to your competitors, you price yourself out of the market. When a business fails to put back sufficient resources into the research and development required to maintain its products in fashion, in technological modernity, why should consumers remain satisfied with the old-fashioned and out of date? The sword of retribution takes a hand unless the scales are once more brought back into balance – see Figure 3.3.

This balance may be upset from such a wide selection of sources that business cannot possibly be fully aware at all times of what is happening in every corner of the environment in which it operates. It must, however, try to maintain a constant vigil in those areas which are most sensitive to change, and be prepared to adapt responsively to external

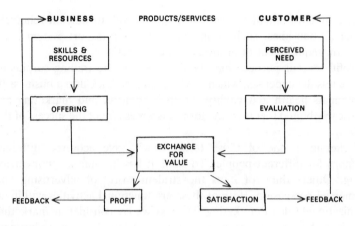

Fig 3.3 *Balancing scales*

---

influences. The absence of such responsiveness is often all too evident. The public is learning to express itself in ways quite unknown fifty years ago. The consumer and environmental movements represent changing attitudes within society giving rise to new values, and hence new evaluations of offerings by producers. The latter ignore these changes at their peril. In the short term they may be resisted as, for example, improved exhaust emission systems are being resisted by motor vehicle manufacturers. But for how long?

When responses fail to materialize, other forces will move into the breach to redress the balance. Typical examples of these can be found in legislation: the Fair Trading Act 1973, the Unsolicited Goods and Services Act 1971, the Restrictive Trade Practices Act 1976 and so on. The alternative is voluntary regulation, either on an industry-wide basis, or by the individual firm. If after all a business fears the reaction of its potential customers, there can surely be no durable exchange relationship; there can be no satisfaction on the one hand, nor profit on the other.

Fortunately the professional associations connected with marketing, to which many practitioners will belong, publish their own Codes of Practice governing the behaviour of members. Breaches can lead to expulsion. Unfortunately marketing and many of its associated activities can be conducted by professionally unqualified people, a very few of whom behave in a manner that can only be described as unethical and, indeed, sometimes criminal.

3.5 Summary

The willingness of people to exchange requires its own system of reward: this is found in profit for business and in satisfaction for the customer. Both must, within reasonable limits and with certain constraints, be fulfilled for durable relationships to be established. Marketing is concerned with the development of durability by the adaptation of business to its total environment, by balancing the scales.

Exercises

1 How was it that we defined marketing in this chapter?

2 Find two advertisements – one for a product/service which you have actually bought or used, the other for a product/service, which you have not bought or used and in which you are not particularly interested.

Compare the 'offering' and your own 'evaluation' of both the purchase and the non-purchase.

3 What do you now understand by the 'marketing concept'?

4 In not more than 500 words, explain which of the two better embodies the spirit of the 'marketing concept': the Trade Descriptions Act 1972 or 'caveat emptor' (let the buyer beware).

4 Pinpointing Markets

4.1 Introduction

Back in Section 3.2 I made the suggestion that one of the limits imposed upon any business is its expertise within a market. We have already demonstrated quite clearly that there are two sides of the exchange coin: the business and the customer. There can be very few exceptions to the general rule that no business is able to continue for long with just one customer. Although each of us as consumers makes many different and individual transactions, a firm is seeking within its market multiple transactions which may be 'first time purchases' by new people entering the market or 'repeat purchases' by those with satisfactory previous experience.

In this chapter we are going to be examining one of the most important strategies within business, namely the one which establishes the direction and management of its market expertise. As we will see there are indeed many different ways in which markets can be pinpointed and once the process has been completed they become known as 'market segments'.

The word 'segment' is defined in the *Concise Oxford Dictionary* as 'part cut off or separable or marked off as though separable from the other parts of something'. From this you will be able to deduce that our examination of market segments will include ways in which markets may be identified and separated, methods we can use to make these subdivisions and the advantages that this gives to a firm in effecting successful exchanges with sufficient numbers of customers. In order to illustrate various methods which are employed in practice, I will be asking you to use your powers of observation, deduction and experience. Once this has been done we will conclude the chapter with a brief discussion on how a business's treatment of its market segments will affect the tools it uses in reaching them effectively.

4.2 Matching Interests

'A million housewives every day pick up a tin of beans and say "Beanz Meanz Heinz".' Do you remember that advertising slogan at the end of the 1970s? Whether it is literally true or not is irrelevant to our purpose at present but a simple projection of that slogan means that something in the region of seven million families consume Heinz Baked Beans every week. A further rough calculation could lead us to suppose that about half of all families in the UK are once-a-week eaters of beans. Half the family population represents a segment.

Self-check

Redefine, in your own words, the term 'segment', and when you have done so refer back to page 36 to check against the dictionary definition.

Bearing in mind the balancing process between business and customer that we were discussing in the last chapter, it becomes self-evident that firms like Heinz which are mass-producing goods in enormous quantities have to find sufficient numbers of customers to maintain the equivalent level of mass consumption. In order to be successful at this level, needs must be identified which require constant satisfaction; all the skills and resources within the business are geared, through the marketing concept, to produce goods providing that necessary satisfaction.

Those companies which have developed market expertise to the extent that they can pinpoint differences in consumer behaviour, and beam appropriate messages to those consumers, are entering into an exchange dialogue. There will be, of course, occasions when these messages miss their target entirely, whatever the precise reason may be. It should be perfectly clear that no business can be 'all things to all people all the time'. Variations in behaviour are so wide that businesses are sensible to seek out those that they can make their own. In so doing they provide a means of carrying out their own market niche, of creating for themselves what is sometimes referred to as a 'mini-monopoly', whereby the worst effects of competition may be avoided. What is important is that these particular behaviour variables are sufficiently large to represent a genuine business opportunity by providing that number of customers seeking their satisfactions through the offerings of the business concerned.

I think it is by now time for you to get involved in a familiar example of the way markets can be split up. To do so I ask you to use both your deductive powers and your general knowledge.

Imagine we are in the latter part of the nineteenth century; the telephone has just been invented. Was there a need for it then, and is there a need for it now?

Quite literally the need for a telephone neither existed at the end of the last century nor exists today. What did exist then, and does now, is the need to 'communicate at a distance'. When we begin to differentiate between what a product is and what it does, the link between needs and people become easier to make. Let us do that.

4.3 Summary

Every time there is an opportunity to separate a part from the whole there is the possibility of creating a market segment. But to be worthwhile for business there must be sufficient numbers of customers willing to exchange for value. The expertise required in a market is just as important a form of specialization as technology and enables business to understand what a product does to meet a need.

4.4 Measuring Markets

In the first two chapters of this book products were divided into two broad categories – consumer and industrial. In this section when we are looking at means of dividing markets into segments these headings will be used again. Criteria applicable to them are sufficiently different to warrant special treatment.

We shall begin by introducing the three main methods of grouping potential customers into a homogeneous market. (Homogeneous means 'of the same or similar kind'. Its opposite is heterogeneous meaning 'diverse in character'.) As we proceed each of these main methods will be applied to consumer and industrial markets. In conclusion we will use a system called 'successive focusing' as a means of combining all three techniques of defining segments, and discuss some actual examples.

Not for one moment must we allow our purpose to be forgotten. Market segmentation strategies are developed for a reason; that reason contributing in no small measure to the success of a business.

4.5 Methods of Differentiating Markets

Location   At one stage or another in a business's relationships with its customers there will be a need for differentiation by location. This is by far the most common method of starting, at least, the segmentation process.

You are a manufacturer of men's suits. Provided you are operating beyond national frontiers, the kind of materials you would use in your suits would have to be different for the colder climates of northern Europe and for the hot one of, say, the Mediterranean. Harris tweed is not the best thing to wear in temperatures above 25°C or 75°F!

Or, you supply machinery for collecting grapes in the wine-growing parts of the world. Your search for customers would be confined, on the basis of location, to areas where the climate, the terrain and the soil are right for vineyards.

These two examples are simple ones and are intended to be suitable only to get you used to the general principle. In real practice the effects of geography would require much more detailed study and can have quite unexpected results.

For example in the 1950s many British cars were exported to countries in the Middle East. At that time plastic technology was not as advanced as it is today, and within a year the coloured clusters of rear lights, i.e. the rear reflectors and brake lights, lost their distinctive red because of the very strong sunlight.

Classification   The second of the three most common forms of differentiating markets is by some classification concerned with the collection of statistics about people under many headings. For example your classification details would include your sex, your age, your marital status, your standard of education, the kind of work that you do, your income level and so on. When nearly all of these things are grouped whole populations can be classified into what are known as 'socio-economic groups'. These groups are given a code as follows:

A – upper middle class (= higher managerial, administrative or professional);
B – middle class (= intermediate managerial, administrative or professional);
C_1 – lower middle class (= supervisory or clerical, junior managerial, administrative or professional);
C_2 – skilled working class (= skilled manual workers);
D – other working class (= semi- and unskilled manual workers);
E – those at lowest levels of subsistence.

The assumption behind classification grouping is that those who fall within a classification will behave in a certain way. For example the main purchasers of discs and cassettes are young people in the teenage and early-twenties age bracket. At the opposite end of the age scale the demand for false teeth is likely to be greater in towns such as Eastbourne, Worthing and Bournemouth, the 'retirement' towns on the south coast, than elsewhere in the country. The socio-economic groups from C_1 upwards are generally regarded as being more interested in home ownership and savings than those in C_2, D and E.

A much more recent and sophisticated form of classification is known as ACORN ('A Classification of Residential Neighbourhoods'). This advanced computerised system groups people according to the type of area in which they live. It makes the assumption that people living in similar areas will, broadly speaking, share common lifestyles.

Lifestyles The third and final main method of putting potential customers into some form of market target is by using lifestyle methods. This is a combination of classifiable and psycho-sociological behaviour patterns, more specifically identified than the broad assumptions made for behaviour under classifications alone. Lifestyle, therefore becomes a much more detailed study of behaviour patterns within certain classes which have been statistically counted and separated. An example of lifestyle segmentation would be the deliberate attempt by a firm to appeal to its customers on the basis of, say, economy or on the basis of quality; any product which has 'status' appeal is based on lifestyle.

Using exactly the same three criteria, but applying them this time to industrial markets, location is critical for many industries: coal mining, shipbuilding, transport systems and many other similar examples.

Businesses can be grouped into size, measured through the number of employees or the value of fixed assets and so on.

Lifestyle differentiation may lie in a business's sensitivity to price, the rate at which it uses or consumes products, the end uses to which it is intended to put products, etc.

4.6 Successive Focusing

Following the last section you will have quickly appreciated that the three major forms of segmenting markets we have used so far are seldom used in isolation but much more commonly in a series of successive stages that we will call 'focusing'. There are two conditions when successive focusing becomes critical:

- when the product is highly specialized and therefore only a few people will buy it, and
- when the firm is small and can only cover a small part of a market (Smith Kendon – boiled sweets).

If the firm has limited production capacity and has no unique product it is a small fish in a big pond; success could come from changing into a big fish in a small pond, i.e. specializing in a subsection of a major market.

The successive focusing illustrated in Figure 4.1 uses two examples, weather forecasting and boiled sweets, to show the narrowing down of

41

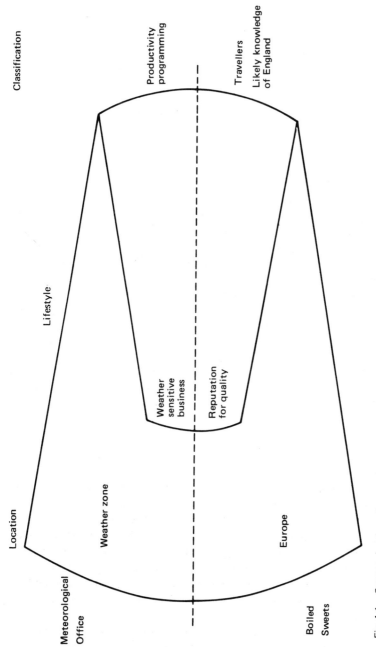

Classification

Productivity programming

Travellers

Likely knowledge of England

Lifestyle

Weather sensitive business

Reputation for quality

Location

Weather zone

Europe

Meteorological Office

Boiled Sweets

Fig 4.1 *Successive focusing*

choice on the criteria of location, classification and lifestyle segmentation.

Weather forecasting Those activities which can be drastically affected by weather (from a local garden fete, major sporting event, or whole agricultural regions) are all potential markets for the Meteorological Office. In order to make the Met Office more cost effective and commercially viable a marketing manager was appointed in 1984. Wimbledon became a particularly important client in the following year during the tennis tournament.

Boiled sweets Smith Kendon Ltd have been in business for over 200 years. In 1964 with a turnover of £250 000 the company decided to attack the European market using a British Week in Düsseldorf as its platform. By 1970 turnover had trebled, exports making up over a half, with Germany becoming the company's biggest overseas market.

With only 130 employees Smith Kendon were just not big enough to attack any mass market but chose the luxury end in Europe where a small firm could specialize. By identifying a particular kind of person the international use of English on the tins of boiled sweets actually helped consumer recognition. Travellers are, after all, easily located. They are a relatively small proportion of populations with a greater likelihood of their being multilingual. Also it is reassuring to find the same products at the service stations on the German *autobahn*, the French *auto-route* and the Italian *autostrada*. 'Travel sweets' had arrived and are still very much with us.

You will understand how abbreviated these two stories are. Indeed both the two finally targeted segments resulted from choice amongst a number of other possible alternatives.

Putting yourself in the position of management in either of these organizations your decision may well have turned out differently. Earlier, in Section 4.2, Heinz was used as an example of mass production, mass marketing and mass consumption: differentiation of market segments is minimal. The logic of this condition is almost universal acceptance of a product from a single source. There are not many products with such an outstanding performance of market domination, and you can imagine how hard Heinz work behind the scenes to keep this position.

Where product differentiation is difficult or impossible (e.g. petrol), market differentiation on lifestyle lines becomes increasingly important.

4.7 European Markets – 1992

Writing this on the 8 August 1988, the birthday of the baby Princess of York, reminds me particularly of significant dates!

In 1992 the United Kingdom will become an 'open' market target for the remaining members of the European Community as all remaining trade barriers and customs restrictions will disappear. Conversely, Western Europe will become totally accessible to UK companies; the use of the word 'exporting' to Europe should disappear. But language will still crudely segment Europe. The principle of successive focusing remains the same; but if the language boundaries are to be crossed multiple languages will have to be incorporated – as they now are on Smith Kendon's tins of travel sweets. And like it or not we British will have to come to terms with learning other languages.

4.8 Summary

In this chapter location, classification and lifestyle methods of segmentation have been used in both consumer and industrial contexts. Successive focusing provides the means of bringing any segment down to a size appropriate to any business activity, from mass markets to differentiated markets. From such targeting strategies, marketing tactics can be developed.

4.9 Ways of Getting Results

The expression 'target market' is very commonly used synonymously with the term 'segment' in marketing. The word target is nicely descriptive; in the discussions so far the description implied is equally useful in identifying a 'separable group of people' which we are attempting to define in segmentation strategy. While this separation would theoretically be possible down to individual level, we are already agreed that firms, except in very rare instances, are looking for many transactions and therefore large numbers of people.

By whatever means is most appropriate the groupings eventually decided upon should be capable of some quantification in order to provide a standard of performance suitable to the circumstances.

Because demographic classifications are based on statistical data, measurement is simple. This is by no means so simple when lifestyle methods have been used. Sometimes it is necessary to conduct market research to obtain estimates of market size and likely consumption. However loose the measurement may be it is certainly better than no measurement at all and can become a standard against which subsequent performance may be assessed.

If an individual market segment is sufficiently different from others to warrant special treatment, marketing must adapt to it. However, if segments were subdivided too much, marketing could become so fragmented in its efforts that it would cease to be effective. A compromise between the needs of a segment and the marketing methods required to reach it often has to be struck.

4.10 **Marketing Techniques**

In Section 3.4 we were regarding marketing as a philosophy more than a technique; this aspect of the subject can be considered as the first level, that containing a conceptual idea permeating the outlook of an organization in the way it behaves towards, and considers, its markets. The 'marketing concept' describes this. The second level of marketing is concerned with putting the philosophy to practical use and application through the functional activities of marketing. These have come to be known as the 'marketing mix'. The expression was coined in 1952 by an American advertising man, Neil Borden. To me it conjures up the image of a number of ingredients being mixed up in different proportions. Any cook will know exactly. The four main ones are:

- *product (or service)*;
- *place – used to describe methods and channels of distribution*;
- *promotion – all the means of communication available*;
- *price*.

Because we have already looked, to quite a considerable extent, at different kinds of product, no further elaboration is required now. The remaining three elements – place, promotion, price – are those which in the end determine the likelihood of an exchange taking place. The fact that we know a market exists does not necessarily mean we can reach it. Although many countries and businesses from them ignored the restrictions, trade sanctions against Rhodesia (before a political settlement was made and that country became Zimbabwe) forbad signatories to the United Nations agreement from trading with the country. Markets existed there, but they were, at least in a legal sense, inaccessible. Petrol prices in rural areas (in the UK) are invariably higher than those in urban or metropolitan centres because the local markets are less accessible, and less profitable by virtue of lower overall consumption levels than the more populated regions. The logistics of moving goods to many places can be difficult and expensive and therefore uneconomic. Given such problems the lack of availability of products denies any possibility of exchange. Rural communities are frequently disadvantaged as a result.

Always assuming that it is possible to deliver the products to a location, the target market still has to be told that they are there, what they may be used for, what benefits they are supposed to deliver, what satisfactions they offer and at what price they may be obtained. If I build a better mouse-trap you are unlikely to beat a path to my door – unless you know about it, unless by one means or another I tell you. In the more colourful words of Charles Tandy, the late founder of the Tandy Corporation, 'If you want to catch a mouse, you have to make a noise like a cheese.'

To decide, therefore, on the practicality of a particular segment we have to be absolutely certain that the goods can be physically brought together with the consumers, and that we can, almost literally, talk to the consumers about them. The combination of this pair, distribution and promotion, constitutes the essentials of making products accessible. Marketing is at its most visible through promotion.

Because product, place, promotion and price are not in themselves sufficient to outline the whole sequence of marketing techniques I would like to add 'information' as that ingredient required at the beginning and end of every management cycle, and 'services' which, increasingly, businesses are having to provide to consumers after an exchange has taken place.

Included in Figure 4.2 is a word which we have met and will meet again indicating the circularity of so much of business – 'feedback'.

In the conclusion to this chapter I must point out that the choice of a market segment, as I think you will have seen, is not self-evident, nor can there ever be absolute guidelines for a correct decision. What so much of marketing is concerned with is first to establish a partnership with customers, then to study and understand the needs and requirements of those customers and finally to build them into a target market chosen from amongst alternatives. The very fact that alternatives exist implies exercising a degree of choice which in its own turn implies risk. But given that a target has been selected, resources are organized to direct marketing activities effectively to instigate, and with luck perpetuate, exchanges. Because the marketing mix itself is so infinitely variable there is an area of risk here as well insofar as the most effective mix may not be employed. Finally business is concerned with results. Information is the prerequisite of producing firstly the standard to be attained, secondly the achievement actually reached and thirdly the discrepancy, if any, between the two. This is, then, both a before and after process essential to any aspect of management.

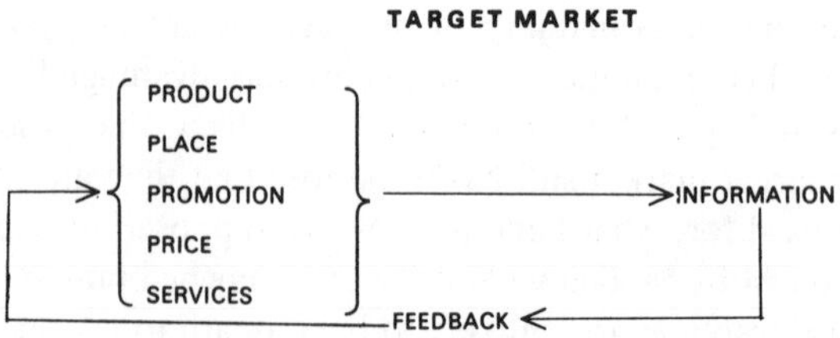

TARGET MARKET

Fig 4.2   *Main elements of the marketing mix*

4.11 Summary

Segmentation strategy is the framework within which marketing tactics (the marketing mix) are organized. Albeit with some risk associated with their selection target markets allow opportunities for real creativity in catering for the needs of particular sections of consumers. This requires a close understanding of them. Thereafter segments give direction to the functional activities of marketing, in particular ensuring their accessibility through distribution and promotion. Finally information systems enable management to monitor past performance and plan for the future.

Exercises

1 Make a list of at least five different kinds of people who have the need to communicate at a distance and explain the different types of need they have.

2 How would you describe the main purpose of carrying out market segmentation strategies?

3 List as fast as you can the four main elements of the marketing mix.

4 Think of a product which you bought during the course of last week, preferably with a value of £5 or more. In relation to that product what price did you pay, where did you buy (place) and how did you hear about it from commercial/business sources (promotion)?

5 Name the three main methods used for differentiating market segments, the sequence in which they have been used in the examples for focusing and how they were applied to the Met Office and boiled sweets. Finally work out in each case a totally different market segment possibility.

6 Assume you are dividing a population into six different divisions on the basis of age (classification), how would you do it?

Part II

The Marketing Mix

5 What is a Product?

5.1 Introduction

If the title of this chapter, 'What is a Product?', may appear to you as being too obvious, I hope that by the end of your reading the next few sections you will have changed your opinion. The answer to the question is by no means obvious, as we shall see together.

Before we launch too deeply into this subject area, may I remind you that earlier in the book I made the specific point that we would use the term 'product' as including 'services'. A little later on in this chapter we will separate these two terms quite deliberately for the first time. But to start with we will still treat them as being the central focus of the activity of commercial organizations; the things if you like, with which organizations enter into exchanges with their customers. Products and services are therefore the core of the commercial apple.

If you accept this proposition it must follow that other commercial activities must be built up directly relating to that core. Nothing could, therefore, be more appropriate as a starting point for our study of the marketing mix than a close scrutiny of the way products and services affect these other activities. The chapter title then is framed as a question because this whole area, very commonly referred to in marketing as 'product planning', is in practice far more complex than it would appear on the surface. The chief objective of this chapter is to provide a framework for us to think through the process of product planning by a means of answering the basic question 'What is a product?' – and linking the answers to the other contributory and overlapping activities in the business. In addition, as marketing operates in conditions of choice, our studies of this area can help to identify the possibilities of creating some advantage over competition or position of superiority in the marketplace; this we will later refer to as a 'differential advantage'. In order to proceed effectively in developing this framework I would like to put you into a particular frame of mind.

Below there is a simple diagram with 'You' in the middle of three blank spaces. By the end of this chapter those three spaces will have words put into them representing the three main attributes of any product, and the two main ones for any service. I will admit to you

..ediately that during this process I am going to ask you to make some very deliberate and, to an extent, artificial distinctions. These distinctions, or separate ways of looking at a product, are designed solely for the purpose of helping us to concentrate our thoughts on one step at a time.

However, in the last section of the chapter we will re-examine the steps and see that in practice they overlap each other, more or less, depending on the product or market. The challenge to you will be to interpret and apply the thinking framework to the situation you may be dealing with.

5.2 **The Physical**

In my left hand I am holding a glass. Let me describe it. First of all it is what I would describe as a 'smoky brown' colour, being lighter at the top than at the bottom; like most glasses it is circular in shape, hollow, 140 mm in height, with a diameter of 68 mm at the top rim narrowing down to 55 mm at its base where it stands on the table. The base of the glass is approximately 10 mm thick and at the top the rim is about $1\frac{1}{2}$ mm thick. In total it weighs 200 grams.

I am no expert in the making or manufacture of glass and, for that matter, I do not suppose you are. However, the brief description which I have just given will, I am sure, be sufficient to give you a mental picture of the object. If, however, we were to assume that we were experts in the manufacture of glass, the information that I have provided could possibly be sufficient to enable you to make such a product. Let us, then, for purposes of illustration take my description as a 'specification'.

What this specification has described are the physical attributes of a product, in this case a glass. All over the world there are people making such glasses or similar ones. You have them in your cupboard. They are a universal object familiar to each and every one of us.

Fig 5.1   *The three main attributes of a product*

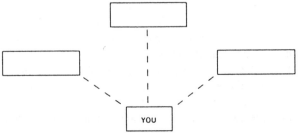

Now imagine that we have written such a specification and passed it on to somebody else who is expert in the making of glass and has a sufficient quantity of both raw materials and the necessary machinery to make such items.

All that has so far been made is a physical object.

As long as the glass remains in a warehouse, on a department stores' shelves, or even in your own cupboard, it is useless and has no value! I repeat: the glass is useless and has no value!

May I, however, remind you that I am to an extent making artificial distinctions in looking at a product in order to help us concentrate our thought processes by taking things a step at a time.

Now let us develop this process a little further, still sticking rigidly to the physical attributes of products in the most literal sense.

Self-check

This time I would like you to go through the process of drawing up a (crude) specification of another product. But in order to be able to help you, allow me to nominate the product, another one which we are all likely to possess or at least be very familiar with: a cheap plastic ballpoint pen. (If you can quickly get your hands on one, so much the better.) Now look at it, examine it, feel its weight, its colour, its shape, its length, the parts from which it is made, what materials have been used, and fill in (at least mentally) the appropriate measurements of the items just mentioned.

Nothing else but a pure physical description is allowed.

Although your 'specification' would probably not be technically accurate (no more would mine) you can readily imagine that you are writing down the instructions to somebody else to make this ballpoint pen, or at least what it would look like when completed. For example:

The one I have has a black removable cap which covers a brass-coloured tapering point with a small ball inside it at the end of a narrow tube containing ink. The tube in total is about 130 mm long and is encased within another transparent outer plastic tube of identical length, which is six-sided in shape, has two small holes in it roughly halfway down its length, has a small black cap at the end opposite to the brass nib, which protrudes from the outer casing about 10 mm. I put it down on my desk and look at it from, say five feet away – it is useless. It is valueless!

Let your imagination roam over other physical objects:

- a gold bar in a Swiss bank vault;
- a Picasso painting;

- the Crown Jewels;
- an architectural drawing-board;
- the local town hall building;
- a pocket diary.

All of these things, and a million others besides, have physical form. In that form alone they are useless and valueless!

All the things listed have in one way or another had their form changed by manufacturing or some other process. Yet you know that all these things have value (in spite of my denial of it), otherwise mankind would not have bothered to make them. The question that arises is 'Where does the value come from?'

Can we, for the moment, return to the glass.

I made the statement that that glass is useless and has no value: I say the same again. It only begins to acquire value when you or some other person goes to it and joins with it. Exactly the same principle applies to the ballpoint pen.

The logic of this argument is that people bring value to products rather than the other way round and, because people are individual and therefore different, they may bring different values to the same product.

Self-check

Way back in this book, indeed in the first chapter, this point was made in the context of a newspaper. Why do you buy them? (There is a discussion answer in Section 1.2.)

At the beginning of the chapter I reminded you that the terms 'product' and 'service' would be normally treated as being one but that 'a little later on' they would be separated. Think back on (or reread if you prefer) this section, asking yourself the question, 'Does the argument apply to a service?'

You will quickly come to the conclusion that it does not. The reason is, of course, that a 'service' has no physical entity; it is abstract, it is intangible.

5.3 The Functional

Before we move on to examine the 'functional' in any detail, you might like to write in the word 'physical' in the top left-hand box of the figure on page 50. If by any chance you used the ballpoint pen which was then lying around, you quite literally gave value to that product by picking it up and using it. In fact the whole purpose of its manufacture was to enable you to do just that. Its component parts had been designed and put together in a certain way in order that, when used correctly, it would write. Apply the same logic to a glass and you have an open-topped container, most commonly used for liquids, but not necessarily; by virtue of its shape the glass enables us to drink liquids from it with relative ease.

Just as I approached the 'physical' very literally, I would wish to do the same with you in this section by treating the 'functional' facet of the product in close association with its physical make-up. In the examples which follow I am therefore concerned solely with that part of a product which can perform a physical function for us; the pen can write.

Self-check

I wear glasses; I have two pairs, one for long-distance sight and the other for reading. On the basis of the 'physical' you can, I am sure, easily provide a mental picture of a pair of glasses – you will have seen them often enough on other people even if you do not have to wear them yourself. What function do glasses perform?

For me, as an individual, I have already intimated that I need two pairs, one for long and one for short distances; literally, then, their function for me is to improve my vision in different circumstances.

Let us now, by way of illustration, turn to things which are probably less familiar. We go into a large modern bakery and at various stages of the bread-making process we will see loaves moving along conveyor belts from one point to another to be baked.

Changing the context, anyone who has flown either on holiday or on business has experienced the wait at the place of destination for the luggage to be offloaded and again placed on a conveyor system from which we collect it. If you have neither flown nor been in a bakery I would be surprised had you not had the experience of being on an escalator either on an underground system, as in London, in a department store or in some other large building.

The technical specifications for the manufacture and installation of any of these types of system would be highly complex and require considerable engineering skills. They all, however, perform the same function of transporting 'things'.

When putting these propositions and examples forward to people involved in marketing I am sometimes challenged to the effect that such functional attributes of a product are what are commonly described in the jargon as the 'benefits'. This I do not accept because, as we will shortly see, there is the third type of facet or attribute to a product which we will be treating separately in Section 5.4.

The 'functional', in that most literal sense in which I am using it, can also be written into a specification and manufactured.

Self-check

Of the six items listed in Section 5.2 which qualify as being functional?

The last three certainly qualify; the Crown Jewels could be included only for those state occasions when they are being worn – but even that is stretching a point beyond which I do not wish, as yet to go. Do you see how literal I am being? Stick with it a while!

Why do I feel that the point made about the Crown Jewels is possibly going too far? Let us come down to earth a bit and consider clothing.

Self-check

Remaining within the strict limits of my argument so far, review those functions performed by clothing. Perhaps you would like to list them, or get somebody else to tell you what they think.

Forgive me for reminding you once more but please re-examine your list and delete any of the functions which cannot be built into the product.

In this paragraph there will be four examples of the functional use of clothing. They are not intended necessarily to cover every possible functional aspect, but I hope will be sufficient to help you to understand quite clearly what I have been getting at in this section. One of the main uses for which clothing is provided is for protection; a mackintosh protects us from the rain. A second very important use of clothing is for the control of body temperature; a sheepskin coat is an essential garment in an Alaskan winter, whereas an Arabian burnous is equally effective in the heat of the desert. Other clothing is also provided for particular safety reasons; the hard hat worn by a miner or special clothing in an atomic power station. A less common example of functional clothing can be illustrated by camouflaged uniforms for the purpose of concealment.

If this review exercise has clarified in your mind my insistence on looking quite separately at the functional attributes of a product, it can be deduced from the example that we have just worked through that these attributes are built in by the maker. Just as in the previous section, when we were looking at the physical, so in this section the functional is concerned with that part of the manufacturing or production process of a product which can be arranged in such a way that a potential user of it can obtain a use from it. By putting it together in this particular way the maker is anticipating that use.

Given that suitable instructions, contained in the physical and functional specification, have been received, understood and implemented by the technical and production people in a business, the article concerned can be made. So would it then be realistic to put the product planning process, so far at least, solely in the hands of the technical side of a business? Undoubtedly the answer must be 'no'.

The reason for my very definite negative against technical people being solely responsible for product planning is that the commercial success of a product is decided in the marketplace by its buyers and users. The link between the inside of a firm and its environment – the market – is one of the roles of marketing. Therefore, at the very least, marketing must have a say in that part of the product specification which reflects the views of potential customers about how they would like to use the product or how a new one could help to solve a particular problem for them – its functional attributes.

Because product ideas can, and indeed should, be obtained from any source, their development or modification must be a matter of teamwork and joint interpretation; indeed sometimes compromise has to be both entertained and practised. Suppose the marketing people were demanding a particularly high quality of performance but at a low price, their technical colleagues could be put into an impossible position. Conversely technical ingenuity often adds on to products performance functions which may not be necessary, would cost more to produce and hence put prices up. The crucial question is: what functions does the prospective customer require and how much value does he or she perceive in them (= price)? The sensible business undertakes appropriate product-testing as insurance, before committing too extensive resources.

Once the product specification has been agreed, the production lines are rolling and the goods are going to the shops, that specification is going to ensure functional consistency in the products; buy one and it will perform its function; buy another it will do likewise. If it does not, there is trouble – and you and I make it by taking it back to the shop, demanding our money back or a replacement in exchange, and so on. Not only does the average customer these days expect a product to perform those functions which its makers claim it will perform, but also there is a legal obligation on the maker (and the seller such as the shop) that it do so.

Let us test out some of these ideas.

Self-check

You have just bought an electric drill with a supply of masonry bits. What function do you expect it to perform? How has the maker matched the specification to the function?

Because they are masonry bits, you will be drilling into walls rather than woodwork. But what do you require of this product's performance? You want *holes*. So long as the drill, plus bits, makes the holes you have obtained the performance required. That's your side of it, what of the maker?

He has an electric motor encased (for your protection) in a 'housing', has a trigger-type switch, a pistol-grip handle, some slots in the casing for air cooling; there is a 'chuck' on the end into which the bit is fitted and locked, which, when powered by the motor, revolves at certain speeds enabling the specially hardened tip of the bit to penetrate into brickwork, concrete or whatever.

You will recall that so far we have been using the terms 'product' and 'service' without differentiation.

At the end of the last section I asked you to decide whether the 'physical' applied to a service, and we agreed that it did not. But does the 'functional' apply to services, such as contract cleaning; TV repairs; dentistry; insurance?

First a reminder: if the function has been built in by the supplier (or the manufacturer) then it has functional attributes.

The functions of contract cleaning, or any type of cleaning, must simply be the removal of dirt, repair (TV or anything else), to put back into working order; dentistry, to prevent or repair tooth decay; insurance, value-replacement of damage to, or loss of, things or people by money. To change the word orientation a bit for services, we can illustrate from the examples that services have been designed and arranged by their suppliers and therefore they are 'functional'.

5.4 Symbolic Meaning

I would be very surprised if you did not feel on occasion some irritation about my rigid and literal interpretation of the physical and the functional in the preceding pages! But this, the third, attribute of a product is the one in which marketing stands alone, no longer supported by technical specifications, more likely distorted through the weaknesses of communications.

You must have heard the expression 'we're not on the same wavelength' (loosely translated as 'we're not thinking alike' – nothing to do with radio!). Do you anticipate my point? If buyer and seller are trying to communicate, which is a two-way process, but are not on the same wavelength all sorts of misunderstandings or misinterpretations can occur.

A major activity within marketing is communication about products and services. You know that already; you see it all around; you are constantly exposed to it. But by now we can clearly appreciate that so much of marketing communication bears little connection with the purely functional attributes. If not that, then what? The symbolic. In this section product planning will not only examine the symbolic meanings of products but use them to begin the process of planning the means of promoting them to the market.

Suppose we examine a couple of the items in the list in Section 5.2 when we were discussing the physical attribute of products:

1 **The Crown Jewels** The Crown was made to fit on the monarch's head (functional); on state occasions it symbolizes royalty, our peculiar constitution – meanings which have nothing to do with the Crown itself, but which have been given to it by society, by government, by people, by us! The Crown Jewels also have many other symbolic meanings, some good, some not so good:

- the state;
- authority;
- continuity;
- history;
- empire;
- exploitation;

- ostentation;
- spectacle;
- tradition;
- craftsmanship;
- personal power;
- and a host of others.

2 **A gold bar in a Swiss bank vault** First question: is it functional? In the way I have been using the term – no, it is not! Second question: has it symbolic meaning? Yes it has, and you can best explain what to yourself by answering this: Why would you like to have one?

- A way of saving for the future, perhaps.
- A hedge against inflation would be nice.
- What a way to boast to my friends!
- Something I could pass on to my children.
- A security for borrowing money to expand, or buy, a business.

When Picasso painted that picture was he making a hedge against inflation?

Let's explore these ideas a bit further.

Self-check

Try to imagine that you are wearing an old-fashioned pair of safety boots: they are ankle length, have lace-up fastenings, the toe-caps are covered in steel, the soles are non-slip with studs embedded in them. They are made primarily for protection so that, if somebody is careless on a building site and drops a scaffold pole on your foot, you will not be damaged while wearing such boots as these.

'Safety boots! They do what they are supposed to do, protect my toes and stop me slipping! But they are ugly, they are heavy, they'll probably give me blisters. I wouldn't be seen dead with them off the building site; I only put them on because of the safety regulations and I'm told by the boss. Yet I've got a date with my girlfriend immediately after work and I haven't any other shoes with me today! It's a good job that the firm supplies them; you'd have a job getting me to spend good money on them. I wonder if I should wear them for next Saturday's football match – there might be some "aggro" there!'

From this small, but real anecdote, we are now in a position to sort out some useful, indeed important, aspects of the functional and symbolic. Go back over the self-check and sort them out under the following headings:

Technology   *Psychology*
Sociology   *Economic value*

Technology: this equates with the functional because it can be built in – steel toe-cap, non-slip soles and boot manufacture.

Psychology: relates to an individual, his or her feelings, e.g. ugly, heavy, uncomfortable (by implication).

Sociology: the links with other people, at work, the boss; the girlfriend, the football crowd.

Economic value: so often put first as a reason to buy or not to buy, but so often in fact last – as in this instance, a result of the others.

If we now assume that many of the negatives could be changed to positives, the reaction to the boots would change dramatically. The limiting factor is the functional: the boots must . . . what must they?

Look above to *Technology*.

Apart from that a manufacturer could incorporate the safety features into fashion shoes, into sneakers, into Wellington boots, into slip-ons, lace-ups – where is the limit? And this is precisely what one firm I know, Fifty Plus Ltd, does do.

By differentiating the attributes of a product through the physical, the functional and the symbolic, marketing is able to link 'product planning' to the remaining elements of the marketing mix: place, promotion and price.

From the anecdote about boots, choose one of the four headings only with a view to turning the negative points into positive ones and then telling people (customers) about the advantages! You will find it very hard, if not impossible, to do it with economic value on its own! Any of the other three can be turned into excellent promotional messages. Mix them up and the possible permutations are countless.

Technology: safety in style.
Psychology: comfort while you work.
Sociology: steel toes are smart.

Mentally add to these examples the opportunity for visualization by drawing, pictures, TV visuals to elaborate and explain your message. In this way product planning cannot help but be linked with promotion and the influence of the potential customer is brought right back into product design.

Nor are the functional and symbolic attributes influential alone on promotion. There is a great deal of symbolism attached to shops; could this conflict with your product? And does the 'value' of your product lie in what it does or what it means?

Figure 5.1 in Section 5.1 can now be completed. See Figure 5.1a.

5.5 The Combination

In one form or another the interrelationship between the technical/ production and the marketing people in a business has been a recurring theme in the last three sections. Suppose we summarize this diagrammatically.

Fig 5.1(a) *The three main attributes of a product*

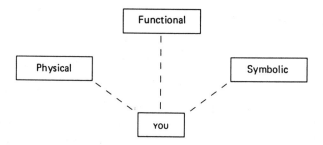

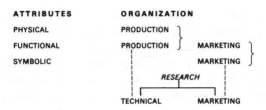

Fig 5.2 *'Product planning'*

The overlapping interest of both production and marketing can be clearly seen opposite 'functional' – to which both contribute. A new dimension, shown for the first time, is research.

By using the 'three attribute analysis' we are coming closest to interpreting 'values' as seen by the consumer. Our interpretation may not be right, or it may be pretty close to the mark; either way it gives us an opportunity to investigate *something* through research in the market.

Although at this stage I intend to do little more than hint at the activities of marketing research, let us consider it as looking for the answer to *a question*: where is the 'needle in a haystack'? If we know the haystack, and that we are looking for a needle, at least we know what we are about! It may be difficult; it may even be virtually impossible; but there is *something* to look for. As soon as you knew that, you could select the right tools – how about a very sensitive metal-detector! Now dismantle a haystack without knowing what you are looking for, what is the chance of finding it? Finding what?

This section now has the task of putting together the process of 'product planning' into a coherent whole, of showing how the organizational overlap works; how the 'functional' and 'symbolic' need to be balanced for both products and markets. Not least we will be examining how my 'mini-monopoly' becomes, more formally, the 'differential advantage', mentioned in the opening of this chapter on page 49.

5.6 Organizational Overlap

In Chapter 3, 'Where marketing begins', I pointed out that 'marketing' should be thought of as a 'business philosophy' on one level and a series of activities or functions on another (see page 33). In this chapter two main functions have been linked – production and marketing – and their respective contributions to 'product planning'. Just as the latter uses marketing research to find out the consumer reactions to the physical, functional and the symbolic, production uses technical research to develop more efficient manufacturing processes, better ways of putting the physical and functional together and improving working methods. These technical processes of research commonly go under the label of R&D (research and development). But the business activities, which go together to make the whole, do not stop here.

Including those which we have already touched upon (production, marketing, R&D, marketing research) we could add administration, finance, personnel; and we could subdivide marketing by advertising and selling, distribution, after-sales service and so on. All of them together make up the corporate effort, and individually are linked directly or indirectly with the business's behaviour in the market. If this idea of teamwork, of everybody working for the common purpose, is real (rather than just paying lip-service to the idea) then anybody should be able to contribute to the product planning process provided the organization gives them the opportunity.

Participation is of increasing importance for several reasons:

- All employees should have a chance to be involved in this central activity.
- Researchers and academics tell us that the failure rate of 'new' products is between 50 and 80 per cent (depending on how 'success' and 'failure' are judged).
- 'New' products are being introduced on to the market at an ever-increasing rate; a business can, therefore, be easily overtaken by its rivals.
- Technology is advancing so fast that even patent rights do not always give protection.
- Technologists change firms and take their knowledge with them.
- Consumer values change over time and new insights into them are constantly required.
- As the world shrinks, competition is no longer (if indeed it ever really was) confined within a country; it is becoming increasingly international.

Organizational overlap is probably greater in 'product planning' than in any other single business activity, and should never be regarded as the particular prerogative of any section of a firm or particular people within it. The more participants the merrier.

5.7 Product Comparability

One of the troubles about today's world is the difficulty of developing, and then maintaining, a unique or distinctive product for any length of time. There are indeed many products, and an even greater proportion of services, which are virtually indistinguishable from their direct competitors.

We can check this by taking a quick look at the list of products and services below. Concentrate your thoughts on the 'functional' and how you would differentiate them. For the moment exclude any price differences.

Product/service
Petrol – four-star
Aspirin
Bank overdrafts
Milk – silver top
Vodka
Window cleaing

I asked you to exclude price differences because, in the absence of any other criteria, price may be the reason why we make a choice, or how we differentiate.

Unless you were a chemist and went to the trouble of analysing the petrol, which no consumer is going to do anyway (chemist or not), how do you tell the difference? It may sound ridiculous but I used to be a Shell man! Looking back I tell myself the reason was because my father had always bought it (or such are my recollections). When my two daughters were young, and Esso was using the famous 'Put a tiger in your tank' advertising campaign, they wanted tiger tails like their friends; I had to switch! Now I tend to go for convenience or price. My car *functions* equally well on any of them. Does yours?

Does an aspirin (using the general term) work any better because it is soluble, because instead of being a normal round pill shape it is in capsule form or because one particular make happens after some trial and error to suit us better? Is the difference real or in the mind?

Do you quiver like a schoolboy called before the headmaster, or a schoolgirl before the headmistress, when you beg your bank manager for an overdraft? My experience is often one of guilt feeling that I have the temerity to ask. Perhaps you are not so sensitive!

I do not think I need to go on elaborating for milk, vodka or window cleaning; you have the idea. When product comparability is identical or even just close, differentiation has to be created in the mind, through the symbolic. That may, or may not, then be differentiated further through price.

5.8 Market Differentiation

By taking the opposite starting point, the market rather than the product, there are many examples to be found of the same product presented in a different way for classes of buyer. According to the newspaper British Leyland (now Austin Rover) took £5m worth of orders for the new Triumph Acclaim within twenty-four hours of its launch – from fleet buyers, e.g. large firms who need many cars for their salesmen and staff each year. Indeed the British motor manufacturers have tended to concentrate their efforts on this market segment, as the private-sector buyers (people like you and me) have been switching to foreign vehicles.

Ford's Sierra and Vauxhall's Cavalier were specifically aimed at these business buyers and the cars themselves, or more correctly the 'offerings' around them, were tailored accordingly. The emphasis was on lower insurance, availability of spares at reasonable cost, adequate if not luxurious accessories, good engine performance without extravagant consumption of fuel.

Another illustration of the influence of the market on a product comes from a publication from the J. Walter Thompson advertising agency in which they tell the stories of eight case histories, three of which were prizewinners in a competition run by the IPA (Institute of Practitioners of Advertising) in 1980. One of the campaigns was about 'Elida Gibbs: All Clear – Introducing a New Shampoo'.

The aim was to capture a 5 per cent share of the shampoo market concentrating on the anti-dandruff sector and competing against the brand leader, Procter & Gamble's Head and Shoulders. Marketing research had revealed that there was a gap for a range of anti-dandruff shampoos catering specifically for different hair conditions for both men and women. The product was designed and developed accordingly – a direct influence from the consumer on the 'functional' attributes of the product. All Clear was presented to the market with a combination of 'functional' and 'symbolic' ideas.

5.9 The Balancing of 'Functional' and 'Symbolic'

Periodically the 'dream machine', a nickname sometimes given to the advertising and promotion industries, comes under heavy consumer attack because of an overemphasis on the symbolic products presented in a manner beyond the bounds of probability. Hamlet cigars, a Bounty bar, lager . . . The list could be endless, but all these fall into the general category of product comparability. The criticisms become more valid when packaging plays deliberately on the optical illusion of size, implying incorrectly that there is more of the product within. No wonder hard-pressed housewives want quantities or weights clearly displayed with the price per gram shown for purposes of comparison.

Are there then any general principles that we can apply to balancing the functional and symbolic? Yes, I think there are; but with due warning that their practical success will be judged, not by the designer, nor the product planner, but in the end by the consumer.

The first principle is 'newness'.

Surely a 'new product' is any product which has not been previously experienced by a potential customer – however long it may in fact have been on the market.

The second principle is one of technology. The more complicated a thing is in the way it works and has to be managed the more we have to be taught how to use it. I remember very clearly the early advertising messages around front-loader washing machines when they were new. Potential buyers had to be informed about how they worked; they tumbled the clothes rather than agitated them; they rinsed as well as washed; they did not work as well with very 'sudsy' detergents. We had to be told a good deal about how they functioned.

Self-check

Imagine (even if you have never had one) that you possess an Instamatic camera. Would you agree they are very simple to use? But now you want to be a bit more ambitious in your photography; friends of yours have been talking about 'depth of field', 'panning for high-speed movement', 'wide-angle and zoom lenses' and so on. You would *have to have* a great deal of 'functional' information about photographic technology. Where would you get this information?

First let us recapitulate: these functions have been built in by the maker. Therefore the first source could be the manufacturer of the camera which interests you. But suppose he is in Germany (Leica) or Japan (Nikon), you might have the odd difficulty. So you would probably go to a dealer for the literature, to see and handle such a camera, to have it demonstrated – to be taught.

Risk, or our perception of risk, is the third principle. I have qualified this by using the word 'perception' because risk has very different meanings and degrees of importance between people. Generally we could associate risk with 'expense'; the greater the outlay (price), or the more important the consequences (changing a raw material for a factory process). In such circumstances we would attempt to project ourselves from an adverse outcome by seeking reassurance on the functional attributes of the product.

None of these principles denies the use of the symbolic. Either individually or in combination they should ensure the use of the functional.

At great risk of causing some offence, I am going to be daring enough to make a sweeping generalization: too many companies marketing industrial products concentrate solely on presenting the functional attributes of their goods to the almost total exclusion of any symbolism at all. 'Oh, that may be all right for consumer people, but not for us.'

However it is also true that public preferences change. Periodically there is an upsurge of criticism about advertising in general: there is too much 'symbolism' and not enough 'information'. These words may not be used but this is what it amounts to! Marketers, who in the end control the advertising, must keep in touch with the consumer feelings in order that their messages persuade effectively and do not put people off.

5.10 **The Differential Advantage**

If this last section has appeared to diverge from what might literally be called 'product planning', it is because our usual conception of that activity is linked to the physical and functional (where production and marketing overlap). In a marketing book we have to look at the totality, and in practice it is the totality which will determine success or failure.

Marketing, we have already agreed, is unnecessary in an environment without competition and therefore choice; or choice and therefore competition. It matters not which way we look at it (see Chapter 3). But that condition is the motivating force to seek differentiation from the competition to gain an advantage in the marketplace – 'differential advantage'.

The functional can always be copied, even if a little time elapses before it is. The symbolic cannot in the same way. In balanced combination they are a key to successful product planning – for a time. Even symbolic ideas decay; people get bored with them; somebody else comes up with a better one. You are left behind!

Self-check

I have just bought (for £9) an intercom set with two 'stations' and installed them, one station on the ground floor and one on the first floor; the system is totally self-contained and battery operated so no real electrical knowledge is required.

In the light of the three principles (newness, technology and risk) consider how you would present such a product, combining both the functional and the symbolic.

Functional	*Symbolic*
Enables speech between people while separated.	Saves shouting – convenience.
A babysitter.	Safety – I can hear my child if it cries from downstairs.
Geriatric help.	An old person, bedridden, can call for help.
None.	I (personally) am pleased with my new 'toy'.

5.11 Summary

In this chapter we have examined a way of concentrating our thinking on different, but interlocking, parts of the product-planning process. The method, if it may be called such, does not solve any problems for us, it merely enables us to be systematic and opens every possible avenue for creativity. The progression from the physical, the functional, to the symbolic also highlights the integrated totality of an organization's contributions to this core activity. In conclusion, by taking the view that marketing works in a competitive environment, business should be seeking for its successful survival some distinguishing feature which gives it a 'differential advantage' in the marketplace.

Exercises

1 First, do you recall the examples used earlier in the chapter of the glass and the ballpoint pen? Describe what it was that gave them value! Now nominate any product and also any service of your choice and identify what gives them value for particular kinds of people.
2 The term 'marketing mix' was first used in Chapter 4. What were its four main ingredients?
3 From your own experience of business, or from your study of it, make a list of what you consider to be the major functions which are involved in the product/service planning process.
4 Generate by yourself, or with some close business colleagues, some *new* symbolic themes around your product(s). Then go outside your firm and do the same with some friends in a nice relaxed social atmosphere; friends who may not have any link with your products at all. Your eyes will be opened and you will resist their thoughts like mad! You will try to make every possible excuse you can to deny their creativity. This is because you have been conditioned by

the culture of your firm, by your 'experience'; your ego may take a battering! Try it!

5 What are the three principles outlined which give guidance on balancing the functional and the symbolic? Apply these principles to a marketing situation with which you are familiar – a product or service from your own firm or one which you consume or use.

6 Goods to People or People to Goods?

6.1 Introduction

The last chapter introduced us to the idea that 'product planning' went far beyond the literal manufacture or production of goods; indeed marketing's interest was primarily one of being able to present that product to potential customers in a way which would appeal to their particular needs and consequently encourage them to buy. We could summarize this process by suggesting that one of marketing's major roles on the business scene is to be able to 'talk about' these products. There is, however, little point in entering into such a dialogue if the other party to the 'conversation' is unable to get physical access to them.

In this chapter we are going to explore some of the major methods by which goods and people are brought together, through what are known as 'channels of distribution'. It is through these that products become physically available to the public. In our normal lives we are likely to refer to them quite simply as 'shops'. However, relatively little thought would quickly bring us to the conclusion that there is an organization structure behind the shops with which we are personally familiar; how deep and complex this structure may be is the main subject of this chapter.

We will be examining distribution from three separate points of view: the suppliers'; the shops' themselves; and their customers'. The reason for this separation is to emphasize the differences of interests, and therefore potential conflict, at the different stages of the 'channel' through which goods flow. There will be no attempt to detail the historical development of various types of distributive system, nor even to illustrate the immense variety of possible channel flows which exist, or could be designed. I am going to assume firstly that your own observations have given a wealth of knowledge already – it may not be organized in any academic sense – and secondly that together we can draw on that knowledge to illustrate many of the key points of this subject.

6.2 Getting Goods to People – the Suppliers' View

For the purpose of this discussion, let us define a 'supplier' as a business which needs the assistance of other organizations to pass on its products or services to its market segments. There are, then, intermediate transactions before the goods reach the final consumer. Indeed channels of distribution are not infrequently referred to as 'intermediaries'; and the word 'channel' conjures up a picture of movement.

Self-check

Define, in your own words, the meaning of the term 'market segment'. (For verification turn back to the *Concise Oxford Dictionary* definition quoted on page 36).

In Chapter 4 we agreed that there were two essential conditions required before a segment becomes an effective target: 'We have to be absolutely certain that the goods can be physically brought together with the consumers and that we can, almost literally, talk to the consumers about them'.

Therefore from the point of view of the supplier the purpose of any distributive system is to make *its* goods accessible to *its* markets; the system is a means to an end, one of the ingredients of the marketing mix. Because the marketing mix, in total, is designed to achieve the suppliers' goal, attempts are made to control the channel system by them – with greater or lesser success.

By their nature suppliers (we could substitute the word 'manufacturer' here if you feel that helps you to identify more closely with the situation) are dealing with a limited range of products – limited by both skills and resources. They also have the intention of projecting their products by a mixture of 'functional' and 'symbolic' appeals; the means by which this is done will be the theme of the next chapter. There is then a problem of matching these products with the intermediary's other product ranges; you will not find a Rolls-Royce in a Ford dealer's showroom. (Somebody will almost certainly be able to prove me wrong!)

The approach of matching products to both the distributive outlet and the other products stocked by it is dependent upon two sets of perceptions – or in other words, the way in which people look at things and interpret them:

- the perception of the supplier; how he sees his products fitting;
- the perception of a customer; how he/she sees the interrelationship of shop and product.

We can dispose of the relationship between the various products quite easily. If you, as a customer, want medicine, you go to a chemist; for nails, to an ironmonger; for groceries, to a supermarket. You know where to expect to find certain types of goods. So too, in general, does an industrial buyer. Therefore if you are the manufacturer of screws, you would not be very wise if you tried to distribute them in chemists! From your own observations you also know that there is a growth of shops dealing in wider and wider varieties of goods. Visualize any Woolworths or department store and you will quickly come to the conclusion that they are organized on product group lines; the principle holds.

For many products the matching process referred to is not a serious one. For some products it may be.

For purposes of practice and elaboration let's examine together the following list of products and services. In each case imagine yourself as the supplier seeking distribution outlets for them. Then by using our judgement we can decide if each one is required to match the other products normally held in an outlet or needs a special type of outlet, or a combination of both.

(a) Alka Seltzer
(b) Package holiday
(c) Roof insulation
(d) Microwave oven
(e) Garden seedlings
(f) Home computer system
(g) A Mercedes car
(h) An Omega watch

As there is some judgement involved in this activity, the 'answer' that am going to give may well not agree with yours; also your experience may have taught you other lessons, which I know nothing of. Nevertheless the thoughts which you and I invest will pay dividends!

(a) Alka Seltzer – this is a product match. We could obtain it in many different kinds of outlets and they would have little influence on us.
(b) Package holiday – this is outlet based. There is an area of specialism here which we, as consumers, would seek out.
(c) Roof insulation – we would probably have to match this one to both product and outlet; a builders' merchant would certainly be a good source, but there are many new distributive organizations entering the home do-it-yourself markets. Sainsbury's is one, a firm we normally associate with foods.
(d) Microwave oven – outlet based. This is the sort of product we would probably expect to find in specialist electrical stores or department stores, for example the Electricity Board showrooms.

(e) Garden seedlings could be any permutation; from a garden centre they would be outlet based (specialist); but we often find them in small domestic hardware shops serving local neighbourhoods – product based, particularly in season.

(f) Home computer systems are appearing in shops only relatively recently (1981). These are very much outlet based because the shops concerned usually tie up by agreement with a particular system: Curry's, Ryman's, W. H. Smith are all entering this market.

(g) A Mercedes car – image of quality and controlled dealerships, therefore outlet centred.

(h) An Omega watch – high quality again and therefore likely to be in selected 'high street' upmarket outlets.

The thought may well have crossed your mind while going through this activity that there are other much more direct systems of distributing products as a supplier – mail order is one, when you buy from a catalogue or from an advertisement; 'direct marketing', a relatively new term, is another, of which Scotcade is a good example (look for their advertisements in the Sunday newspaper colour supplements); the question is, are they suppliers in the manufacturing sense? I do not actually know, but I would guess not. There are also things known as 'tied outlets' or 'tied houses'; oil companies and breweries are both good examples of organizations which exercise control over distributive systems by ownership. This is what an economist would call 'vertical integration' where the whole network of moving goods from producer to consumer is owned and controlled by the one business.

Although these are generally the exceptions in terms of trade volume in the advanced western economies, they illustrate well how new developments take place. There is no end to the ingenuity that can be employed by suppliers to reach their markets. This alone can be the 'differential advantage' for success. But we must try to simplify; examine these systems for any general rules, guidelines or principles which may be the launching pads for original designs.

Let me remind you that we are still taking the supplier's viewpoint.

6.3 The Two Ss

Suppose we set out a scale:

Selection ⌊＿＿⌋＿＿⌋＿＿⌊＿＿⌋＿＿⌋ Saturation

Using these words as representing two extremes, as suppliers we may seek the maximum possible number of outlets: saturation; alternatively the nature of our product dictates a degree of technical knowledge in the outlet, it is prestigious and we do not want it to rub shoulders with every

Tom, Dick and Harry! Milk is probably the extreme example of saturation; it is brought daily to our doorsteps.

Not far from where I live there is a neighbourhood which I would describe as 'becoming elderly'; there is an unusually high proportion of senior citizens. There is also a shop, run by an old lady well into her eighties, dealing in feminine underwear! Most of the products stocked are dictated by the fashions of fifty years ago. (There are great opportunities for suppliers in this age segment all too often still neglected.) This gives an extreme example of selection not based on technical, nor prestigious grounds, but on specialization.

6.4 The Cost

Do you recall that we began this chapter by defining the word 'supplier' and introducing the word 'intermediary', the latter being a separate organization? Supposing we introduce a simplified system for purposes of illustration consisting of a supplier (S), a wholesaler (W/S), a retailer (R) and finally the customer (C), it might appear as in Figure 6.1.

Each link in the chain adds to the cost a margin to cover its operations and, at the end of the day, to provide a profit. The consumer (C) sees the price as £15, but does not necessarily know or even appreciate that this is 50 per cent higher than the price at which the same product was sold by the supplier (S). The supplier should know the final selling price and the margins in between; if he does not he can easily price himself out of the market. Similarly he should know to what extent the increase in his original price is genuinely adding value to the consumer at the end of the chain. After all the intermediaries do not alter, or add directly to, the product in any way; they sell the same things as they buy. But if they do not add value they are economically wasteful and unlikely to survive for long. (If you have ever picked your fruit or vegetables at a smallholding, rather than bought at the local greengrocer, you will appreciate how much money you can save – but conversely how much time and effort you have to spend.)

A closer look will be taken at this expression I have used of 'added value' in the next section, when we look at distribution from the

Fig 6.1   *A simple 'intermediary' system*

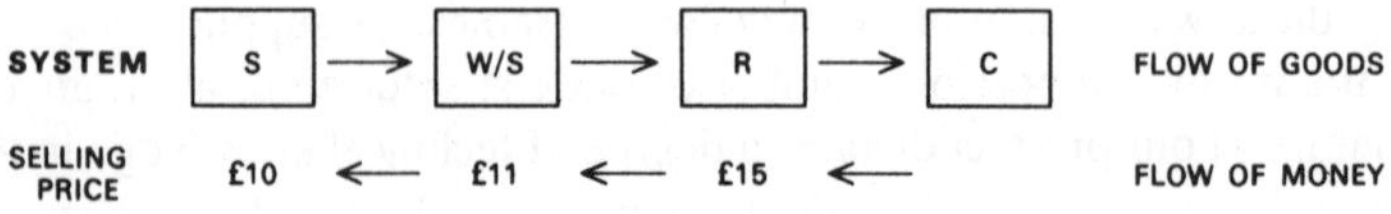

| SYSTEM | S | → | W/S | → | R | → | C | FLOW OF GOODS |
| SELLING PRICE | £10 | ← | £11 | ← | £15 | ← | | FLOW OF MONEY |

intermediaries' point of view. For the moment we can accept the simplified version, that they serve some function in the movement of goods to people.

The supplier of goods and services is concerned with moving his goods to people through a system which will be, if not permanent, then certainly durable. Outlets cannot be changed quickly. What is more outlets have their own characteristics, can be separately classified and grouped and frequently require special treatment. This last sentence should take you (mentally) straight back to market segmentation!

In 1981 the *Sunday Times* management wanted to lift their price per copy from 35p to 40p to cover increased costs of production. The wholesalers earned 30 per cent per copy = 10.5p at the 35p price. At the proposed 40p price, 10.5 = $24\frac{1}{4}\%$, relatively, therefore, the wholesalers were losing on their margin, but absolutely it remained the same. They rebelled on the grounds that their costs were also going up, and the *Sunday Times* had to withdraw its price increase. This anecdote illustrates how dependent a supplier is on his channels and vice versa; they are parts of the same overall system, yet are separate and independent organizations, sometimes with very distinct and conflicting interests. No supplier can ignore with impunity his channels of distribution.

6.5 Moving People to Goods – the Intermediaries' View

At the beginning of Section 6.2 we introduced the term 'intermediary' as a means of differentiating between that and a 'supplier' in the total system of distribution. Perhaps now we should be a little bit more formal in our definition of an 'intermediary'.

For our purpose we should consider them as being organizations independent of their sources of supply. They therefore have separate interests, different goals or objectives and separate functions. They are, as we already appreciate, in the middle, buying in goods from sources of supply in order to resell those goods, either further along a channel, for example a wholesaler to a retailer, or direct to end consumers, be they private individuals or industrial and commercial concerns. By being situated part of the way along the process of moving goods from makers to ultimate consumers the perspective of the intermediary must be different from that of the supplier.

There are, of course, some occasions when the channels of distribution are controlled by the supplier as a matter of business policy. When a manufacturer organizes his own distribution from source to consumer, this would normally be called a system of 'forward vertical integration'. Instead of going into a lengthy explanation of this term, let me give you an example of an industry which has been very tightly vertically integrated for a long time, although in the last twenty years, for entirely different reasons, there has been a tendency for the chain to have parts removed from it; this we shall explain.

The industry I am referring to by way of example is the oil industry. The major international oil companies have concessions for extracting the raw oil from the fields, transporting it by pipeline or tanker to other parts of the world; refining it at the ports of destination; distributing it by rail and road tanker fleets to depots strategically located in certain geographical areas; and finally moving it a further step to the service stations and petrol pumps where you and I buy it. At virtually every level of this system the supplying organizations, e.g. the major oil companies, have total control to the extent that even the service stations are owned by them with their own managers operating them. This does not of course exclude the fact that there are other service stations in private hands who work with supply contracts in conjunction with the oil companies. You will readily appreciate how much power such a system can put into the hands of the industry. The reference I made earlier to this system being broken up relates of course to the changed political situations in those countries in which the oil deposits are to be found, in the Middle East or parts of Africa. The original concessions have been considerably renegotiated and many of the nation states have nationalized the oil fields; any extraction by the oil companies has to be paid for on a royalty or some other basis.

In the area of activity in which the intermediaries are primarily concerned a more common form of integration is that known as 'horizontal'. This means that previously independent organizations carrying out the same kinds of activity (in this case distribution) join together, either by voluntary arrangement retaining a degree of independence (known as 'symbol' groups, to be elaborated on a little later), or by merger where formal and legal integration takes place, or by takeover when one party may be a reluctant victim. This can happen at any stage of the chain between supply and consumption. For example at the manufacturing end the merger of Cadbury and Schweppes brought two major companies together. In the distribution field a similar example would be the merger between Boots the Chemist and Timothy Whites. The purpose of such integration is ultimately to provide further strength in the marketplace.

As an intermediary gets bigger, and therefore more powerful, it may well enter into the process of 'backward vertical integration', in other words obtaining control, or at least very strong influence, over its sources of supply. The takeover of ownership may not be necessary. Many of the major retail groups we know, such as Woolworths, Tesco, the Co-op,

Sainsbury, have extremely close links with their suppliers to the extent that they are in a position to dictate quality, terms of delivery and other contractual obligations between the two; the supreme example in the UK is probably Marks & Spencer. These organizations are at one extreme of size – at the large end. At the other end there are the small independent outlets whose only protection against the increasing domination of the big store groups is to band together on a voluntary basis to obtain some of the advantages of size. These have become known as the 'symbol' independents, of which Spar or Mace shops are examples. In essence they are a group of independent shops, all of whom operate in the same trade, e.g. groceries, ironmongers, chemists, who cluster by agreement around a wholesaler and who undertake to buy a minimum quantity of their annual turnover, usually about 60 per cent, from that wholesaler. The latter is then in a position to buy from suppliers in bulk and obtain the favourable terms that accrue to such arrangements; he is also given a virtual guarantee of resale volume to the members of the group, and therefore can plan ahead and provide other services to the membership which individually they could not obtain. These would include such things as special promotions, management expertise in stock handling or financing, and often the provision of training both for staff and for management.

A fairly new term which has come into the distributive world is that of 'franchising'. This, in a way, is a development of the symbol independent groups but is usually set up by a supplier who provides considerably more of the capital equipment, possibly even the premises, certainly the procedures to be adopted, the provision of the goods for resale and other services. Such examples would include launderettes, Wimpy Bars, hairdressing and other trades. There is indeed no real limit to this kind of development. The major difference is that a person wishing to enter into a franchise arrangement very often has to pay for the privilege at the beginning and is more closely controlled throughout the whole operation, than would be the case under a symbol group.

Whatever the form of organization, and I am only hinting at some of them in the preceding paragraphs, our main concern in looking at the whole area of distribution from the intermediaries' point of view is to identify such differences as are commercially significant for them. What differences of perspective exist between them and suppliers that justify separate investigation and treatment?

If we regard the intermediary as the middle section of a tripartite system, our thoughts can be focused that much better on the problem. What we are here attempting to clarify are the various activities conducted by the intermediaries, unique to them, which 'add value' to the product, and their relationships with suppliers on the one hand and customers on the other. What do they do in relation to the preceding stage and the following one?

One activity undertaken by intermediaries is to collect an assortment of goods from their suppliers; so what have I done? I place the words 'collect assortment' under the column headed 'From suppliers'. Just let us pause for a moment here to imagine how difficult our lives would become if shops did not do this essential task for us! The main activity towards customers is to 'sell'. But the shop will in most cases, buy in far larger quantities from the suppliers than will ever be sold to an individual customer; therefore one activity is breaking bulk.

By continuing this process with a few more quick examples and then following them up by some discussion in the next section, we will quickly see some of the 'added values'; that intermediaries can supply.

	From suppliers	*Intermediaries*	*To Customers*
Example:	Collect assortment	Break bulk	Sell
	Anticipate demand	Communicate	Offer choice
	Market information	Interpret	Offer expertise
		Take risk	Offer credit
		Legal liability	Delivery services

6.6 'Added Values' of the Distributive System

A 'shop' serves a static geographical area which can quite easily be mapped on the basis of access by any form of public transport, bus, tube or rail; by private transport, on foot, by bicycle, by car. Therefore it must first attract: it *brings people to goods*. The population within that geographical area may change and its needs alter; then the shop must change too.

The attraction must be based on making goods *available* within a locality in such a way that the *convenience* provided for the customer is worth his money. One of these is choice; surely another way of expressing an 'assortment'. We have to be made aware, however, of the choices that confront us, we have to be told. The shopkeeper does this by display, by signs, by telling us if we ask: so he is also a *communicator* on behalf of his suppliers. To be successful in buying in he has to be an expert *interpreter* of the needs of his community.

To achieve all these things he has to take *risks*; the greatest of these, for the health of his business, may be in the *extent of credit* he gives us. In recent years the shopkeeper has been greatly helped here by 'plastic money' – the credit card, whereby the risk is transferred. He also has to *finance* the assortment of goods in anticipation of selling them; he has to hold them in stock for a period. For many goods, particularly the more bulky items, *delivery services* may be essential; how are they paid for – within the price or by a special charge?

In his relations with his suppliers, the intermediary should be a lucrative *source of market information*. He is also *liable* for the 'merchantable quality' (to use the legal expression) of the goods he sells; if you buy a product which does not do what is claimed for it, you have redress against the person from whom you bought it in law. Please note that this does not apply universally, for instance in a private sale it may not be relevant. In any cases of doubt reference should be made to the Office of Fair Trading.

To conclude these examples let me revert to the tip I offered you to start with. How badly off we would be if all these services for 'added value' were removed!

In the previous paragraphs I have italicized eleven examples of 'added value' by an intermediary. We cannot deny, therefore, that they perform an essential part in the marketing of a product. But because they are businesses with their own identities and interests, these will be interpreted for their own benefit not for that of their suppliers. There may well be a distinct conflict of interest.

6.7 Conclusion

I think we can be fairly clear by now that where the interests of suppliers and intermediaries coincide in bringing an assortment of products to the public, there can be, and indeed are, harmonious relations. But also we cannot escape from the fact that both types of organization are essentially looking after their own interests by their interpretation of the marketplace and their internal goals. That these should sometimes come into conflict is not to be wondered at. The intermediary is a marketing organization in a much fuller sense than a supplier or manufacturer. Intermediaries only have the 'added values' to offer.

Distribution channels have been, and will continue to be, the subject of evolution, and on occasion totally new methods will be invented for the movement of goods. However these may develop in the future they will be successful only to the extent that they give 'added value' to their customers for which the latter are prepared to pay. Whatever new organizational forms may develop, the functions of distribution will still have to be performed somehow; and from the intermediaries' point of view people have to be attracted to those goods they deal in.

6.8 The Customers' View

At this stage of a book about marketing it may seem superfluous to reiterate the point that the customers' view must never be lost sight of; in practice how easy it is to do just that. In the world of distribution channels some intimation of customer behaviour was given in Chapter 1 in order to illustrate (albeit somewhat superficially) the complexity of a purchase decision.

Although it is my intention during this section to expand on the word 'convenience' as it relates to the customers' viewpoint, it should be worthwhile considering it first briefly in the context of either a supplier or an intermediary. The reason for this is that customers generally react to commercial offerings from whatever source. The offering on the other hand is as a result of a deliberate managerial decision. This means, does it not, that any product offered to us, or any particular form of added value surrounding it, is not a matter of accident but one whose purpose is to achieve a particular business goal. These goals as we have also seen are the result of trading with, not one customer, but many customers. Added together these many customers represent society at large and, when we subdivide it, separate market segments. Whichever term we choose to use, any change in behaviour is the result of a lot of individual decisions caused by some alteration in attitude, or in life style, or any other reason, which is then reflected in social change. Let us attempt to be more specific by way of starting you off with an example.

Self-check

If you could conduct this self-check as a discussion with somebody else I think you would find it both more revealing and more fun. This may not always be possible, however, so I will ask you to think the implication through on your own. What we are trying to identify are ways in which our shopping behaviour has changed as a result of certain social influences or forms of social behaviour which have become widespread:

Example:

Cause of social change

More women working and bringing a second income into the household.

Effect on shopping behaviour

Less time available for the physical act of shopping due to the commitment to work: demand for speed results at the point of shopping – self-selection and supermarkets. Within the home this gives rise to opportunities for products such as TV dinners (for example semi- or fully-prepared foods which only require

heating before putting on the table)
because the housewife no longer has
the leisure to spend on the lengthy
preparation of meals.

Drawing this part of the discussion to a close it would be no exaggeration to say that the vast majority of us find 'convenience' the most important single factor in our shopping behaviour. Conversely it could be argued that those shops which pay especial care to supplying 'convenience' to their customers and by identifying new ways of doing it are likely to maintain a competitive edge.

Because 'convenience' on its own is probably too wide a word, I am going to suggest that we juggle our priorities when shopping between the time and money we have available, and the amount of effort we are prepared to invest. Sometimes one of these three takes total precedence.

It follows from this that the relative shortage of time available to shop around and look for bargains may lead to paying slightly higher prices. For example, where the car gives greater mobility, there are occasions when quite a lot of time and effort is expended to reach places, say out-of-town shopping centres or smallholdings for picking one's own fruit and vegetables, in order to save money and obtain good price bargains. There can also be no doubt that DIY effort generates a major saving of money, but not of time.

6.9 Summary

Because I stated categorically earlier that intermediaries are marketing organizations, it is in their interest to aid by whatever means are available to them the transfer of their goods out of the shops into the hands of customers; they are moving goods towards consumption through the distributive system. They will only carry out this function successfully if they add value to the products they handle and their customers are prepared to pay for it. Just as they have to contend with the competing offerings of their suppliers, and choose between them with their limited resources, so too must they recognize that customers are also juggling with limited resources which we can now refer to as 'time, money and effort'; at the beginning of this section we combined these three into the single word 'convenience' but that may be regarded as too wide a term to enable us to focus our attention effectively enough on its components.

Exercises

1 From your own observations and experience trace the vertical integration process in the UK of the brewing industry and explain the reasons why such distribution policies have developed.

2 Assume you are a shopkeeper. How would you react in the following circumstances? Would you buy into stock, or not?

You are approached by a supplier of:

	Buy	Not buy
(a) a well-established product in good demand		
(b) a new product from a large well-known company		
(c) a new product to be supported by an extensive advertising campaign to launch it		
(d) a new product from a small unknown firm, with no advertising support, but demonstrably superior to competition		
(e) a product similar to a range you already have in stock		
(f) a product range to which you are given exclusive rights within an area		

3 One of the words used in the text to summarize a major form of added value by the distribution system was 'convenience'. But the text also added that it was too general a term to give much guidance; it was sub-divided into three further words – what were they? Consider and explain a personal example of how these three words operated for you.

4 Identify from the examples below ways in which our shopping behaviour has changed as a result of social influences or forms of social behaviour which have become widespread:

Mobility provided by much wider ownership of motorcars.

The increasing cost of hiring skilled tradesmen for work in the home, e.g. decorators, plumbers, carpenters.

National Health prescriptions for medicines.

5 Imagine that you work for a soft drinks manufacturer. Design at least three distribution systems that will move your products to three different end user market segments.

7 What We Call Promotion

7.1 Introduction

What we call 'promotion' is that part of marketing most visible to public gaze and the one which, as a result, comes under most criticism. It is by no means unusual for the average person to equate marketing with selling and advertising. By now the reader of this book should be thoroughly aware that this is not so.

In this chapter we will be looking at that part of marketing which deals with 'the promotion mix'. These are the tools available to a marketer to communicate; for our purposes they may be split into two major parts:

- non-personal communication, which is 'one way' only, for example messages sent in print from a business to a consumer;
- personal communication in which a human being takes part with another human being, where 'two-way' communication can take place by the interaction between people. This second category will be looked at in detail in the next chapter.

This chapter will be concerned solely with non-personal types of marketing communication.

Therefore I am going to assume that you have been the target of a great deal of commercial communication and that you recognize it for what it is. I am also going to assume that you have been exposed to a considerable amount of other communication, which was not being directed at you as a potential member of its audience; it is often these latter messages which give us plenty of opportunity of being critical about the quantity, the content and the frequency with which we are bombarded by apparently irrelevant messages from businesses. Quite frequently we judge all commercial promotions on this latter basis and come to the conclusion, therefore, that they cannot possibly be of much influence either upon us or, because we assume that we are like other people, upon others.

The purpose of this chapter is to illustrate the main communication techniques available to business, how they may be used, interact and support one another.

7.2 Communicating Over Time and Distance

Before we get down to examining in any detail particular techniques used by business for promotion, we are going to journey along what I will call a 'communication route'. The journey started at the end of Chapter 1 Figure 1.2, 'Steps in the buying process'. Several pages earlier in Chapter 1 (in fact in Section 1.5) I told you the story of my purchase of a replacement fluorescent tube and linked this example with the figure, step by step.

You may already have noted that increasingly I am having to refer back to examples in previous chapters in addition to those contained in the current one.

7.3 Stimulus Source

You will recall that there were three main sets of stimuli in the large box at the top of the figure namely:

Personal   Social   Commercial

The stimuli we are concerned with in this chapter are quite definitely 'commercial'.

A few paragraphs ago I also used the word 'journey'. Now any journey will have two main characteristics; it will be between two points – distance; it will last over a period – time. Business communication is designed to help us, guide us, persuade us to make the journey. Often it is successful; often it is not!

If you now think of each step in the buying process and relate the kind of information you would need for each one, you will come to the rapid conclusion – there are differences.

In the example of the fluorescent tube I was not exposed to much new commercial communication; I drew mostly on my previous experience. So let us take a different illustration and this time angle it specifically from a manufacturer's point of view.

We belong to a large company and one of the products we make is garden fertilizer. What are the communication tasks that we would have to carry out to persuade potential customers to buy our products rather than anybody else's?

Step 1 Perceived need
Step 1 must surely be concerned with timing; we would generally fertilize the ground before planting, that might mean either the autumn or spring according to the kind of plant. Furthermore some reminder of the need would have to give time for the idea to get into the customers' heads in competition with a lot of other priorities.

Step 2 Internal/external search
Internal search of step 2 would be irrelevant; external is what matters for us as a supplier. Where do gardeners look for information? In appropriate magazines or during TV or radio programmes. So we would have to ensure that the information was available; and in this case, because the need had already been identified, the kind of information would probably be different – instructions for use would be relevant.

Step 3 Evaluation of alternatives
Step 3, when customers are evaluating the alternatives, means that our product is in competition with others; will 'functional' or 'symbolic' messages be more effective, or a combination of both?

Step 4 Purchase decision
Step 4's purchase decision may require that extra inducement of some special offer or advantage by buying our product. How and from where does the customer get to know about it?

Step 5 Experience recall
But if our customer had used our fertilizer last year, had run out and was replenishing his stocks, experience recall (step 5) may take him rapidly to our product, from our company, from that shop in the high street, at a certain price (which will probably have gone up from last year because of inflation). That always assumes of course that his previous experience had been a happy one – his blooms had bloomed!

All this takes time and the buyer is physically separated from the product, distance. Just because you are reminded about the need for fertilizer for your plants, do you immediately leap to your feet, go tearing off to the shops, rush back to your garden and start digging frenziedly? Of course you don't; nor should we as a supplier expect anyone else to.

Let us approach the problem from a different direction.

Stay with the fertilizer example. What means has the maker to communicate at the greatest time and distance from the potential purchase? What other means does he have getting steadily closer to the point of sale? Can you identify a series of steps from the most remote to the closest? Let me see if I can guide you through this stage by stage.

1 How many firms can you name that make fertilizer? (How do you know? Where did you get the information from?)
2 Could it be important that you know the firm? Because of its fertilizer, or because of its general reputation? If the latter, would this affect your purchases of other products from the same source? If the former, would your satisfaction with the use of their fertilizer possibly influence you to use another of their products?

3 Can you name the fertilizers from each of the firms you knew in the first question? Perhaps they have not got a special name of their own – a 'brand' name. Does this make it easier or more difficult to identify and buy them?

4 Do you know how to use the fertilizer? For which plants, at which time of year? How do you know – from commercial communication sources?

5 If you went into a garden centre would you recognize the product on display? (If it was on display).

6 A competitive product is linked with a money-off inducement; would you switch?

These questions could go on for a long time; you would have no difficulty in adding to them. But for the moment let us summarize.

1 and **2** are about reputations: they take time to build by a firm and, if successfully done, can be carried out while you are in your living room or office – you do not need to be buying, do you?

3 is about product identity. This may be very important to differentiate your product from the competition, to give it some personality of its own, to help people talk about it, ask for it, even demand it! It's easier than 'thingamebob' or 'whatyoumaycallit'. You still do not have to move from your living room to get this message.

4 gives you information, and probably persuasion. Have you left your armchair yet?

5 is much closer to buying time and place: you are in or near the shop. If the previous communications have persuaded you that you know what you want before you go in, they have succeeded so far. But do you remember how I chose that fluorescent tube? Yes, the shopkeeper did it for me. I had not been adequately preconditioned.

Finally **6** offers, and draws your attention to, an alternative. Would you be dissuaded from your first choice by the inducement at the very last point in the sequence of purchase? A display notice in the shop or on a package itself could make the difference.

I hope you got the feeling of getting nearer and nearer to that packet of fertilizer over time and distance. Suppliers want us to get to know them and their products before we even enter a shop, hence the repetition of messages on TV and radio, in newspapers and magazines, on posters, buses, trains, leaflets, displays, packages – wherever ingenuity (and the law) allows.

In this section I have deliberately avoided using the titles for these various communication or promotion activities. This I can maintain no longer. In the sections that follow the correct terms will be used and defined in relation to the idea of time and distance.

7.4 **Public Relations and Publicity**

Most promotional activities have been, and indeed still are, defined as
what they are; I am going to use a different approach. My definitions are
going to be concerned with what they do! This means that if you, as a
student or businessman, wish to know what the official definition of
public relations is, you will not find it in this book. You can ask the
Institute of Public Relations (and all the other institutes for the other
activities). My reason is simple. Descriptive definitions get out of date
very quickly in marketing, as ingenious marketers find new ways of using
old tools. If, however, we place the promotional activity titles into
categories which cover their purpose, what they are used for, you should
find fewer exceptions proving rules. There is nowadays too much overlap
between activities to maintain clear distinctions. I shall illustrate the
point with some examples at intervals throughout the next few sections.

What we will be aiming at in this section is to look at two of the
commonly used titles – public relations and publicity – and determine
what they do in the communication process on the time and distance
principle; indeed this principle will be the common core running throughout our discussions of promotional techniques. There is some confusion
about the two terms mentioned, partly brought about in the UK by the
widespread use of American terminology, through their marketing
textbooks. They tend to use 'publicity' in the way we would use 'public
relations'. In my opinion there is justification in using both terms but
with different meanings and uses.

7.5 **Public Relations**

On our journey through the communication route, PR is the most
remote from the point of any purchasing. Firstly it is not concerned with
a public (and we have been thinking almost exclusively about a consumer
public or segment) but with several publics; in fact with any public for
whom the reputation of a business may be significant. Forget marketing
for a moment, and consider which publics may be of importance to a
firm. Let us approach it by considering with whom a business must deal,
either directly or indirectly, to carry on its business.

You are in business and you must relate to a variety of publics:

1 You buy goods in from your *suppliers* who are concerned with your
reputation for credit worthiness.
2 If you are quoted on the Stock Exchange the *shareholders* will watch
your activities closely and your reputation for profit and dividends.
3 You may be very concerned with labour relations and therefore the
trade unions and their members could be important to you.

4 Given that you may want to expand and enlarge your premises, relations with the neighbourhood population and the local council may be significant.

5 And always there are your customers to consider: they will have an interpretation of your reputation – which incidentally may not be the one which you hope for! There may also be consumer associations, *Which* magazine, and other forms of consumer organizations.

Four out of the five are nothing to do with the sale of your products, but have a lot to do with enabling your business to operate! And there are of course other publics which may affect, and be affected by, your business which I have not illustrated.

The most important word I have used in connection with PR so far is 'reputation'. By focusing on its purpose, my definition of public relations would be:

● *any communication activities designed to create, or maintain, a planned reputation among one or more publics.*

A key word is 'planned'. PR is not accidental, or should not be. It is an element of the whole of the communication mix available to a company, but because of its variety of audiences (publics) has more concern with the 'corporate image' than with products. If we relate this idea of PR to some well-known companies you will recognize it in practice.

Self-check

What planned reputation have the following companies earned for themselves amongst the publics listed and – because this book is about marketing – amongst potential customers? (Please note that there is always some danger in using illustrations like this, as they may rapidly become out of date.)

Marks & Spencer	employees	BP	financial
	customers		institutions
Philips	suppliers		government
	customers		customers
House of Fraser	shareholders	Tate & Lyle	shareholders
(e.g. Harrods)	customers		customers

There is every possibility that the answers we have given about the reputations of these companies may differ; you may have your own view, and I may have mine. The degree to which they coincide will be one measure of the success of the organizations' PR activities!

Surely M&S are renowned for treating their employees well and providing good quality products. Philips, as a multinational company of Dutch origin, would be regarded by its suppliers as sound, a good credit risk and a healthy business to have as a customer; to you and me the slogan used by Philips of 'Simply years ahead' must be familiar. 'Tiny' Rowland's Lonrho Group was stopped by the Monopolies Commission from taking over the House of Fraser; a bid of that kind usually favours shareholders by pushing up share values. I would doubt if Harrods' customers would change their opinion of that store's reputation. BP the British oil giant, was recently 'privatized – the latest word for denationalization. You may remember the share issue to the public which flopped badly with the Stock Market crash in the autumn of 1987, in spite of a great deal of public relations, publicity and advertising.

Nevertheless this flop really had nothing at all to do with the trading reputation of BP.

I wonder if you remember the now famous battle of 'Mr Cube' against nationalization (it was some years ago), but the shareholders reaped the benefit and customers have always been well served by Tate & Lyle, a company with almost a monopoly in sugar in the UK which has never abused its economic power.

7.6 Publicity

Some people say that there is no such thing as bad publicity! I wonder. But of course not all publicity need be bad, it just always seems that way! Whichever way it goes, it can enhance or diminish a reputation, and therefore has close links, indeed overlap, with PR. There are some essential differences, however.

By no means all publicity is planned by the business concerned; it appears in the media at the discretion of editors because it appears to them to be newsworthy to their publics – viewers, listeners or readers. This is not to deny that many legitimate pieces of news are published because they have been supplied to the media by the firms. Pick up any technical journal, for example, and there will be 'stories' about new products, inventions or people relevant to the readership. Do you ever watch *Tomorrow's World* on TV? The items featured on that programme did not appear out of thin air! The creation of publicity for a firm can be a highly creative and ingenious job. I wonder how many of you readers have ever tried to get reports of some local association's activities into the press.

A further distinction that I would like to make about publicity is that it may be about anything connected with a business including products; whereas PR is much more concerned with corporate image.

In a way 'publicity' could be regarded as the 'poor man's PR'. In practice it is only the larger organizations that come to our public notice through PR because of their large resources, and hence power. Many more operate PR in their own circles about which you and I will never know. But any firm can attempt to gain publicity by being newsworthy. So publicity is:

- *the planned, or unplanned, appearance of some newsworthy item about any aspect of a business*

7.7 Summary

The key to PR is the 'public' concerned; the key to publicity is the 'subject matter'. There is no doubt, however, that these two communication techniques overlap.

7.8 Advertising and Direct Mail

Because everybody I have ever met has an opinion, good or bad, about advertising, I propose to start this section with my definition and use that as the basis for discussion. The purpose of advertising is:

- *to influence product-related behaviour through planned messages in hired media.*

You will note that I am still defining these relatively familiar terms on the basis of what they attempt to do, not what they are! I repeat the distinction here, because frankly I consider it most important in enabling us later to handle the complexity of integrating a variety of communication techniques for marketing purposes. An immediate illustration would be of value.

In the last section I quoted a slogan formerly used extensively by Philips on all its advertisements – 'Simply years ahead'.

But that slogan was used by me to illustrate PR; now I am putting it into advertising! It is just this sort of conflict which I wish to avoid by defining communication techniques by their purpose rather than what they are. To elaborate further:

'Simply years ahead' (the Philips slogan) appeared in all advertisements planned by that company; advertisements for razors, TV sets, recording equipment and so on. The question is, what purpose does the slogan perform? Is it specifically related to the product in the advertisement, or does it apply to the reputation of Philips as a company? Surely the latter. In my terms, then, that part of the advertisement containing the slogan is PR, the rest of it (product-related) is 'advertising'. The medium and the vehicle by which the message is sent are identical. What I am getting at here is that most definitions imply that anything inserted into 'bought media' is advertising; this is what marketers play havoc with!

How could Philips possibly keep getting their slogan across to their publics (note the plural) without using the media? We should now take a closer look at my definition of advertising.

'To influence'

Being a lecturer I have the great advantage of meeting many people connected with marketing, from many industries and firms, who believe the myth, no delusion, that advertising sells; it does not! *It does not!* If it did, marketing, indeed successful trading, would become so easy – just advertise! Spend more, sell more. How simple! A moment's thought shows that this is just not true. Another moment's consideration, however, also tells us that advertising must 'work', for if it did not then business is being extremely foolish in laying out money for it.

What must be recognized about advertising, indeed about all marketing communications, is that there are too many things that may come between the sending of a message by a firm (advertising) and the actions of a consumer in a shop or a buyer in a factory. If you are unconvinced, stop right here, go back and reread Chapters 1 and 2.

Nobody has yet been able to say how advertising works for any one individual, and because advertising *can* only work on the individual, even though there may be many of them, nobody really knows how it works. What we do know is that it is part of a communication process; that if a person actually 'gets the message', metaphorically it goes 'in one ear', is mixed up with what is between the two and then comes 'out the other' in some form of behaviour. Where most communications go wrong in terms of their effectiveness is between the two ears!

Self-check

1 Why have you, or have you not, joined the Forces from their advertising? (The army, navy and air force advertise extensively. What goes on *in your mind* when you see such advertisements makes them effective or ineffective.)
2 When you last bought flowers for your wife or girlfriend was it advertising that made you do it? Most likely a desire to please or a guilty conscience!
3 Now be honest with yourself and decide what advertising has influenced you, and what is more, why it did so. There is only one real answer – *because you wanted what it offered.*

'Behaviour'

The behaviour advertising attempts to influence is buying behaviour; this is what makes it 'product'-related' (may I remind you that the way I am currently using the word, 'product' and 'service' are synonymous). This being so, advertising is open, sometimes strident, certainly unambiguous in what it is trying to do, and we know it. But because behaviour may be the end result of a communication process, there are also the preceding steps which have to be negotiated. Of all the tools available to marketing, advertising is unquestionably the most versatile and the most widely used. Its overriding virtue is that the message it conveys is entirely in the hands of its designer.

'Hired media'

I have chosen to use the word 'hired' in this context because to me it conveys a more temporary feeling than 'bought', the latter word being more generally used when talking about advertising. One hires for a short space of time and then returns the object to its owner. During that period of hire, however, full use may be made of it. 'It' in this context is time or space.

The media for advertising are any means by which a message may be conveyed to an audience so long as it has been paid for and is not in the direct ownership of the sponsor of the message. TV and radio readily fall into this category; newspapers and magazines also; outdoor and indoor, stationary or mobile, posters on hoardings, on buses and trains can all be included as hired space. When the hire contract has expired the time or space becomes available to someone else.

7.9 'The Shotgun and the Rifle'

Although many laymen ascribe powers to advertising which in reality do not exist, there is no question that it is the least expensive form of communicating with large numbers of people. That is not to say that the communication is necessarily effective; nor that it reaches all the people at whom it is directed. A great deal of waste takes place. However, if in the end a meaningful result is obtained, the advertising may be described as effective. Waste is caused by a number of things, and the student of advertising should be aware of the most important of them, if only because a number of different measurement criteria can be constructed which may conceal rather than reveal the true value of the advertising. In the self-check I asked you if recruitment advertising for the Forces had inspired you to join the colours. For the sake of this discussion we'll assume that advertisements seeking officer recruits for the navy, or for the army or the air force, appearing in any one of the Sunday colour supplements, will each be printed approximately $1\frac{1}{4}$ million times. Assuming that all copies are successfully distributed and sold, this figure would become known as the 'circulation'; for purposes of advertising and media planning, and to establish appropriate charges, circulation figures are important to the buyers of space. Similarly the numbers of people viewing or listening to broadcast media are also regularly monitored.

Supposing a business is prepared to pay £5000 for a single advertisement in one of the Sunday colour supplements with a circulation of $1\frac{1}{4}$ million, each individual copy would cost the advertiser 0.4p. If we further suppose that each copy is read by two people (in practice it may be considerably more) the cost is halved to 0.2p per reader. On such suppositions advertising can be fantastically cheap. You must, however, have already spotted the flaws in these two examples. Because circulation figures, and costs, are changing so rapidly, please do not take the figures used above as anything more than illustrative. In practice any advertiser would need to find out exactly the claimed circulation and the accurate costs of media space and time for any planned insertion.

The first major flaw is the hypothesis that either the circulation figure, or the readership figure, in any way represents the number of people who actually see the advertisement! A media salesman might interject here with some indignation that I am misrepresenting the case. I am drawing attention to a form of 'erosion' in advertising that is underestimated (by students and businessmen). I will pursue my argument diagrammatically.

Note that the residual 10 000 may be all that is required. But at which point, or points, is a measurement taken for control purposes? Obviously circumstances will vary; but if the advertising is to be properly managed some attempt must be made.

At each stage of the diagram I have reduced by half; this was purely arbitrary. Research should be undertaken to determine both the stage and the rate of the erosion.

Fig 7.1 *'Erosion' in advertising*

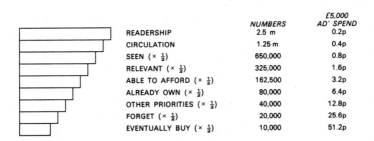

		NUMBERS	£5,000 AD' SPEND
	READERSHIP	2.5 m	0.2p
	CIRCULATION	1.25 m	0.4p
	SEEN (× ½)	650,000	0.8p
	RELEVANT (× ½)	325,000	1.6p
	ABLE TO AFFORD (× ½)	162,500	3.2p
	ALREADY OWN (× ½)	80,000	6.4p
	OTHER PRIORITIES (× ½)	40,000	12.8p
	FORGET (× ½)	20,000	25.6p
	EVENTUALLY BUY (× ½)	10,000	51.2p

An actual example of this sort of process was published in *Marketing* on 25 February 1981: Sir Clive Sinclair launched his ZX80 personal computer in January 1980 at a price of £99.95. The target cost of the advertising campaign per order was set at £15 with double that figure being an acceptable maximum – £30. At the time of publication of the article the promotional cost per unit was £12.50. This kind of control is relatively easy for a mail order operation; you know exactly how many units you are selling. The criteria could not be the same for a Yorkie chocolate bar.

Self-check

Have a quick look back to the diagram and identify for yourself that point beyond which the advertiser can have no further influence upon the effectiveness of his advertisement. While you are doing this bear in mind that the advertiser has absolutely no control whatever over the reaction to his message of any reader. Think of your own behaviour as a reader when thumbing through a colour supplement, or for that matter any other magazine. How many of the advertisements do you actually look at? When we think of it that way, would you agree that all the advertiser can in fact do is to 'expose' his message to his audience? Surely then the key point is that of 'seen'. The advertiser can only give readers an 'opportunity to see' (often referred to as OTS).

Continuing to review the situation still further, the example I used preceding the diagram was that of a single insertion. One advertisement, even costing £5000 in full and glorious colour, does not frankly give many 'opportunities to see'. Supposing you were choosing a new electric lawnmower, estimate for yourself how many times you would need to see some form of marketing promotion, including advertisements, before you began to be persuaded which one to buy, or between which ones to choose. It will not take a great deal of further thought for you to realize that the kind of product concerned with the advertising may largely determine the required opportunities to see for a potential purchaser.

It is a regrettable fact that a great deal of advertising expenditure is wasted because companies fail to appreciate the amount of 'exposure' required to give the requisite number of OTSs to a target audience.

The closest connection to advertising for the vast majority of us is the insertion of a few lines into the classified columns of the local paper, or possibly the London evening paper, in order to sell our car privately. If we attract ten inquiries out of a circulation of hundreds of thousands, or possibly even millions, we are almost certain to make the sale. But it gives a very graphic picture of the amount of erosion. In this way advertising has a very 'shotgun' approach: it scatters its message as widely as it can hoping that within the scatter it will reach its target audience. The four things helping it to succeed will be the correct design and combination of:

- *message*;
- *media*;
- *timing*;
- *frequency*.

7.10 Direct Mail

Direct mail has a pinpoint accuracy denied to advertising; it is the rifle! Its purpose is:

- *to influence product-related behaviour through planned messages delivered to an individual at his home or place of work*

The word 'mail' should not, therefore, be taken literally; the key is the individual, and his letter box. Anything shoved through it can be classed as direct mail.

Within limits advertising media can be reasonably specific; for example not many people other than architects read the *Architects' Journal*. But it may be difficult to isolate, shall we say, the Greater London area; direct mail could, always provided there is a list of addresses. This is its major problem. Building, then keeping up to date, a direct mail list can be a difficult and time-consuming problem; it must therefore be worth the expense. That it so often is has been proved by the fact that specialist agencies have grown up for the purpose; many professional bodies, including the Institute of Marketing, have membership lists which can be used for mailings. Every business has available its own customer list, and probably one of prospects!

Apart from the different method of delivery all the rules applicable to advertising apply. If the 'mail' is personally addressed it is the more likely to reach its target; but a lot of it is not. The addressee may be a job title, for example 'The Training Manager'; sometimes the name of the firm is deemed to be sufficient. Whilst any weakening of the addressee will lose accuracy, the cost of personalized addressing may be regarded as uneconomic.

7.11 How Much to Spend?

For some reason, and I do not know what it is, a special piece of jargon has grown up around the amount of money to be spent on advertising. It is known as the advertising 'appropriation' – at least in a great deal of the

literature. Individual firms may have their own names. Similarly textbooks dealing with advertising will illustrate a number of methods by
which the 'appropriation' may be set. Theory and practice differ. If not
invariably, then very close to it, the amount to be spent on advertising,
indeed a whole promotional budget, will be decided on the basis of
financial constraint offset against an anticipated reward – the ratio of
input to output.

There is frankly no real formula, although a great deal of learned
research, computer stimulation models, operational research techniques
and so on have been devoted to attempting to find one. The trouble is
that there are far too many unknowns about the effect of advertising for
any real accurate cost measurements to be laid down in any set of rules.
However, in individual cases every business advertising should attempt
some model of its own, peculiar to its products and its markets, in order
to accumulate some 'wisdom' beyond pure hunch! The best way to set
about doing this is to be quite certain from the outset what the
advertising is attempting to achieve.

In brief, marketing communication objectives may be summarized by
'three As'.

- changing or maintaining *awareness*;
- changing or maintaining *attitudes*;
- changing or maintaining *actions*.

7.12 Sales Promotion and Packaging

Our journey along what I have called the 'communication route' has so
far been fuelled by the four techniques of PR and publicity, advertising
and direct mail. Assuming that they have been reasonably successful they
should have transported us to the first two general objectives, which I
summarized in the last section by calling them the three *As*.

awareness – attitude – action.

The next step is to introduce you to that technique whose main purpose is
to generate action or purchase behaviour. This technique is called sales
promotion.

During the course of this chapter I have used the rather formal word of
'communication' quite a lot; let me become more colloquial. Let us
imagine two people talking to each other about somebody else – a
pastime most of us indulge in from time to time. Would you not agree
that it becomes much easier if we know whom we are talking about and
we can refer to that person by name? Much the same applies to a

company or product. So if you are a company wanting to talk to consumers it makes it easier for both if you can call your product something. Taking the opposite approach – it is easier for a purchaser to ask for something by name or to be able to recognize it either by name or by appearance. This is known as 'branding' or giving a product a 'brand name' – something which I referred to in Section 7.3. One of the ways by which marketing keeps continuity links throughout the variety of techniques used in the promotion mix is through the name and the appearance of a product. In this way sales promotion can be linked 'backwards' to advertising and 'forwards' to packaging in our journey.

We are now ready to define sales promotion, whose purpose is:

- *to offer an inducement by temporarily attaching additional value to a form of behaviour.*

Like the previous definitions, this one is a little bit cryptic and needs some elaboration around its key components, of which there are four.

- *Form of behaviour*
  Sales promotion is directed at trade buyers (industrial or intermediary) and consumers to induce them to buy; it is also used to encourage and reward sales personnel.
- *Additional value*
  Taking each of the three targets in order, a salesman will receive, say, a bonus or a holiday in the Bahamas for two, if he exceeds by a certain amount his sales quota. A wholesaler or retailer could receive a 'baker's dozen' (thirteen cases for the price of twelve). The consumer may get almost anything from a plastic daffodil to a double pack or some other inducement.
- *Inducement*
  In the previous paragraph the behaviour is rewarded by the added value, something is obtained for nothing provided a purchase has been made. The inducement is the offer of that reward before the behaviour has taken place.
- *Temporary*
  No inducement must be allowed to become permanent; as soon as it does, it ceases to be one.

Sales promotion is seldom mentioned in the context of industrial marketing; its practice in industry is just as valid as in the consumer world. The inducements may be different but the purpose is identical. There should, however, be no ambiguity at all; sales promotion is not a 'slush' fund! Some industries, pharmaceuticals being a case in point, are severely regulated as to what they are, and are not, allowed to do. Nor can taking a customer out to lunch (entertaining) be disguised in the accounts as sales promotion. The inducement is obligatory and linked to the behaviour; there is no discretion to the offer.

Self-check

One of the classic advertising and sales promotion campaigns, which will live long in marketing history, was Esso's 'Put a tiger in your tank'; you may remember it. If so, separate the advertising from the sales promotion.

The advertising, you will recall, was to be seen everywhere, on TV, on posters, in newspapers and magazines, using the cartoon tiger in all the illustrations. This was a major break with tradition for the company, who have again reverted to the real and natural animal. However, it caught the fancy of children! On that basis the sales promotional link appealed to the young, who in turn badgered their parents for tiger tails, cuddly tigers and other paraphernalia when filling up the car with petrol. Esso began a sales promotional war between the oil companies at the filling stations. For the next couple of years the range of offers varied from the useful to the useless. Those days are a far cry from the present when competition is almost exclusively based on price.

Unfortunately sales promotional offers have generated so much ingenuity that a special language has appeared with all sorts of titles to indicate the type of scheme being offered to the trade or through trade channels; money off, coupons, bingo labels, redemption offers, banded packs, self-liquidating offers and so on. I do not propose to dwell on this voluminous terminology, except to say that they all relate directly to products at the point of sale. Other examples with which most people are familiar are 'sales' by the big stores, extra bonuses to a sales force on a special drive for the launch of a new product, and, say, an additional discount to industrial customers for the clearance of a line becoming obsolescent.

7.13 Packaging

Packaging is the last chance, in consumer marketing at least, for a business to 'talk to' a potential customer. In the promotion mix packaging communicates; its other tasks of protection and handling relate to distribution. Obviously one has influenced the other. The advent of self-selection and self-service in retailing, and in cash and carry, greatly increased the need for point-of-sale promotion around the product – packaging. The purpose of packaging is:

- *to provide visibility for the product amongst competing brands.*

To obtain the visibility, and its opposite from the customer's point of view – recognition – every technique of 'catching the eye' must be skilfully used. But even more is required: the customer must be made familiar with the appearance of the packaged product by advance communication, usually through advertising, so that in the store he or she is confronted by friends not strangers.

Self-check

With the number of electrical gadgets around these days, batteries are not an uncommon purchase. Some years ago Ever Ready were upset at the suggestion of designers that their typeface should be modernized (to what it is today). The company believed that the former type had been the main factor giving recognition to customers; in fact research had indicated that the real visibility of the products lay in the colour combination of blue, orange and white. The next time you go into an electrical shop or a service station (anywhere that sells batteries) see from what distance you can identify the makes.

The visibility/recognition factor calls to the consumer's mind all the associations that may have been learned about the product, in the past, some good, some bad. If the balance is generally on the favourable side, these associations are enormously helpful to the promotional efforts of the maker.

7.14 Merchandising and Display

All the techniques we have looked at so far in this chapter could be confined to use by a producer; I do not mean that in practice they are only used by producers, but we could isolate them in this way. This section, however, deals with two more communication activities that can take place only at the point of sale and, therefore, are much more commonly associated with distribution or the intermediaries between producer and customer.

Self-check

In the previous chapter I was careful to describe 'intermediaries' in a certain way, and then developed by discussion and illustration the terms 'vertical' and 'horizontal' integration. Perhaps if I remind you of oil and brewing you will recall the distinctions made about different types of distributive organization. (If you have any problems, refer back to Section 6.5.)

Then we considered intermediaries to be 'independent of their sources of supply', and went on to discuss the various types of integration when a supplier sets out to obtain control, in lesser or greater degree, over the channels. Because merchandising is an activity conducted at the point of sale, those channels integrated to their sources of supply can be much more easily organized and managed. So what is merchandising?

Because, as you are now fully aware, I am relating all definitions of these promotional activities to their purposes rather than their content, I must first explain that merchandising has, historically, always been considered a part of sales promotion. In recent years its importance has grown to such an extent that it warrants separation.

If I am going to make a distinction between sales promotion and merchandising, can we first check our definition of sales promotion? Do you remember the most important key word of all? (Refer back to the definition in Section 7.12.)

The word was 'inducement' connected with some form of behaviour. So from our point of view merchandising must be something different from that, must have a different purpose. The purpose of merchandising is:

● *to give customers information about, and easy access to, products near or at the point of sale.*

Using an excess of imagination close your eyes and 'wander into a store that you know well'. Now blot out every sign; remove every person whom you might be tempted to ask; and find your way to the section selling coffees, powdered milk, sugar, etc. What (apart from people) have you blotted out?

Perhaps we can share a couple of experiences, and as we go relate them to merchandising.

On relatively rare occasions I accompany my wife on some shopping expedition which takes us into a large department store in my home town. Because these visits are infrequent, I do not know the geography and frankly find the place confusing. I am constantly having to search for direction signs, look for escalators or staircases or lifts, seek out the products when, at last, I find myself in their vicinity and then finally, if in spite of my exasperation I have actually bought something, search for someone to whom I can give my money! Now believe me I am not a typical shopper and I know people who thoroughly enjoy going to such stores, find their way about with ease of familiarity and love the atmosphere.

Merchandising is just about everything you blotted out. Can I do it with you? Several weeks ago we ran out of Coffeemate in my staff room.

So during an interval in teaching I crossed the road to a large super-market which I had never been in before. Through the swing doors and into the mighty hall I went without the faintest idea where to find what I wanted. I was surrounded by information in abundance (sometimes the abundance becomes so great as to be confusing!). In the middle distance there was a sign announcing 'coffee', so assuming an association I headed in that direction. Negotiating rows of identical shelving, stuffed with products from floor to above my head, I sought my powdered milk! How often do you find that you cannot see for looking? By the time I had negotiated the checkout that purchase had taken me ten minutes – ridiculous isn't it? The next time I did it in three! But if we change the product to something much more complicated from the electrical department of a major store, the information required assumes greater importance.

A Black & Decker drill with sanding attachment was the object of my search. Two local stores were known to me (through local press advertising) offering this range at reduced prices. Once in the shops I had to locate them; then I had to obtain the necessary technical information and make comparisons between different drills; which model would best operate the attachment. For this I needed technical literature and leaflets or a close look at the packaging giving the details of performance, wattage, price and so on. All this means access by a customer like myself.

In the definition above I used the word 'products'; this was because the individual customer is looking for a product. Take the role of the shop or store manager, he will think less of products but more of merchan-dise – the range of products that he offers, how it is displayed – and therefore help his customers reach it.

7.15 Display

You must at some time or another have heard somebody use the expression 'He (or she) keeps making a display of himself!' Let me ask you to substitute another word for 'display' – what would it be? 'Exhibi-tion'? The meaning implicit in such a remark is not intended to be flattering when associated with a person's behaviour. Why not? Probably because in our society we do not consider it appropriate to draw attention to oneself in normal circumstances. For an actor or a model in their professional roles, however, such behaviour would be both ex-pected and entirely appropriate.

Following the last paragraph a definition of 'display' must be fairly obvious. Its purpose is:

● *to draw attention to a product by making it conspicuous at the point of sale.*

There should be absolutely no inhibitions in a store! However, no product can be held permanently on display, any more than a sales promotional offer can be. The result would be self-defeating. Similarly only a few products can be 'on display' at any one time; relatively the others must remain in the background. Now there must be the danger of some conflict of interest here; the supplier wants his products brought before the customers as often and as conspicuously as possible. The store manager may want to promote, through display, some special lines, some obsolescent stocks (to get rid of them), a competing brand or for that matter nothing particular at all. A chain of stores may well decide that they will have a corporate display and merchandising policy that is uniform; wherever a customer may see it recognition is instant.

What should be very clear by now is that merchandising and display are two promotional activities outside the control of suppliers but rather controlled by the intermediaries. This does not mean, however, that the suppliers let it go by default, far from it. After all, any means of influencing a potential customer is a legitimate area of interest for the marketer – even if that customer is, so to speak, at second remove. So in order to do this suppliers seek to help the shops in their merchandising and display activities with personnel, materials, money and in the case of the bigger stores by providing specially designed promotional aids to order.

Self-check

What product display characteristics are common to stores like Woolworth, Marks & Spencer, Littlewoods and British Home Stores? Does a department store (like Selfridges, or Debenhams) have the same kind of product layout? How does it differ? Do the same signs appear in the windows of the big stores as in the local suburban shop? Why do shop chains appear to favour uniformity? Does merchandising policy of an organization like Sainsbury differ from that of Tesco? In what respect? To what extent can suppliers influence in-store activity?

From this review you will certainly find some of the common denominators of merchandising and display. For example Woolworth, M&S, Littlewoods and BHS are rather special kinds of store with distinctive open-top counters for the products – they are sometimes referred to as 'bazaar stores', an out-of-date term which reflects their origins from the market stalls. Department stores have their uniqueness in the separation of products into distinct areas (departments) with a multiplicity of display appropriate to the variety of stock. Their window displays are probably artistically the best in the country; this may be because they are big enough to employ really professional people to carry out the window dressing. Nor are we likely to find permanent banners in these windows as we so often can in a suburban parade.

The question of uniformity of shop chains will usually relate back to segmentation policy: an organization appealing to a part of the population. Shall we test this idea? Do you believe that Sainsbury and Tesco appeal to the same people? I do not. In spite of the fact that they will both stock the same nationally branded products, that they both have their 'own brands', that they both deal primarily in food, they have a different 'atmosphere', a different 'feeling' – generated by totally different merchandising and display approaches.

If you remember, until a few years ago Tesco used to have Green Shield Stamps; in the high street competition of the late 1970s they were beginning to cost too much. Amid a lot of publicity Tesco discontinued the stamps; it made a major change in its merchandising policy. Since then its policy has been 'pile it high and sell it cheap' (and please accept some oversimplification). The appeal was, and is, broadly to very price-conscious, generally working-class customers. Sainsbury by contrast is usually considered to be more subdued, conservative, good quality, middle class and appeals accordingly.

A supplier can influence only those with some freedom of action. In a big organization a branch manager has not the discretion to exercise outside the policy of the head office; as a result any agreement on merchandising is usually negotiated at high management levels and implemented at local level. The organization of the supplier has to be tailored to meet these circumstances.

7.16 Summary

Merchandising has grown in importance to such an extent that it deserves to be separated from what used to be an 'umbrella' term – sales promotion. We have drawn clear distinctions between the two. The former is still part of the total communication system available to marketing for the benefit of the customer, but is almost totally a technique available to intermediaries rather than suppliers. Merchandising is concerned with the environment around products at their point of sale. Similarly we find display also at the point of sale – making products conspicuous.

7.17 Integrating the Promotion Mix

Altogether we have examined during this chapter eight different promotional techniques spanning a marketing system from supplier, through intermediaries, to consumers; all of them have been non-personal and therefore one-way. There is no direct feedback of their results or their effectiveness. Indeed one of the great difficulties in marketing is how to identify the effect of each promotional tool or of all of them operating together.

The trouble is in practice that the vast majority of firms cannot possibly use all the techniques we have discussed. Really only the very substantial businesses mass-producing large quantities of products have to employ mass marketing in order to maintain the corresponding levels of consumption.

By putting the eight non-personal promotion technique into a diagram, the way they complement each other can be shown by overlapping them as they move customers through awareness, attitude and action over time and distance.

Bearing in mind what I was saying a couple of pages ago, namely that few firms can afford to use all these techniques, the one that is most common, most versatile and most effective is advertising. After all, advertising can create awareness about a product, can generate (favourable) attitudes and, when the message connects with a potential customer's genuine need, can lead to action. However, there are millions of products that are never even advertised! Their manufacturers rely solely on visibility at the point of sale, either of the product itself or of its packaging, through the cooperation of the outlet. Members of the public would expect to find these products in the right kind of shop: biscuits in a supermarket, nails and screws in an ironmonger, writing paper in a stationer's.

How would you put together an integrated promotional plan in the story which follows?

Fig 7.2   *Overlapping effect of promotional techniques*

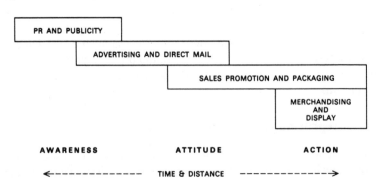

In 1978 a young businessman in Ontario, Canada, commissioned the building of a windjammer (or a three-masted schooner – sailing ship) for use on the Great Lakes. She was to have a crew of four, and able to accommodate ten passengers for a sailing holiday; they could help the crew or take it easy as they chose. A year later the boat was launched amidst a great deal of *publicity* with the Lieutenant Governor of the province and most of the other local notables in attendance. The news media had a field day as the *Challenge*, the first ship of its kind ever to be launched on the Great Lakes, went into the water. She was to ply her trade in the summer months on Lake Erie or Lake Ontario, and in winter sail down to the Bahamas and continue operating there.

Through that first year and into the second *Challenge* continued to attract publicity, but not passengers! At least not in sufficient numbers. A limited amount of cash remained after the high capital cost of building the boat, and only a small amount of advertising could be afforded. In the spring of 1981 the boat was nearly sold. At the time the owner could not really understand why all the very favourable publicity had not 'worked'. Do you?

Given that your funds are pretty strictly limited, what would you have done?

1 Identify your market segment.
2 What do they need that your 'offering' will match?
3 How do you reach them?
4 What promotion techniques would you employ?
5 How would you help them to take action?
6 How would you measure the results?

In the latter half of the 1981 summer season, *Challenge* was carrying her quota of holidaymakers and bookings for the Caribbean winter were going fine. But the whole promotional mix had been changed.

Windjammer Sailing Ltd was the name given to the small private company running the *Challenge*. The intention was to convey an image; but note that the word 'holiday' did not appear – it would, after all, have made the name a bit long. Initially, apart from normal holidaymakers, attempts were made to appeal to parties of children for which there was some, albeit limited, success. But who are the normal holidaymakers and how does one reach them in the mass of a population running into millions spread over an area as large as Europe? In spite of the publicity of the launch and the limited amount of advertising, applications for a week's cruise were minimal. Of the three *As* – action seemed to be missing. Why?

The publicity was 'newsworthy' but did not tell people how to book, or even encourage them to do so. You might say, 'But surely people could think that out for themselves.' Why should they? There is always a great deal of competitive activity which makes things easy; they do not have to think; they follow the direction signs that are given to them, for example:

Fill in a coupon with name and address for a brochure.
Telephone a booking and follow up with payment (as instructed).
Go to a holiday travel agent (names, addresses and phone numbers listed).

By trying to go it alone, the limited advertising by Windjammer Sailing gave insufficient numbers of OTSs (for reference see Section 7.9) to overcome the erosion, and gave insufficient guidance to make inquiry easy.

An anxious first year of operation compelled the company to review its promotion for 1981. The major change was to put the *Challenge* on to the books of a travel agent specializing in waterborne holidays and joining up with a sailing fleet, through the same agent, in the Bahamas. Of course this arrangement cost commission to the agent; but it is better to pay commission from a profit than to pay nothing from a loss. Promotion could now be increased on a shared basis, and it was. Posters, brochures and leaflets could be circulated by mail through the agents' customer list, both in Canada and in the USA. Put in summary form: the merchandising of an intermediary made a major contribution to the action part of the three *As* sequence.

Unfortunately *Challenge* had to be sold as the financial struggle became too great for the young businessman and his family. She is, however, still sailing the Great Lakes but only after considerable adaptation and lengthening by her new owners.

7.18 Chapter Summary

This chapter has covered eight major techniques of what is commonly called the 'promotion mix'. All of those illustrated were 'non-personal' in which human interaction was not involved and therefore the effect of the communications could not be immediately gauged; there is none of the 'feedback' possible when people are talking to each other. The techniques were defined around their purposes, rather than the more usual practice of defining them as a particular activity. It was done this way because ingenuity is such that marketers will often find new uses for old techniques distorting the formal definitions and rendering them rather more confusing than illuminating.

The chapter also continued the framework laid down early in the book that a consumer approaches a purchase in a series of steps, which I have summarized by the principle of 'time and distance'. Different kinds of communication are appropriate at different stages of the approach in order to prepare a consumer for the act of purchase: this preparation is embodied in the three words 'awareness', 'attitude' and 'action'.

Exercises

1 You are planning an advertising campaign to launch a new drug to doctors, starting with 25 000 general practitioners before moving on to hospitals. Your previous experience in the field tells you that each doctor really needs four OTSs, and a good previous mixture has been two direct mail shots to the 4000 doctors with whom your twenty sales personnel keep in regular touch, and three insertions in medical journals, the two media complementing each other. Finally a sample of the new drug is either to be left with the doctors by the salesmen or included with one of the direct mail letters.

Through market research it is known that each GP prescribes, on average, similar competing drugs 140 times a year; your target is to achieve 40 000 prescriptions in the first year. Your costs are estimated as follows:

Samples £1
Each direct mail letter £0.25
Three advertisements £5000

1 Calculate your target market share of the prescriptions.
2 Would you send the samples and the direct mail letters to (a) all GPs or (b) the 4000 GPs only?
3 Calculate, according to your choice in question 2 the total cost of samples and direct mail and then add the total for the three advertisements.
4 Calculate the promotional cost per target prescription. Note: bearing in mind that the outcome will always be uncertain, you are hoping to contain your promotional costs between 20p and 30p per prescription.
5 If this mixture is successful, how many prescriptions would you obtain if the promotional costs were 20p each, and how many at 30p each?

2 I gave each of the eight techniques listed below a definition relating to its purpose: can you fill in the space provided the key word(s) from each definition without looking them up? Have a try. Remember the order I took them was governed by the principle of 'time and distance'.

Promotional technique		*Key word*
Public relations		_____
Publicity		_____
Advertising		_____
Direct mail		_____
Sales promotion	Branding	_____
Packaging		_____
Merchandising		_____
Display		_____

3 Which of the following examples would, according to my definitions, be classed as public relations and which as publicity?

1 The publication of a company's annual accounts and chairman's report in the financial press – space paid for by their company.

2 A Member of Parliament opening a new factory in his constituency with write-up and photographs in the local press.

3 A television report of a workforce voting on an industrial dispute.

4 The joint announcement by government and a firm of agreement on a major project, such as the Thames barrier at Woolwich (for flood control).

4 Advertising objectives were summarized in the text as:

● changing or maintaining _____

● changing or maintaining _____

● changing or maintaining _____

Can you fill in the blank spaces? To what principle are these three words related?

5 Exercise **2** and **4** identify the information required to reproduce the diagram illustrating the overlapping effect of promotional techniques: given that information can you reproduce the diagram?

8 The Personal Touch

8.1 Introduction

We are now ready to approach the second major part of the 'promotion mix', which was introduced at the beginning of the last chapter as:

- *personal communication in which a human being takes part with another human being, where 'two-way' communication can take place by the interaction between people* (see Section 7.1).

This description is still much too loose to be applied as it stands to the main function of personal communication in marketing: this chapter will tighten it up.

In this Chapter we are going to examine the reasons why personal communication for promoting goods and services is more or less effective than other methods. We will attempt to identify certain principles which should guide us in those situations where human intervention is necessary; where the tasks are such that only people can effectively overcome the difficulties.

Once the question 'Why use people?' has been answered, we shall go on to ask how they may be best employed to provide the required results. In this section of the chapter we will be defining a number of difficulties that must also be considered when using people as the main communicators. And finally there are occasions when both the non-personal and personal forms of promotion come together to give the marketer even greater opportunity for blending the elements of the whole promotion mix.

8.2 Why Use People?

My communication to you is non-personal, through the written word (like an advertisement in a paper); I have no feedback. But if I had been talking to you face to face, using the identical words, I could have seen their effect (or lack of it) by what you did. The communication would have been *two-way*. And if you had not responded I could have altered my communication by repetition, change in words, tone of voice, volume, expression and body language to obtain better effect. You only have to think of some recent conversation, discussion or argument with someone to appreciate how much you adjusted to the continuous feedback taking place throughout it. This flexibility, or adaptability, to a situation is the key advantage of human communicating ability over all other methods.

The main objective of this section will be to determine business situations where this flexibility is a necessary ingredient of successfully concluding exchanges. For this is what 'selling' is all about. Its purpose is:

- *personal persuasive communication to generate directly or indirectly purchase behaviour in another person or persons.*

'Directly or indirectly'

These words quoted from the definition are especially important in comparing selling with those promotion techniques covered in Chapter 7.

Because of its flexibility personal communication is capable of all (and indeed more) of the variety of aims of the non-personal ones. Through word of mouth any kind of message may be 'sent'. Put another way, a human being can convey all the messages of all the promotion techniques; but there are some things that people can do that cannot ever be done by non-personal means. It is this potential for substitution that may lead to considerable difficulty in putting together a complete promotion mix.

'Persuasive'

A comment is often made that selling does not start until somebody says 'No'. If we accept this, at least for the sake of illustration, then the process of changing that 'No' to a 'Yes' is what persuasion is about. Somebody already motivated to buy a product hardly needs to be 'sold' – it could be argued that he has been 'presold', possibly by non-personal promotion techniques.

Any such change implies some movement of position by the receiver of the communication – and in this context that person is the potential buyer. For the time being I am going to ask you to play the role most familiar to you, that of a buyer rather than the seller. (I suggest this role as being familiar simply because everybody is a buyer, but not everybody is a salesman).

Self-check

Let us concentrate on the word 'flexibility'

(a) You are in a jeweller's shop looking for a ladies' wrist watch which you intend giving as a 21st-birthday present. You have not yet decided on the type, the price, the movement or display and so on. What do you have to do before any salesman can begin to help you?

(b) You are on a package holiday in North Africa, let us say Algeria; you are walking through the local native bazaar intending to buy a souvenir for yourself to take home. Do you pay the price asked?

(c) You are in the market for video equipment, which some of your friends already have. You have seen a number of different kinds as well as any number of advertisements. You go to a good store to see a variety of them, to examine them and to find out all you can. How do you do it?

Suppose we now take each of these three examples in turn.

I wonder how many of you thought that in answer to **(a)**, the ladies' wrist watch, you should say 'make up your mind'! I hope you did not because by so doing you would exclude any consideration of the role of a salesman. Surely the real answer here, and what happens in practice, is that you have to give the salesman some information; it's often hesitant at first, is it not? But gradually you loosen up as you talk about it, as he makes suggestions (and observes your reactions – feedback) and as the discussion goes to and fro. Now reverse the process. What is the first thing that the salesman must begin to do? Ask questions; in other words – investigate.

Taking you to North Africa is enough on its own to give the right clue. You would probably be very unwise to pay the price asked! Contrary to our western customs of fixed pricing, many parts of the world expect bargaining to take place before a sale is made. Buyer and seller negotiate. You do the same when you trade in a car in the process of buying a new one. A professional industrial buyer or store buyer will negotiate the best terms he can from a supplier.

Although we are getting more and more used to technology, most of us would want to learn quite a lot about expensive video equipment before we bought. The literature is all very well, but sometimes difficult to follow, often hard to read and anyway inhuman! Much nicer to ask a helpful assistant in the store; he has (or should have) all the comparisons at his fingertips, can demonstrate the advantages and disadvantages of each; he can respond to you.

To sum this up so far, there are three 'flexibilities':

- to investigate;
- to negotiate;
- to explain technology.

There is another situation where human flexibility is supremely important but may not be as easy to identify with. We have imagined business organizations before in this book and at this point it is necessary to do it again.

In Section 2.12 five roles were identified in a Decision Making Unit. Do you remember what they were?

In Chapter 2, the section was entitled 'Who buys in business?' and we were, you will recall, looking at things from that point of view. Now we are on the other side of the same coin. Would you now look up Exercise 5 at the end of Chapter 5 and remind yourself of the scenario.

Between the end of the first conversation and the meeting 'some months later' a number of different people were involved, in their several roles, before any decision was made. To what kind of promotion, non-personal or personal, had these people been exposed?

The only certainty likely in any such list is

Buyer--- Salesman

However, a good salesman would have been doing his utmost to:

- identify the important members of the DMU;
- try to see them;
- if his firm's marketing activity was not trying to influence them anyway, he might ask for direct mailing to be sent.

Everything hinges upon *identification*.

In practice it has been found that salesmen seldom, if ever, are able to see all the members of a decision-making unit in industrial purchasing: the number is usually between two and three. Therefore other means have to be found to influence them – non-personal means. From this must come the logical conclusion that 'selling' can be, and should be if the resources are available, and often is supported by other promotional techniques. In fact the logic can be taken a step further:

If messages can be delivered to target audiences effectively, and more economically, by non-personal means, selling should be reserved for those particular flexibilities for which human intervention is essential.

8.3 **Summary**

We have found a number of reasons why personal communication should be used as part of the promotion mix. We can summarize these reasons by using the letter technique again – the three *Is*. They are the flexibility of

- *investigation*;
- *identification*;
- *interaction in*: negotiation, technology.

Whenever we may find situations where one, or more, of these appears to be significant, the greater the likelihood that we will have to employ human (personal) promotion.

Fig 8.1   *The 3-I 'flexibilities' in personal selling*

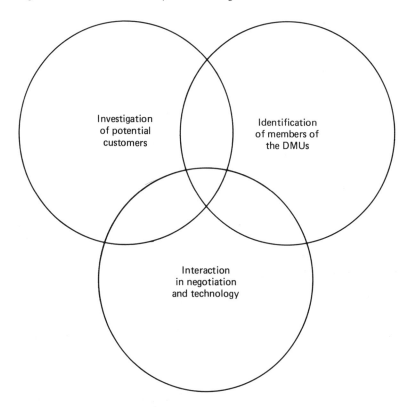

8.4 **A Foot in the Door**

Because we are very quickly going into some calculations, it would be advisable to have a calculator handy.

The *Financial Times* conducts surveys to find out and publish the total cost of a travelling salesman. The average figure is now approximately £20 000 (1979 = £16 183) of which less than half is under the heading 'Remuneration'; the remainder was accounted for by expenses, vehicle costs, supervision, clerical and so on – eleven separate headings in all. Therefore please note 'total cost', not merely direct operating costs.

Mr Average Salesman spends 48 weeks a year 'on the road'; five days in each week and eight hours in each day. Calculate his cost per hour (48 weeks allow for 3 weeks of annual holiday and for Bank Holidays.) During the course of each day, he averages 10 'calls' in which he is face to face, and selling, to a customer. Calculate the cost per call. Finally his total costs represent, say, 7 per cent of his total turnover, e.g. the total invoiced value of the orders he takes in a year: how much turnover must he generate in total, and how much per call?

Cost per hour   _____
Cost per call   _____
Total turnover   _____
Turnover per call   _____

These calculations bring us very quickly up against some of the most crucial realities of personal communication: it is expensive and therefore must produce an adequate return. Unproductive salesmen cannot be tolerated in the 1990s! Naturally the figures that I have used in the example will vary in practice from company to company. The principle of using such controls should not vary. We will be returning to the figures, and answers to the calculations later in the section.

Because a number of readers will be familiar with sales personnel only in shops, I am going to use as illustration for this section the example of a medium-sized manufacturer of decorative paints. The salesmen 'represent' the company to its various customers – hence the term 'representative' (now much more commonly used than 'salesman'). The company has three distinct types of customers: architects who may 'specify' the paint (that is, give instructions to decorators which type of paint is to be used and from which manufacturer); trade decorators, usually larger ones working on building contracts; and wholesalers who will supply the smaller decorators and some retail shops. All of these are called on by the 'reps'.

Bearing firmly in mind the content of the previous section, in which we discovered the reasons why personal communication is better than non-personal, we can now continue to elaborate some of the limitations or constraints which apply when using people as the main means of promotion.

8.5 Number of Customers

You are one of the reps for the medium-sized paint manufacturer; how many customers can you handle? We know how many hours you work, how many calls you make on average, but what we have neither asked nor answered is how frequently you have to call on your customers?

Suppose we decide, for the moment, that you need to call six times a year on each customer. That means that you would call every eight weeks – known as a 'journey cycle' (6 × 8 = 48).

Work out with the previous, and this new, information how many customers you could handle. I make it 400. Do you agree from your calculations? (Don't take mine for granted as being correct!)

Now cross-check your figures to the previously calculated total turnover:

400 customers × turnover per call × number of calls = turnover £ _____

Using UK national figures there are over $\frac{1}{4}$ million potential customers in the three categories combined. To cover them all our paint company would require 625 representatives! At that rate it would no longer be medium sized, nor would it be able to achieve average turnover figures; such an operation, against competition, would be totally uneconomic.

8.6 Frequency of Call

As long as we use average figures, you will appreciate that extremes will be concealed; there will be high-turnover customers ranging right down to quite infrequent purchasers spending a minimum. Do they all warrant the same call frequency throughout a journey cycle?

Undoubtedly not! Therefore most managements require their sales representatives to arrange their calls at different time intervals according to customer need. They will also require a certain amount of 'prospecting' to be done. Prospecting is looking for new business, or opening new accounts. Remember all these differing call rates and prospecting have to be managed within the overall limit of total calls, which we set at 400.

Just to take this situation a little further, let us now suppose that there is, on average, a 10 per cent erosion of business from existing customers each year. (The figure is illustrative only but should be known by every sales manager!) This means a reduction of turnover from £258 000 (see original figures on page 112 = £18 061/0.07) by £25 800 to be made up from the 20 prospects called on six times in a year at the average order values of £107.50 per call (£258 000/2400), which equals £12 900 – not enough!

All this leads us to a fairly simple formula which should be calculated regularly for every salesman:

	Actual			Forecast
Turnover	£258 000		b/f	£258 000*
Erosion		@ 10%		£25 800
New business		@ £107.50		£12 900
Net turnover c/f	£258 000			£245 100

* No other considerations taken into account in this example.

It stands to reason that if the above figures represent the picture with a reasonable degree of accuracy the deficiency must be made up from some alteration of the relationships:

1 More business from existing customers.
2 A reduction in the erosion rate.
3 A higher volume of new business.
4 A mixture of 1–3.

This leads us to the next major question. What tasks should the rep be performing?

8.7 Sales Objectives

One of the reasons that I chose to use a paint manufacturer as an example is because of the variety of customer segments served. You will recall that I mentioned three in this case; architects, decorators and wholesalers. (There could be many others.)

We know that the purpose of all promotion is to bring consumers through the three *As* – awareness, attitude and action. We know also that personal communication becomes more and more important as the three *Is* assume greater signification – investigation, identification and interaction. Finally we agreed that a human being can communicate all those things which non-personal promotion techniques can also do.

But salesmen are very limited in the number of consumers they can reach, and, as we have seen, are an expensive resource.

Architects (and other specifiers) What makes architects a special category of customer? First, they do not buy themselves, they specify. Second, because they are only one member of a DMU, they may themselves come under pressure from the main building contractor. Third, when products are very comparable (as in paints) why should they stick to one source? Fourth, any specification may be prepared two or three years before the paint is actually applied on to a new building. Fifth, the location of architect (say London) may be far removed from the building site (say Manchester).

Reps who are used to, and like, selling for orders find this kind of selling very difficult; so a certain type of person may be required to do it.

Builders and decorators (the trade) These customers both buy and use. They are as a rule tough negotiators on price and are often in need of technical advice or assistance, given that they are big enough to have some bargaining power. Ideal types for using salesmen.

Wholesalers and intermediaries They sell on to other customers. They may have their own salesmen to do this or, less frequently, rely on customers coming to them. How much are the paint manufacturer's promotional messages diluted in this process? Who are the rep's friends? The manager who may place the order, or the counter assistant who deals with the public? Do they need any training, and if so who will do it? You as a supplier or their own training staff?

I hope you can see how much variation there can be in the communication job to be carried out without my developing the technicalities of this particular 'trade' too far. Each industry has its own peculiarities, which must be properly identified; but general principles should have fairly universal application.

8.8 Summary

Sections 8.4 to 8.7 focused to begin with on the costs related to personal selling and revenues which should result. Further calculations were made to provide examples of broad control measures of performance. Arising from these figures, several constraints emerged: the number of customers that could be handled and the number of calls that a salesman may make. How often should salesmen call on different types of customer was then considered. Because different customers had different requirements, there may be the need to employ a variety of types of salesmen: specifically architects, builders and decorators, and wholesalers were mentioned.

8.9 Specialization in Selling

The Chapter so far has isolated for us those areas in which personal communication will always be more effective than the non-personal techniques; we summarized these under the three *Is*. We also emphasized how personal promotion was able to use 'feedback', adapting instantaneously to a two-way flow of words and ideas between people. The question this section will be asking is how far this principle can be carried out in practice; how adaptable are salesmen? Is there any limit and what may cause it?

Sales management always faces a choice between using a 'generalist' or a 'specialist'. We will be exploring the five main criteria which should govern that choice: the kind of purchase; the people involved in the purchasing decision; the types and number of products; the ability of the salesman; and the cost of the personal promotion task (which 'must' be carried out by a human being). By considering these five you will be able to decide what kind of sales force you would operate in different circumstances; because you would be expecting *results* from the *resources* employed. So incidently would your superiors.

8.10 The Kind of Purchase

If selling is primarily about persuasion, those purchases where none is necessary need no salesman; what kinds of purchase are these?

Self-check

From the following list of purchases tick which ones need no selling, need a little or need a lot.

	None	A little	A lot
A replacement colour TV			
A loaf of bread			
Ovaltine (for the first time)			
New gas heated hair curlers (e.g. new on the market)			

All these examples are with customer products, so let us elaborate further with some industrial ones.

	None	A little	A lot
Extending a contract to supply further steel pipes for North Sea oil			
Installing a new car-wash system, including hot wax and polishing			
Topping up the supply of envelopes for a direct mail company			
Replacement of an existing production line by robots			
Switching from a natural to a synthetic chemical raw material			

Of course the three categories of 'none', 'a little' and 'a lot' are somewhat arbitrary, and we cannot use them to make fine distinctions. They should be sufficient for our purpose, so perhaps we should now compare notes.

Those which are often labelled as 'repeat purchases' are likely to be the ones which you have marked under 'none': a loaf of bread (consumer) and the envelopes (industrial). The ones which I would mark under 'a little', would include replacements and extensions with the qualification of the three Rs: as risk, resources and results assume greater significance, the more selling is likely to be required. This is because of the kind of people involved in the purchasing decision, which we shall be looking at in greater depth in the next section. However, we can illustrate what I mean from the list of products.

A replacement colour TV, a replacement ('switching') of a raw material and extending the pipeline contract are all based on previous experience of some kind. Total persuasion, in other words from a 'No', is not necessary; persuasion towards selection may be. Which TV do you choose? It is most unlikely to be the same model that you had previously. There are certain to be new features to choose from. Although there is always some risk in changing any raw material, not only from a natural to a synthetic one, testing it would answer many of the possible questions and doubts about it: the selection of which synthetic, or which supplier, may be the important one; the extension of the contract to supply pipes would be one of choosing the supplier, as all of them would be capable of making to the required specification.

Which items am I suggesting that we qualify under the three R criteria? From the consumer list consider Ovaltine, which may have been bought for the first time as a night-time drink for the growing children, to help settle them down for bed. A relatively inexpensive and not all that significant, purchase: selling? I think some would be required, probably not personal though, so let us say 'a little'. Would you accept that? By contrast consider the replacement of a production line by robotics. Here the implications are enormous and 'a lot' of selling would be required.

Suppose we label the second category as 'renewals' (and the first one 'repeat purchases'). Now what about the third?

We are left with new gas-heated hair curlers from the consumer list, the robotics and the new car wash from the industrial one. Each of these products is 'new': so we have a third category. They need 'a lot' of selling.

Self-check

We now have three levels of selling and three kinds of purchase: with 3 × 3 we can easily make a matrix for ourselves. Will you please make one showing how selling escalates across the three purchases.

8.11 People Involved in the Purchase Decision

We know by now without thinking about it very much that as soon as we start thinking of the people involved in purchasing, decision-making units pop up.

We also know that as we move from a repeat to a new purchase, in other words from something quite routine to one requiring, shall we say, considerable investigation, greater involvement by senior management will occur. As there is also a relationship between 'kind of purchase' and types of product with DMUs, we can now ask ourselves – with how much of this could a salesman cope?

Let me illustrate this in three dimensions.

8.12 Substitution of Types of Product

The product types illustrated above are industrial 'converting' ones.

Fig 8.2　*Product/purchase/sell model*

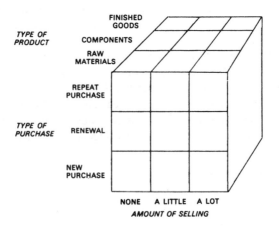

They can be substituted as follows:

	Industrial	
Consumer	*Converting*	*Enabling*
Consumer Durables	Finished goods	Capital
FMCG	Components	
	Consumables	
	Raw materials	

Please remember that 'services' by their nature can compare with both consumer and industrial goods. Using Figure 8.2 we can make up two 'triple combinations'; one being as easy and straightforward as possible and the other as complex as we can devise.

Easy and straightforward: repeat purchase/FMCG/none = a pint of beer. Complex: new purchase/capital/a lot = an advanced gas cooled reactor for an atomic power station.

In the introduction to Section 8.9 I used the words 'generalist', or 'specialist'. Let me exaggerate to make my first point: can you imagine the same person selling beer into pubs and reactors to the Central Electricity Generating Board? I think your answer must surely be 'No'.

8.13 The Ability of the Salesman

Now we have come to the fourth of the criteria. We have already agreed that the three *I*s govern the need for human communication, rather than non-personal.

We recall that they demanded flexibility, something that only people can adequately provide: flexibility to investigate, to identify (what? the members of the DMU), to interact in negotiation and technology. Now relate to beer and reactors. Both of these products will require the three *I*s to a greater or lesser extent: it is the extent that matters, and the greater it is, the greater the skill required by the seller.

There are few salesmen, of whatever seniority, who will have a new product to offer on every call they make. Suppliers therefore sought to find ways of offering services to their intermediary customers to ensure adequate stock levels, a good share of shelf display and the integration of special promotions that either company or store may be running. You should not pay a top rate senior salesman for work at that level.

There is an activity, however, on the supermarket floor, linked to selling, which we have not yet mentioned: merchandising.

The merchandiser will operate at individual store level; the senior salesman at the purchasing department at head office or regional office. Merchandising developed as a means whereby the supplying company could provide a service at store level, and through that service a reduction in the latter's administrative costs. Not unnaturally he too gained by ensuring stock levels were maintained, adequate display space was provided and any promotions were being properly used. These tasks are relatively mundane and will most likely be carried out by junior personnel. In the whole spectrum of personal services that are offered to customers merchandising makes a valuable contribution.

During most of this chapter the emphasis has been on the communication role of personal selling, but in the third of the three *I*s there is also the technological part. We now have to ask ourselves, are technical and communication skills capable of being integrated into one person, or is more than one required? You will agree that to some extent it will depend on the person; indeed it may be easier to find somebody technically qualified than one who is demonstrably a communicator. What is beyond dispute is that many selling situations demand an amalgam of these two. How much can be embraced by one person? Let me illustrate how one company – IBM – divides its sales force by way of illustration:

Division 1   Main frame (big) computers
Division 2   Micro- and mini-computers
Division 3   Office machines (e.g. typewriters)

The higher the technology the greater is the need for technical expertise – in the salesman *or* in a sales team.

8.14 Technical Service Back-up to Selling

There are two parts to these services differentiated by time:

• Presale technical service: although the result was unsuccessful it is not hard to imagine how many different people were involved in attempts to sell Concorde to the American airlines. A lot of those people were highly technical.
• After-sales service: this is the familiar one to most of us, for example whenever we get our cars serviced, when the TV set breaks down and so on.

Self-check

Put yourself in the position of the buyer in each of the following situations and judge for yourself how they would affect you.

1 You, as a distributor of electrical goods, have been approached through a representative of a Far Eastern business and have been asked to handle their microwave ovens which are new to the UK market. When you ask whether or not the products have an approved British safety standard, the representative tells you that for technical reasons he would have to refer your question back to his head office.

2 You have a foreign car, which is currently making a horrible noise somewhere in the back axle. Your usual service station tells you that there are no spares available from the main import agents, and you are going to have to wait until the next shipment arrives. 'When will that be?' you inquire, 'Oh, we have no control over that, that's up to the main agents.'

3 Your Xerox in the office packs up and your operator cannot put it right (there is more wrong than just getting the paper mixed up). Within twenty-four hours it is back in working order under the service contract.

4 You are a keen watcher of Wimbledon tennis and your TV is on for unusually long hours in the heat of June. It expires in a cloud of smoke. The service operator from the rental company tells you he cannot repair it because it is an old model. 'If you had any sense you'd rent a new one,' he tells you. (This actually happened to me and I need hardly tell you what I did about further renting from that company.)

Do I need go on? Hardly I think. We can summarize the ability problem like this – communication skills and technological skills must be matched when the product/market situation requires it. At one extreme they can be combined in one person; at the other, teams of people may be involved. The more that is being combined the stronger the demand for a 'generalist'. On the other hand, when tasks can be broken down, or perhaps need to be, the more need there is for a 'specialist'.

8.15 The Fifth Criterion – Cost

Would you accept that the word 'specialist' implies a degree of 'expertise'? If so, can we go one stage further and suggest that expertise costs money, and the person that possesses it can command a reasonable salary? So his employer will be looking for his money's worth. We're back full circle – let the specialist specialize.

That means that other tasks have to be carried out by others.

Self-check

Let us combine ability and cost in the following situations. I am going to put forward three scenarios; make up your mind about the key figure – the salesman – and whether he should be a 'generalist' or a 'specialist'.

1 You have been appointed the sales manager of a small company making very accurately engineered components for naval marine engines. You want to appoint a new representative and are wondering if he should have any engineering qualification. He will be joining a team of four other salesmen.

2 Your marketing director has suggested to you that two sales forces covering the same geographical territories are uneconomic. One force sells pharmaceutical products to wholesalers and retailers; the other sells to specialist doctors in hospitals, hospital pharmacies and general practitioners. Would you argue for, and on what grounds, the maintenance of the two forces?

3 You see an advertisement for an export manager whose main duties are described as 'setting up a network of agencies in India, Pakistan and the Middle East'. No product details are given in the advertisement. You wonder if you have the 'qualifications' to apply for the job.

Now which of these five criteria apply to the three scenarios?

1 Kind of purchase – all three are possible.
DMUs – could be extensive.
Types and numbers of products – varied/technical.
Ability of salesman – *engineering qualification*.
Cost – small company, not a lot of back-up.

This one is really quite complicated: some criteria are calling for a 'generalist' approach, others for a 'specialist'. Given the small company with limited back-up, you, as the sales manager, should probably go for a person capable of generalizing within a specialist field. I'm not trying to have it both ways; this is a genuine and common dilemma.

2 Kind of purchase – repeat and new.
DMUs – limited.
Types and number of products – finished goods.
Ability of salesmen – medical knowledge to doctors; product knowledge sufficient for channels of distribution.
Cost – amalgamating both forces would increase costs. Reps to distribution channels need not be as highly paid as the others.

Although both forces are handling the same products, the degrees of skill required differ considerably. They may be covering the same geographical area, but are not duplicating the customers: 'specialists'.

3 Kind of purchase – service.
DMUs – variable.
Types and number of products – not known.
Ability of salesman – negotiation.
Cost – high.

The job looks as if it will be demanding extensive travel and, as not everybody is willing to undertake that, it will have to be paid for in both salary and expenses. The key thing here is without question an ability to negotiate: 'generalist'.

8.16 Summary

We have now explored five criteria of looking at the sales task and, from that starting point, the kind of people needed to carry it out. It began by examining a kind of purchase and a type of product against degrees of selling effort, from 'none' to 'a lot'. We also reviewed the importance of DMUs. Finally the ability of the salesman was considered and his cost; the more wide ranging his activities, the more he could be regarded as a 'generalist'; conversely the more narrowly based they were, particularly on technical grounds, the more the salesman will tend to specialize.

8.17 Combined Operations

By this time it is as clear to you as it is to me that the promotion mix must be a 'combined operation', the title of this section. However, I am using the expression to introduce something that has not yet been considered, that is widely used and often misused! Something also that will help to reinforce the theory and practice of integrated promotion: the exhibition.

Under this heading I propose to include international 'trade fairs', such as motor shows at the Exhibition Centre, Birmingham, or the ones held in Paris and Frankfurt; ones to which the public have access such as the Ideal Homes Exhibition at Olympia, London; trade shows like those at Brighton and Harrogate for toys. If these are examples of some of the big ones, we must not forget quite local events: for instance exhibitions of agricultural machinery at country horse-shows. We can afford to encompass such a range of events under one main heading because they all follow the same general rules – an essential mixture of personal and non-personal promotion techniques before, during and after.

Following our previous practice in defining activities, the purpose of an exhibition is:

• *to attract relevant people to a particular short-term location in order to promote, display and demonstrate products or services in the pursuit of business goals.*

'To attract'

Do you remember Chapter 6 on distribution channels and its title? We took two opposite approaches: 'moving goods to people' and 'moving people to goods'. Now deduce which approach is relevant to an exhibition: the second surely.

'Particular short-term location'

The reason why we have to move people (not to goods but to exhibitions) lies in this paragraph heading. The duration of an exhibition is always short and there will only be one important one going on at a time: for example the toy fairs mentioned above, at Brighton and Harrogate, are held at different times.

'Pursuit of business goals'

These may, of course, differ widely from one company to another at the same exhibition. It does not matter particularly what the business goal is so long as there is one. A businessman, and a marketer in particular, should consider the following common reasons given for exhibiting as totally inadequate:

. . . because our competitors always do.
. . . we always have, so we just continue.

The kind of goal that should dominate the thinking behind promoting through exhibitions can be illustrated by:

to bring a new product to the notice of buyers (in a particular trade).

to establish contact with new potential customers for subsequent follow-up.

to support local dealers by giving out their addresses to members of the public.

The reason then that I have called this section 'combined operations' is because non-personal and personal promotion techniques come together quite literally during the exhibition itself (sales personnel on the stand), but also precede it and follow it. Therefore I am now bringing into the open an area of neglect – too many exhibitors stop when the doors close!

That is not really surprising if there is any truth in the inadequate reasons for exhibiting mentioned a little earlier. The professionals in this area of marketing will claim that an exhibition lasts for twelve months: six for planning and designing it, the exhibition 'week' (or 'fortnight') and six months for following up on the set objectives. The latter six months are the ones which suffer from neglect.

'Promote, display and demonstrate'
These words embody the particularly unique aspect of exhibitions: the products are subject to all necessary and suitable promotion techniques, first to get visitors along, then to show them off, but finally (and possibly most important) actually to see them working or show them working in a way which may not be possible for a representative calling. Let me illustrate what I mean:

Self-check

You are the makers of lifts, for both passengers and freight, moving walkways, escalators and so on. Your business might be defined as 'being concerned with moving people and goods in and around buildings'. How would you be able to demonstrate such products at an exhibition, which would not be possible in sombody's office?

Closed-circuit television would be one way of doing it. But you might argue that it is possible for representatives to take CCTV to potential customers; I would agree with some reservations at the present time but not for much longer. Film is less portable but is frequently to be found at exhibitions. But probably the greatest opportunity which the exhibition gives above all else is the use of models. One of the features you wish to bring to the notice of customers is your new electronic control panel. You could easily have the full-sized working system for visitors to play with linked to models of lifts. This sort of thing enables an exhibition visitor to participate in some of the action: and that is one of the best forms of persuasive communication!

You are going to go through the process of planning an exhibition. So you are going to need a piece of paper and pen or pencil. If you are all set, let us start planning!

1 Decide on the business you are in and the products you are going to exhibit (Chapters 1–3).
2 Decide who your customers are (Chapter 4).

3 Decide at what time of year and in which major location(s) you will be exhibiting.

4 Decide why you are going to exhibit – set your precise exhibition objective(s).

5 Draw up your promotion plan to get visitors to your stand.

6 Plan how you will meet your exhibition objectives (4 above) once your visitor is on the stand – what are you going to show him?

7 Depending upon what your objectives are, what follow-up methods will you use to ensure that you reached them?

8 Over what length of time after the close of the exhibition will you require to follow up (7 above) before you know whether or not the exhibition has yielded up all its possible results?

This looks quite a formidable list – and indeed so it is. Let me remind you of the two main stages, (a) getting people to visit and (b) getting some result once they have visited.

MY EXHIBITION

Because I have never been to one and therefore, like many of you, have nothing else to draw on than imagination, I am going to choose the Boat Show, and the products I make are navigational instruments. My main target market (for the purpose of this particular exhibition) is that of boatbuilders; I want my products to become standard components. My subsidiary target will be dealers in navigational instruments. So I am interested in 'trade' customers, not the general public. Timing is not unique in any way; I am governed by the timing of the Boat Show itself. Location – London.

Objectives: To attract at least thirty boatbuilders to the stand from companies big enough to require fifty sets of my equipment in a year; to obtain two thirds of these as 'prospects' for my sales staff to follow up after the exhibition; to obtain during the follow-up at least ten new account customers. (And something similar for dealers.)

To get these people to my stand, I would include in all my advertising directed at both the trade and the public a notice of my presence at the Boat Show. I would attempt some joint publicity with boatbuilders who also intend exhibiting and who use my instruments. I would investigate amongst boatbuilders, and make a list of those companies big enough to meet my 'objective' criteria; these I would direct-mail and include free tickets to the Boat Show. The best fifty would be invited to a specially commissioned film preview of my instruments under severe weather on board two boats in the transatlantic yacht race; light refreshments would be offered and a well-known yachting personality would be present. (I honestly have not a clue whether or not such an approach would be adequate! This does not matter; firstly I am only illustrating, and secondly if you or I were doing this for real, we would know, or we would certainly find out!) Assuming that I am boss of the business (its managing director), I would spend as much time as possible myself at the exhibition talking to potential customers and backing up my salesmen also present on the stand.

On the stand I would have plenty of audio-visual material and a yacht cockpit simulator for 'boys' – of all ages – to play with! There would be a photographer on permanent hire for possible publicity (after the exhibition) should any celebrities come on to the stand – Ted Heath (?). There would be a system for recording the names and addresses of all visitors; the sales staff would be firmly briefed to obtain entries into the visitors book. This is an essential preliminary to any subsequent follow-up. Obvious really but not always used!

Orders would be taken on the stand, but this would not be a prime task. *Awareness* and a favourable *attitude* would be the communication objectives; *action* can come at the time of follow-up.

After the exhibition all visitors would receive a direct-mail letter offering a special introductory discount on any purchase above a minimum value; the offer would be firmly linked to both the Boat Show and the visit to the stand. This letter would in turn be followed by a visit from a rep.

At the end of six months after the close of the exhibition, an analysis would be made of:

1 number of visitors actually visiting from original short list invited;
2 number of other visitors;
3 number of direct-mail letters sent after the exhibition to classes 1 and 2 above and resulting inquiries or orders;
4 number of rep calls on classes 1 and 2 above, with and without direct-mail letter, leading to orders;
5 cumulative £ sterling value of orders received from classes 1 and 2 above, and other new accounts;
6 any noticeable increase or decrease in business from previously existing accounts, which show a marked variation since the Boat Show. Investigate the variances;
7 calculate whether or not the exhibition 'paid' in terms of communication, possibly goodwill, and new business;
8 draw any other relevant conclusions for future exhibitions (if any).

8.18 Summary

We have used the term 'exhibition' to cover everything from a major international event to a local one: they differ only in degree. By looking closely at the three stages – planning, the exhibition, the follow-up – it becomes clear that this technique must be considered as a part of a total promotional plan, with its own specific objectives. Sufficient time must be allowed after the event to obtain the full benefits and draw the necessary conclusions for future reference. The exhibition also demonstrates how it draws on and in turn supports other promotional tools.

8.19 Technology in Selling

During the course of our discussion about selling and the people who carry it out a number of difficulties have appeared. Personal selling is an expensive resource to use and must therefore be highly effective in costly competitive conditions. Any aid which can improve the results or economise on costs is a bonus. As selling is about communication we should be looking for technology to improve that process, always provided the technology more than pays for itself in practice.

Some aids to communication:

• the car telephone;
• the miniaturization of television and the flat screen;
• the portable battery operated computer with messages transmitted by telephone

and many others already in existence or still to be invented.

I remember when I was a representative in the London area how important it was to know two things: the location of all public lavatories and telephone boxes. British Telecom have been severely criticized in recent years over the number of public phones out of order. Quite apart from that problem, there is also always the one about parking the car! Just imagine the amount of time that can be saved by car telephones.

Most sales managers will want to be certain that the products being sold by their sales forces are getting across with the right and most effective message. New miniature or flat screen television is now so portable that it literally fits into a briefcase. Battery operated it does not even need plugging in and can be used in any situation, an office, a building site, in an aeroplane or car – glorious colour! The communication effect can be far stronger when backed up by personnel; because what was a one-way communication medium can be converted into a two-way one.

One of the chores most sales people loathe is the administrative paperwork, usually worked at well into the evening. Mastery of a small computer can be used to great benefit by substituting paper with magnetic disc and transmitting the data by telephone to the master system in the office.

In Section 8.6 the 'frequency of call' by representatives was discussed. One of the points raised then was the method of altering the number of times poor, or small customers were called on. Not dissimilar to this situation is the one where a customer is only likely to be a 'one off' – once bought there will be no repeat purchase. Examples of the latter situation would be central heating, double glazing, fitted kitchens, bathrooms and so on, all for domestic consumers. Many of us have been at the receiving end of telephone selling!

Now calculate the cost efficiency of this method against a personal call from a representative; link it with the three *A*s (awareness, attitude and action). Conversely, there are now systems linking personal computers with direct ordering to shops.

As we began, so we may summarize: any technological aids to the communication process must become part of the armoury of selling and managements must constantly examine the possibilities.

Exercises

1 Take the situation exactly as it is recorded in Exercise 5 at the end of Chapter 2: list below that promotional technique you currently consider most appropriate to reach every member of the DMU. For this purpose do not list more than one for each position and, after thinking carefully, tick those who could be reached by personal selling.

	Non-personal	*Personal*
Chief executive		
Marketing manager		
Design engineer		
Production manager		
Personnel manager		
Accountant		
Buyer		

2 From the following workload table, how many total customers and prospects can a rep handle in an eight-week journey cycle with a maximum of 400 calls?

	Number	Call rate	No. calls	Cumulative
	20	2 weeks		
	80	4 weeks		
Existing	40	8 weeks		
Customers	75	12 weeks		
	100	16 weeks		
Prospects	?	8 weeks		

3 When choosing between a 'specialist' or 'generalist' sales person five main criteria were explored to help in the selection: what were those five criteria and how would they apply in the following situation?

Product type	Situation
FMCG	Straight rebuy
Consumable durable	New buy
Consumer service	Modified rebuy
Industrial component	Modified rebuy
Capital good	New buy
Raw material	Modified rebuy
Industrial service	Straight rebuy

4 In determining the need for personal as opposed to non-personal means of communication with potential or actual customers three '*I*s' were offered as a means of judging. What were the three '*I*s' and why are they significant?

5 You have just been appointed to a new post as a senior salesman responsible for key accounts on behalf of the wines and spirits subsidiary of a major brewery. (Key accounts are those regarded by the company as warranting special attention, usually because of their size or purchasing importance.) What would your roles be in relation to your company's total promotional effort?

First of all work through the small questionnaire below, ticking the items where you think you would have a role. Later I will ask you to elaborate on those roles – but let's find them first!

Would you play any part in the following promotional activities on behalf of . . .

		Your own company	(code)	*Key account company*	(code)
Public relations	Yes	. . .	1a	. . .	1b
(reputation)	No	. . .	2a	. . .	2b
Publicity	Yes	. . .	3a	. . .	3b
(newsworthy)	No	. . .	4a	. . .	4b
Advertising	Yes	. . .	5a	. . .	5b
(influence)	No	. . .	6a	. . .	6b
Direct mail	Yes	. . .	7a	. . .	7b
(influence)	No	. . .	8a	. . .	8b
Sales promotion	Yes	. . .	9a	. . .	9b
(inducement)	No	. . .	10a	. . .	10b
Packaging	Yes	. . .	11a	. . .	11b
(visibility)	No	. . .	12a	. . .	12b
Merchandising	Yes	. . .	13a	. . .	13b
(information/	No	. . .	14a	. . .	14b
access)					
Display (make	Yes	. . .	15a	. . .	15b
conspicuous)	No	. . .	16a	. . .	16b
Selling (generate	Existing		Yes	. . .	17
purchase	products		No	. . .	18
behaviour)	New products		Yes	. . .	19
			No	. . .	20

9 How Much Shall We Charge?

9.1 Introduction

No discussion of any competitive business situation can last for long without the question of price arising. Indeed on occasion, so far in this book, mention has been made of it in passing. This chapter takes a much deeper and formal look at a crucial aspect of the marketing mix. It has been left until last for such consideration because those activities already covered – products, distribution and promotion – affect, or are affected by, price decisions.

Both products and promotion incur costs; research, development and production costs for the former, communication costs for the latter. Join these to all the other costs and expenses necessary to run a business, then there is a total cost which in the long run must be covered by revenue or income. This income is the multiplication of all the goods sold by the price charged.

Distribution generates costs in two ways. There are the expenses of moving goods from, shall we say, a factory to a shop by some form of transport, which would usually be a charge on the supplier. Then there is the difference at the shop between the price paid for buying in and the price charged for selling out. This difference we referred to in an example in Section 6.4 as the 'margin'. No supplier of goods through distribution channels can afford to ignore the effect of the margin on the ultimate price paid by the consumer, cost has to be contained and a price charged with this in mind.

There is unfortunately great danger in approaching the subject of pricing in the arithmetic fashion just described: add up revenue add up costs, take the latter away from the former and you are left with profit (or loss). In this chapter we are going to be looking at price first from a consumer's point of view. If we can understand and appreciate that, and we ought to be able to because we are ourselves consumers, then it should be easier to consider the meaning of price to a business. That meaning should be firmly set in the context of marketing objectives, and we will be asking ourselves the questions 'How does this or that approach to price contribute to achieving these goals?' However, in fairness to fluctuating fortunes and other disciplines in business apart from marketing, let me admit before we go any further that I do not advocate that all price decisions be the exclusive preserve of the marketing function. Nevertheless the approach taken in this chapter will unquestionably be biased in that direction.

Also we will be considering some usefui tools to help us choose amongst price alternatives. Finally it is very common for external factors, over which neither consumer nor business has control, to intervene in pricing: a quick example to show what I mean – the level of VAT (value added tax), currently at 15 per cent.

9.2 What Does Price Mean to the Buyer?

When you see the price of a product, it sets off one part of a communication process; you contribute the other part. Your part is the variable one; that is to say, you will bring your own individual reaction, which could be quite different from mine. We are going to explore this variability in this section. At the end of it we should have a basis for changing our role to that of the businessman making price decisions. For these to be most effective he (and you) must know what has to be taken into account from the human and sometimes unpredictable point of view of the consumer.

Self-check

How would you answer the question, 'What is a price?' It seems almost silly to ask! We all know what price is! In which case it should be fairly easy for us to explain! But it isn't, is it? So having got myself into this situation, I had better have a go at doing just that! Well, why not?

9.3 What is a Price?

I am going to define price in the same sort of way that I have used definitions in the previous chapters – by looking at what it does. On that basis, the purpose of price :

● *to provide a means of assessing value and/or making comparisons of value.*

Answering the question more directly, price – like money – is a means of measuring. This argument is based on the premise that money has no value. As we use it money gives us purchasing power and, through that, satisfaction. Twice before we have stressed the use of the word 'value'.

Self-check

'Profit and satisfaction' were the balancing ingredients of the marketing concept brought together by 'exchanges for value' (refer to page 34, Figure 3.3). Later, on page 52 we employed the words 'people bring value to products'. How often have you said, or has someone said to you, 'Why on earth did you spend your money on that?' (I am sure that this will 'ring a bell' with all parents!)

The fact that our individual monetary judgements differ illustrates precisely how we bring different values to purchases. It is, of course, true that the purchase may be regretted, for whatever reason, later; at the time it was made, however, there was sufficient expectation of value to exchange money for it. This is one way price is used by a consumer – a means of assessment.

All of us have certain priorities of what we want and whether or not we are prepared to pay for it. This is a constantly changing situation; our priorities cannot remain the same for long. After all as soon as one has been met, the remainder 'move up a place', rather like waiting in a queue. Or something may intervene to rearrange the priority entirely; for instance you just remember someone's birthday and have a present to buy. In this way we are constantly making 'comparisons of value', weighing up one kind of purchase against another or comparing one product with another.

Those people who were the first to study the effects of price and of behaviour were of course the economists; and although many of the earlier theories have long since been superseded, they made a major contribution to modern understanding of the subject. A continuing problem for marketers is determining the extent of 'rational' consumer behaviour around prices. The early economists put the view that people were essentially rational and, assuming that they had the necessary information, would spend their money to 'maximize utility'. For a long time, although no longer, this idea concealed many other influences which apparently indicated 'irrational' reactions to price. Both the words 'rational' and 'irrational' are always applied in these contexts by people other than the purchasers themselves! They are, in effect, judgements, and I always ask myself, 'What right has anybody got to judge my spending habits?' Indeed have I any right to judge yours?

The use of the word 'utility', from economics, is very similar to my use of the word 'functional' in Section 5.3.

Another term which has come from economics is that of 'disposable income'. We can explain this as being the amount of money left to us after the necessities of life have been paid for. Some of you may also have come across the term 'discretionary income'. I am not going to make any distinction between the two, except to suggest that the latter is rather more descriptive. (I mention them both because everybody may not be familiar with them.) For our purposes, whichever term we may be used to, let us interpret it as money over which we have complete freedom to spend as we choose. The limits of this income operate as a brake on our spending, however rational or irrational our approach to prices.

Self-check

Because price is so intimately tied up with value, whether of 'utility' (functional) or symbolic (psychological, sociological or even technological), there are examples of apparently extraordinary purchasing behaviour:

1 In the late 1950s, when television was very much a status symbol, many people bought roof aerials (they had to be that kind in those days) to display 'ownership'. Often there was no television set at the end of the aerial!
2 Continuing the theme, studies in the USA showed that in the decade 1958 to 1968 sales of television sets were more closely associated with social values than with the level of disposable income. In other words purchasers put the priorities for TV high above many other things.
3 Any of the older computer companies could give you examples of very costly installations being made for reasons of prestige by the managing directors of many businesses.

9.4 Summary

The keynote of price from the consumer's point of view is, then, one of value, however that may be interpreted by an individual. The interpretation is assisted by money, or the price, for measurement or comparison. Because personal characteristics and external circumstances are infinitely variable, observations of other people's purchasing behaviour may lead to totally erroneous judgements about them; price behaviour never was, nor ever will be, totally 'rational'. Priorities, of whatever kind, govern!

9.5 What Does Price Mean to the Business?

In the introduction to this chapter there was early warning that we would be looking at price 'firmly set in the context of marketing objectives'. This is what we will now be embarking on. Just as I qualified it in the introduction, there must also be consideration of other aspects and functions in business which have a bearing on the whole relationship of revenue, less costs, leaving a surplus that we call profit. But for us the main consideration will always be the marketing one, if only because it is in the market that exchanges for value take place.

We are therefore going to explore a number of situations related to both products and companies in the context of pricing. We will examine the policies pursued by them to see if any special lessons can be drawn; is there anything of universal application which might guide our decisions when we have to make them? Perhaps we could start by looking at some of the 'traditional' names given to some price policies.

9.6 Some 'Traditional' Names

There are occasions, some of which we shall illustrate shortly, when companies decide that they want to capture a slice of a market. Now markets have a habit of not remaining too constant for any length of time! They can be growing, they can be shrinking or they can be static. The probability is that at one time or another they will be all three; which means that the marketer has to keep in touch with what is going on 'out there' in the marketplace. I used the word 'capture' earlier deliberately because it implies, rightly in this case, that you want either to take a share of the market away from somebody or get hold of it before somebody else does. You are competing hard, making it more difficult for the opposition and easier for your potential customers. So what do you do? You lower price. This would be known as 'penetration' pricing.

The opposite is usually known as 'skimming'. Figuratively you are taking the cream off the top of the milk; going for a small proportion of the whole but at the quality end of the market. This equals high prices. Naturally there are all the possible permutations between these two extremes. Quite a lot will depend on how a business may view price: is it something which should be related to the firm itself or should it reflect the position of the market? The former might be called 'cost oriented', the latter 'demand oriented'.

At its extreme a cost oriented approach to pricing is often also referred to as 'cost plus'. In normal competitive industries this is not very common, but it was frequently used during the Second World War for defence contracts. A firm would calculate its costs and add on a fixed percentage over and above giving the 'price'. Quite obviously this approach gives no encouragement to finding cost economies, rather the reverse!

Whenever a business prices its products on its interpretation of conditions in the market, it is using a demand orientation approach; costs have to be contained within the dictates of the market. Consumer values are the basis on which prices are set. In times of recession, as in the early 1980s, total incomes diminish, necessities rise in price (through inflation

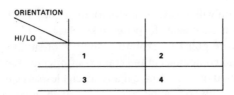

Fig 9.1   *Price orientation – 1*

for example) and disposable incomes are dramatically squeezed. Any attempt to keep prices in line with the altered consumer values and still remain profitable forces businesses into drastic cost reductions. In times of boom the reverse may take place; pressure on prices diminishes, profitability becomes easier and there is less pressure on costs.

We have considered two extremes of pricing, at the low end and at the high, and two orientations (or points of view) taken by firms when setting prices.

The 'boxes' in Figure 9.1 above are numbered so that the case studies that I am going to tell you about below can be easily related back to the matrix, first by you and then by me.

I am going to tell you a number of stories (or what I have just referred to as 'case studies') in order to relate real events – practice – to the theories. After each story I will ask you to give it a number from the matrix; put another way, I am going to be asking you to place it in the right box.

A *Societé BiC, SA*

You and I will know of this company primarily through its ballpoint pens, disposable razors and lighters. In 1958 a Frenchman, M Marcel Bich, decided to become an international leader in the low price disposable ballpoint pen market. Low priced cigarette lighters and then razors followed in the 1970s. There were two main keys to success: mass production techniques were developed to enable manufacture to take place at high volume but minimum cost per unit produced; mass marketing was planned, including the lowest possible prices. (Which box? **1, 2, 3** or **4**?)

B *Bechstein*

You are an up-and-coming concert pianist and have just signed a contract for a European tour. You are looking for a new piano for yourself and go to visit a West End dealer in musical instruments. How would that dealer classify you within the market and what sort of 'value' would he imagine you put on the piano? (Which box? **1, 2, 3** or **4**?)

C *Commodore Business Machines*
'A leading computer company shows that with prices from £200 to £9000 their micros can fit anyone's pocket . . . ' says an advertisement (*Daily Telegraph*, 23.2.82). The £200 model, it goes on to explain, would be the 'home colour computer' – what are becoming known as 'personal' computers. Where would you place this one in relation to the Sinclair ZX81 at £69.95? (Which box? **1, 2, 3** or **4**?)

D *De Lorean*
After putting in £80 million of investment in the late 1970s to establish the De Lorean plant in Belfast to make stainless-steel sports cars for the American market, the British government finally appointed the Official Receiver in February 1982 to take over. Originally it had been hoped to make and sell about 20 000 cars a year; in practice less than half that number were sold. Conversely prices being charged in the USA were twice that originally intended at £14 000, which put the car into a much higher price bracket and therefore different market than its quality warranted. (Which box? **1, 2, 3** or **4**?)

E *Skytrain and Virgin Atlantic*
By offering the 'no frills' walk-on-walk-off transatlantic air fares at much lower rates than those charged by the international cartel IATA, Sir Freddie Laker broke down restrictive air fares across to North America. He will always be remembered as the man who brought cheap travel to many people and greatly expanded the market. But as recession bit into the western economies, the competition hit back hard to retain their share of a shrinking market. As we all know, Laker collapsed. But low price airfares were not for long held at bay by the major airlines; Virgin Atlantic has now entered the market although still operating on a much smaller scale – so far. (Which box? **1, 2, 3** or **4**?)

F *ABC Cinemas*
There are few large cinemas left; most have been split into two or three small ones and it is on these that we shall focus:

(**a**) an ordinary 'run of the mill' film distributed throughout the chain;
(**b**) a special international box-office 'hit'.

What price policies would be pursued for (**a**) and for (**b**); would they be different? (Which box? **1, 2, 3** or **4**?)

If, working through these six examples, you have not had cause to think rather carefully, I would be surprised. Have some 'ifs' and 'buts' reared their heads in your mind? I am sure they have; because the matrix is rather too simple to take account of all possible variations of

Fig 9.2   *Price orientation – 2*

prices. Nevertheless, let me also use it to start with, just as you have, and then elaborate a little further. (See Figure 9.2.)

There are two points that I must make before we go any further. The first is that the case studies are so highly abbreviated that many other contributory causes have been ignored in relation to the price policies illustrated; because of this brevity the second point is that different interpretations of the box placings are possible. However, there are several conclusions that we can draw from the examples, and this can be done with the aid of another matrix.

Self-check

This time we will look at the six products again but sort them out on different grounds; instead of taking the firm's pricing point of view (cost or demand orientation) we will consider the product – is it in the 'necessity' category or the 'disposable' one?

In Figure 9.3 what sticks out like a sore thumb is a gap in box 1! Does this indicate that there are no such things as high-priced necessities? We only have one example in box 2! In both cases this is frankly because of the products used, and I did not want to make the first list too long. But there is no reason why it cannot be lengthened now. And with your help it will be.

9.7 High-priced Necessities

A key characteristic about necessities is their stability of demand; because we have them there will always be a number of businesses ready to supply, in competition with each other of course. But competition usually forces prices down. So high-priced necessities will usually be

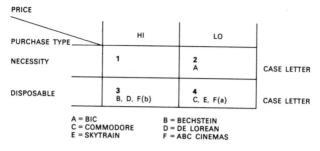

Fig 9.3 *Price orientation – 3*

those products and services where there is an absence of severe competition. Can you think of any examples? What about rates (local government taxes)? Would fares on public transport fall into this category in your opinion?

The Greater London Council 'Fare's Fair' scheme Until it was decreed by the Law Lords that the scheme was illegal, the GLC (now abolished) decided to reduce London Transport fares by subsidies which would be paid for by ratepayers. Fares had been considered high (box **1**), were reduced by subsidy (moved to box **2**) and now back again (box **1**).

9.8 Low-priced Necessities

Think of the stability of demand for ballpoint pens! Men, too, will always have to shave – unfortunately! But before BiC came along there were well-known names (some of which still survive successfully) in both product areas: Waterman, Parker, Conway Stewart; Gillette, Wilkinson; and for electric razors, Philips, Remington, Ronson.

The number of products which could be put into this box is enormous; think of foodstuffs, groceries, cosmetics, with their wide range of choices. Of course, in bad times people can and do economize by consuming less extravagantly – or buy a less expensive product. In other words even necessities are not absolutely stable in demand; we can all trim back a little, but not completely. So if a company can capture and retain sufficient volume, this kind of product/market is a good one to be in.

9.9 High-priced Disposables

All disposable spending is much less predictable and therefore risky! High-priced is possibly less so than low-priced because such products are aimed at, and appeal to, a small proportion of the population – the wealthy! There is no question of attempting to create a volume market, but what volume there is can, in severe economic conditions, contract hard. Our Bechstein piano example would be a case in point.

The De Lorean car illustrates a rather different condition. It was never the intention that this car would be high priced relative to its competition, rather the contrary. What put it into this box, number 3 rather than number 4, was a miscalculation of the volume to be sold. You will recall that less than half of the anticipated 20 000 have been sold. An attempt had to be made to cover costs. (Do you notice how the word 'volume' is cropping up?)

9.10 Low-priced Disposables

This is the most dynamic, and perhaps exciting, area for marketing; it is also full of risks! In the long run many low-priced disposables have a tendency to become necessities, often starting at the top end of the wealth scale and gradually coming down into the mass markets: kitchen equipment like refrigerators, freezers; TV sets; cars of course; transistor radios; electronic calculators and so on. Prices start out high, but reduce as competition enters the market (moves from box 3 to box 4). But if for any reason disposable income contracts, most of such purchases can be postponed, or the existing one made to last a little longer! Demand can be unpredictable; and if there is at the same time an overabundant supply, companies get into trouble!

This is what happened to Skytrain. Sir Freddie Laker by reducing prices dramatically for transatlantic flights expanded the whole market for air travel; new people came in for the first time. As long as demand was expanding this was fine, but as soon as it shrank (people had other priorities for spending their money) there was a surplus of seats in too many aircraft. The other airlines had to retaliate against Laker and slashed their fares even to the extent of making deliberate losses.

Can we compare this to the personal computer? Yes, the differences are these: there is an increasing demand for personal computers – at the moment – and Sinclair, like Freddie Laker, is increasing the total market by bringing such products within the price range of a lot of people. By February 1982 he is reported to have sold over 260 000 ZX81s. The £200 Commodore is more expensive but still pretty cheap. But there is still an overall shortage against strong demand even in a period of recession.

Entertainment – ABC Cinemas – is something that can very easily be cut out when personal budgets are tight; not that we want to, but our priorities dictate it. Therefore general 'run of the mill' films have to try to keep their prices down (box 4) to remain any kind of attraction. But if a really good box-office hit is available up goes the demand to see it, the market is expanded from the usual one – the young – to families: *The Sound of Music* and *E.T.*, would be examples where prices could be increased or the runs extended into second or even third weeks to get extra (guaranteed?) revenue.

It should be very obvious how much the state of the market affects the price decision. Inevitably this must reduce the freedom of action of any decision-maker when attempting to set prices; simultaneously he should be aware of contributory causes of the market situation.

As a market declines or shrinks a business must become more cost oriented in order to prevent potential losses as volume decreases; when the market is growing profits are much easier to make.

9.11 Summary

By now a lot of ground has been covered: at the beginning two extremes of low and high pricing, known respectively as 'penetration' and 'skimming', were discussed. From there we took two points of view that may govern a firm's price decisions; we called them 'cost' and 'demand' orientation. Using these four variables, six small case studies relating to actual and, for the most part, well-known companies and events in their histories were used to illustrate some of the opportunities and dangers that may hinge around a price decision, depending upon the kind of product. Borrowing from the terms used in economics (and in the previous sections) products were related to simple classifications – namely were they 'necessities' or 'disposable' (the latter having a special meaning).

Using the case studies for working purposes two matrices were used to help clarify our thinking, and for differentiating the examples one from another. These led us into the development of other considerations affecting price such as output volumes, the state of competition and the availability of supplies.

9.12 How to Decide and Subsequently Verify

In the end a price is a definite figure – whatever the currency. Because this is so calculations around its components can be done mathematically and tend to give us a spurious impression of precision and accuracy. Hence the second half of the title of this section – 'subsequently verify'.

We are going to look at a method of manipulating prices for decision-making in order to achieve predetermined levels of profit. We are going to be brief. That will lead us into the danger of excluding certain variations, which a more comprehensive study would include. If, therefore, you wish to pursue this technique I would advise you to seek further information from accountancy textbooks. We are, of course, going to be dealing in money.

9.13 Profit-Volume Analysis

You will remember that in Section 9.9 I drew your attention to the way the word 'volume' kept cropping up. The technique of 'profit volume analysis' is a means of manipulating the following variables:

- number of units (or products) multiplied by
- the price(s) at which they are sold equals
- the 'revenue';
- the total costs, which are made up of
- 'variable' costs, e.g. those directly linked to the level of output and
- 'fixed' costs which have to be paid regardless of the level of output;
- 'contribution', which is the difference between price and variable costs.

In order to get the picture a little clearer in your mind, particularly if you have never come across this before, let's clarify by illustrations the terms 'variable' and 'fixed' costs.

Variable costs . . . those directly linked to the level of output. You are making a plateful of scrambled eggs for yourself: you use two eggs, some milk, salt and pepper, possibly some spicy herbs, and butter in the pan; you will also be using some power to cook it, gas or electricity, and your own labour. Three variable costs – materials, power, labour. Now suppose you were making scrambled eggs for six people, you would use more of everything, not necessarily in direct proportion though. But you would be able to calculate (if you went to the trouble) the relationship. Now translate this principle to a carpet factory: the more carpet produced the greater the variable costs proportionately. This is called a 'linear relationship' and is a principle of this technique as well as being one of its weaknesses, e.g. changing costs of raw materials, and changing wage rates due either to overtime or wage awards.

Fixed costs . . . which have to be paid regardless of the level of output. Rent and rates have to be paid; so do salaries of directors and employees who are not linked to production, e.g. all clerical staff; power used in the offices. These items are sometimes referred to as 'overheads'. In the short run they cannot be changed.

Contribution . . . which is the difference between price and variable costs. Each time we sell a product this difference 'contributes' towards

How Much

The Marketing

144

Now we c
see wha
alrea

covering the fixed costs and, after that has beer
profit.

If price is £1, variable cost is £0.75 and fixed cost
(products) do we have to sell to pay for our fixed
how many contributions do we need to make up £.

Contribution = £1 − £0.75 = £0.25, or 25p. Your a
£5 divided by 25p.

So if you sell 20 units you have recovered all yo_ ⌐sts, both the variable ones (75p) and the fixed ones. The point at which all costs are covered by revenue is known as the *break-even point*. Once you reach this point every additional 'contribution' goes to profit − because all your fixed costs have been covered.

You want to make £1.50 profit. How many more units do you have to sell over and above the 20 already sold to reach your profit target?

Divide £1.50 by 25p = 6. So in total you would need to sell 26 units.

Now that is all pretty simple. But the figures are a little unrealistic for a business; I agree. So we will correct that in a future example. But remember, even though the numbers may be bigger, the principle remains exactly the same.

9.14 Using Graphs

Before we go on to use different figures let me illustrate the graphic approach first. The data remains the same: price = £1; VC = £0.75; FC = £5. Therefore:

Revenue = 26 × £1 = £26.
Total VC = 26 × £0.75 = £19.50.
Total contributions = 26 × £0.25 = £6.50 (or £26 − £19.50 = £6.50).
Total costs: VC + FC = £19.50 + £5 = £24.50
Profit = revenue − total costs = £26 − £24.50 = £1.50

As you can see from the chart − Figure 9.4 − the fixed costs are shown below the line preceded by a 'minus' sign (−), because, as you will recall, they have to be paid regardless of the level of output; they are thought of as 'negative'. Where the sloping line, which represents the successive erosion of fixed costs by the contributions, crosses the horizontal one is the break-even point (where total costs = total revenue). We have shown the horizontal line with values of units; multiply these units by price and this line can also show revenue at various points along it.

Given that the price and cross relationships remain constant, we can read off profit or loss anywhere along the horizontal scale; and as we have seen, we can also calculate it arithmetically.

begin to explore making changes in the figures in order to happens. In the table below the middle column lists those charted, as Figure 9.4. The right-hand column shows some different figures with a change in price and, in consequence, some other changes.

	As per PV chart Fig. 9.4	As per PV Chart Fig. 9.5
Price per unit	£1	£0.95
Variable costs per unit	£0.75	£0.75
Contributions per unit	£0.25	£0.20
Fixed costs	£5	£5
Profit target	£1.50	£1.60

Questions to be answered
1 What are the two break-even points in units?
2 How many units have to be sold at each price to reach the profit targets?
3 Calculate the percentage change in price and the percentage change in units to achieve the equivalent profit targets.

The combination of our profit target and the number of units we have to sell to reach it is the *profit volume point*.

Therefore the calculations can be made as follows:

$$\text{Break-even point} = \frac{\text{total fixed costs}}{\text{unit contribution}}$$

$$\text{Profit volume point} = \frac{\text{total fixed costs} + \text{profit target}}{\text{unit contribution}}$$

Fig 9.4   *Profit volume chart – 1*

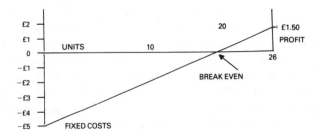

Therefore:

	PV chart Fig. 1	PV chart Fig. 2
BE =	£5/£0.25 = 20 units	£5/£0.20 = 25 units

$$PV = \frac{£5 + £1.50}{£0.25} \qquad \frac{£5 + £1.60}{£0.20}$$

$$= 26 \text{ units} \qquad = 33 \text{ units}$$

Therefore, a 5 per cent *reduction in price* would result in a 27 per cent *increase in volume* to obtain the equivalent profit!

Note: this relationship is not a universal one. In other words it applies to the illustration and the relationship of costs and prices in this example.

I suggested a couple of pages back that the figures we were using might appear to be a bit simple for a real business situation. Well, imagine that we are marketing executive jets at £1 million each, we have sold in the past year 26 of them at a total cost of £24 500 000, of which £5 million were fixed costs; draw up a profit volume chart and you would be reproducing Figure 9.4 all over again.

9.15 Verification

It is all very well planning prices, and even publishing them for all to see, but do they work out quite so neatly in the end? The answer to this question will be dependent upon the relationship between buyer and seller.

In Section 8.2 I sent you on an imaginary package holiday in Algeria where you were wandering through the native bazaar looking for a

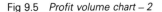

Fig 9.5 *Profit volume chart – 2*

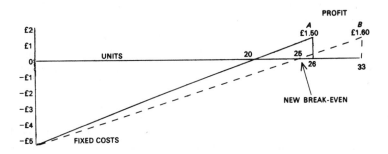

souvenir; did you pay the price asked? Suppose that souvenir had been
an imitation Arabian dagger to be used as an ornament or a paper-knife
and the street vendor sold quite a lot of them but at different prices
depending on how gullible the tourists were, he would have difficulty in
calculating his unit 'contributions'! He would have to have enough 'feel
for the trade' to ensure that over a number of sales he would come out on
the right side – profitably. When you are that close to both goods and
customers traders will cope, usually adequately. As soon as a business
gets to any reasonable size rather more formal methods than 'feel' need
to be used.

Most businesses also have not one but a variety of products all selling
at different prices and with different cost structures. That will muddle the
picture up a bit too. It is therefore essential for 'average' prices and costs
to be calculated on historical records in order to see what difference
there may be between 'actual' price (the one really obtained) and 'list'
price (the one quoted before negotiation).

Also referring back once more to the previous chapter, Section 8.3
illustrated the 3 '*I*s' – investigation, identification and interaction. The
last of these was subdivided into 'negotiation' (and also 'technology' – not necessarily relevant in this discussion).

This was one reason why people are so important in selling; so if we,
for instance, were to imagine ourselves as being sales managers, we must
be allowing our salesmen to negotiate – on prices, on volumes, on
technology!

Given the chance most salesmen will try to sell through price negotiation, and in practice that means cutting. And when competition gets
tougher they will try to use it more and more. If you as the sales manager
let it happen your average price can come tumbling down with disastrous
results as 'contributions' fall.

9.16 Summary and Active Review

By now I think we are ready to draw some of the threads together and by
so doing review a number of points in both this and other chapters. But I
will ask also for your active collaboration!

The name of our company is Executive Jets Ltd and we have a
problem! Our list price for each aircraft is £1 million; variable costs per
plane are £750 000 and we have to cover fixed costs of £5 million. (If
these figures are apparently familiar to you, so they should be – refer to
the table in Section 9.14.)

The present state of trading, based on an estimate of sales for the year
of 26 aircraft, is that we have sold 18 at list price, have firm contracts for
a further three also at list price and are negotiating with a large

multinational corporation for the sale of five for delivery and use in South America. The general situation is summarized below:

	Facts	*Considerations*
Type of product	Capital good, technical – spares and maintenance	'Disposable' – purchase could easily be deferred
Competition	Three other firms in running	Comparable
State of market	Static	No supply shortage
Location	South America	Company has stronger spares and service network than competition
List prices	From £915 000 to £1 220 000	£1 000 000

EJL must negotiate their way through this one! The only specific advantage lies in a previous policy decision to specialize on geographic market segments and build up after-sales services within them, before moving on hard to other areas. South America is one such segment and therefore should give the company a competitive edge.

From our previous calculations we know that we break even at twenty aircraft sold at list prices (see profit volume chart, Figure 9.4, Section 9.14). At 21 certain sales then we have a contribution to profit from the twenty-first of £250 000. And now we have the opportunity of selling five more to a single customer. If we lose this one there are no other orders in sight. We should probably have to put the plant on short-time working, which could lead to industrial relations problems, some loss of skilled staff – all of which we would want to avoid. But at what cost? In view of the strength of the customer, it's pretty obvious that we are going to have to negotiate! So we must look at some options.

Options
1 The company's records indicate that servicing and spares, on average flying hours a year, would amount to £30 000 per aircraft in its first twelve months of service. If we could offer a free spares and service contract for twelve months in South America for these five planes, would that be enough to swing the order our way? If it were, the cost would be deferred into the next financial period, which could be very useful. The total cost would amount to £150 000 (£30 000 × 5), which is only three fifths of the contribution from a single aircraft.

2 Our next position could be to offer the free service as in **1** above, plus an additional inducement (remember which promotional technique this was? See 'Sales promotion', Section 7.12) of a £52 000 reduction off list price. *Calculate* what the profit for the year would be for all 26 aircraft and their average price.

3 Suppose that we forget the servicing offer and stick to price only and offer a reduction of £104 000 per plane. *Calculate* what the profit for the year would be for all twenty-six aircraft and their average price.

In the first option, as has already been mentioned, the cost would not affect the current year, so the total profit would remain as £1 500 000 (see Section 9.13).

Do you remember how to calculate 'contribution'? You do? Good! Price less variable costs: £1 million − £750 000 = £250 000.

Option **2** would give us, in the current year, a contribution per unit of £250 000   less   £52 000 = £198 000 × 5 = £990 000 + £250 000   (the twenty-first plane) = £1 240 000 profit.

Option **3** gives us in the current year a contribution per unit of £250 000   less   £104 000 = £146 000 × 5 = £730 000 + £250 00 = £980 000 profit.

Average price for twenty-six planes	Revenue	Price
Option 1	£26 m	£1 m
Option 2	£25.74 m	£0.99 m
Option 3	£25.48 m	£0.98 m

On, option **3**, for example, it means that EJL is 'losing', or 'has lost', £20 000 per plane during the full year's trading. It is the equivalent of a 3.8 per cent profit on revenue as opposed to the original target of 5.8 per cent; that is quite a substantial price to pay. But it could make the long-term difference of staying in profitable business or departing from it altogether. A very crucial matter of negotiation!

Exercises

1 Prices do not remain permanent; assuming that the state of the market is either 'shrinking', 'static' or 'growing' how would you alter prices in the following circumstances?

<table>
<tr><td></td><td colspan="3">*Markets*</td></tr>
<tr><td></td><td>*Shrinking*</td><td>*Static*</td><td>*Growing*</td></tr>
</table>

1 At which extremes would you put 'cost' or 'demand' orientation?
2 For a necessity like stationery would you increase, hold or reduce price?
3 For a necessity like postage stamps would you increase, hold or reduce price?
4 For a disposable like a fashion dress would you increase, hold or reduce price?
5 For a disposable like garden bulbs (for spring flowers) would you increase, hold or reduce price?

2 What did we have to divide into fixed costs to obtain the break-even point? And how did we find out how many extra units have to be sold to reach a given profit level?

There are occasions in business when unit contributions are not available; then the following formula can be used.

$$\frac{TR \times FC}{TR - TVC} = BE \text{ } £$$

Try it and see if you get the same arithmetic result for the break-even. The data are taken from the table in Section 9.14 'As per PV chart Figure 9.4'.

Total revenue £26
Fixed costs £ 5
Total variable costs £19.50

3 If you look carefully at the profit volume chart, Figure 9.5, you will see the letters *A* and *B* above each of the two profit volume points: *A* for the first price of £1 and *B* for the altered price of £0.95. In each of the case studies on pages 136–7 we can make an example of using the charts, by imagining price movement from *A* to *B*, from *B* to *A*, or no movement at all but stationary on either *A* or *B*. Would you then refresh your memory of what happens in each case and fill in the proforma below.

(tick appropriate column)	*Movement* *A to B*	*B to A*	*Stationary* *A*	*B*
1 Société BiC, SA				
2 Bechstein				
3 Commodore				
4 De Lorean				
5 Skytrain				
6 ABC Cinemas (a)				
(b)				

4 'Cost orientation' and 'demand orientation' were represented in a matrix in Section 9.6, Figure 9.2. If we add 'competition' we can convert these into the '3 *Cs*' – Cost, Customers and Competition – all having an influence upon price.

From your own experience identify products/services which have their prices constrained by one or more of the '3*Cs*'.

10 What Do We Know?

10.1 Introduction

Most of the books on the subject include a chapter on marketing research before discussing the marketing mix. In this book I have done the opposite because the approach I am going to take relates research very much to the mix. By dealing with that part of marketing first you are now familiar with its main ingredients. Therefore the sections which we have already covered are going to act as an agenda (almost) for this chapter.

This constraint on the content of the chapter should be recognized early; it poses a limitation on a large and complex subject area. I therefore make no claim that the chapter is comprehensive. Indeed it is not. What I aim to do is provide some easily recognizable areas for the student of marketing to cover and identify with. I would go even further and attempt to limit techniques and examples to those which could possible be tried out – given both the interest and the need (say for some course project).

10.2 What is 'Research'?

Even if you are not absolutely sure of the difference, you are almost certain to have heard of 'pure' and 'applied' research! Our subject matter is almost always 'applied', which means that it is directed at finding some kind of solution to a known and defined problem. Also research is associated with what is known as the 'scientific method'. This too has its own important and specific meaning: it requires objectivity, precision and certainty. To achieve such demanding standards the disciplines which have to be applied are rigorous.

There is another aspect to research, of all kinds, that should also be remembered: it sets out to challenge preconceptions. A great many of the ideas which were once taken as true have subsequently been disproved by the challenge of new research. Each piece of research should therefore be reproducible, given the same conditions. This poses immense problems for the behavioural sciences like marketing (as opposed to the physical). Controlled laboratory conditions are seldom available.

Because of these difficulties a specialist industry has evolved for marketing research. Highly sophisticated techniques have been developed by statisticians, operational researchers and behavioural scientists to deal with the multiplicity of problems that arise from marketing. These should be left to the experts.

10.3 D-I-C-E

Whenever we use dice in some game or other, we are in fact employing chance; there is considerable uncertainty and that in turn can be interpreted as risk. Now we have used the word 'risk' in connection with 'resources' and 'results'. So the implication is that risk exists before those resources (whatever they may be) are allocated. Nobody in business likes risk, so steps need to be taken to reduce it. This is where marketing research comes in.

For our purpose the main elements of marketing research can be represented diagrammatically by D-I-C-E.

The very first, and most significant point of all, is the connection with decisions, or more accurately, potential decisions. This is why I mentioned earlier that we are talking about 'applied' research. Unfortunately all too often research is used (and good money spent) without any potential decision having been made. From the limited examination of the subject in this chapter, may I ask you to keep this point firmly in mind; it will be further developed later on.

The remaining 'arms' of Figure 10.1 introduce us to the three main areas of marketing research activity:

Fig 10.1   *D-I-C-E*

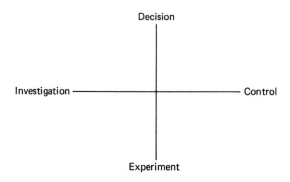

1 Investigation into some defined problem connected with marketing in order to minimize the amount of risk. This is a 'before' situation.
2 Control is concerned with 'after' an event. To what extent has the original plan met its target?
3 Experiments are usually about trial and error, the outcome of which is unknown. Once it has been clarified action can be based upon the result.

10.4 **Planning and Control**

To transpose the words 'before' and 'after' into a managerial situation brings us quickly into the context of planning, often represented as a cycle as in Figure 10.2 below.

Planning is concerned with making decisions about the future use of resources (inputs) to achieve certain results (outputs) over a given period of time. It is not difficult for any of us to accept that this needs information; marketing research is one way of getting it.

If you imagine for a moment that you are behind your office desk making decisions about product, place, promotion and price (inputs), you have total control of what is going to be done! The product will be red, packed in polystyrene, advertised in colour supplements, distributed to certain retailers, aimed at teenagers, and priced at £5.99. These points are 'controllable'.

The reaction (outputs) are not 'controllable'. How do you know that the teenagers want red? Is the price of £5.99 attractive? Do they frequent the type of retailer that you have chosen? Now obviously experience is going to tell you a great deal of what to do and what not to do, particularly if you are closely in touch with the buyers. But the further removed you are from them the more need there is to close the gap. The local corner shop can react very quickly to its customers' purchasing behaviour. But can a major multinational company? Do you remember when Coca Cola changed its flavour and what happened? There was an

---

Fig 10.2   *Planning cycle*

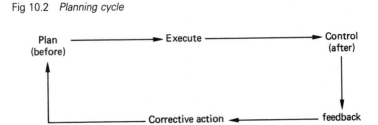

international 'hoo-ha'; but months elapsed before the company was convinced that it had made a mistake and reverted to the old formula. What had happened to the research?

There are many stories in the history of marketing research when, after spending considerable sums of money, companies still found that their decisions were mistaken. So there are no guarantees; the 'certainty' demanded by the scientific approach is not in fact always applicable because of the dynamic nature of the 'uncontrollable' environment. The future can never be predicted with certainty.

The warning in the previous paragraph must not be taken to imply that, therefore, marketing research is a waste of time. Far from it. First we must recognize that it has its limitations; it serves the purpose of reducing risk, never of eliminating it. Therefore a good way of thinking about it is as insurance. Which is wiser – to go full speed ahead with all the investment and execution of a marketing programme at great cost, or to spend a limited sum of money to assess the probable outcome of a plan? The difference may be £1 000 000 or £10 000.

10.5 *'Ad hoc'* or 'Continuous' Feedback

In Figure 10.2 above the word 'feedback' is used. Let us now think of that part of the system as being either an occasional event (*'ad hoc'*) or a 'continuous' one. Each of the three 'arms' in Figure 10.1, after Decision, – investigation, control and experiment – should be designed to be one or the other. The likelihood will be:

Investigation – *ad hoc*
Control   – continuous
Experiment – *ad hoc*

10.6 For Whom?

You will have realized by now that everything so far in this chapter has been about marketing management, not research. Decisions are taken by executives not researchers; so where do the responsibilities divide?

To avoid possible confusion about functions, let us agree to use only two titles, marketing management and research management. The former will be held responsible for all marketing activities as elaborated in the 'mix', and the latter for all research activities. In practice you know that there would be separation amongst a number of people.

The marketing manager is the decision maker. He has executive responsibility for getting things done. In his planning for the use of some resource(s) he has some doubts which he would like resolved. For example someone in the Coca Cola company began to have doubts about the correctness of the original flavour. Pursuing this analogy (and I have no inside information) let us assume that Pepsi was encroaching on Coke's sales. Put at its simplest Coca Cola's marketing management had only two real choices:

1 Remain with the existing (original) formula.
2 Alter the formula with a new flavour.

At the time of the first doubts, the second alternative was nothing else but an hypothesis:

'Given that we (Coca Cola) could find a new flavour acceptable to the consumer, we could retain our existing share of the market and recover sales lost to Pepsi.'

Only at this point does the researcher get involved. Marketing management has arrived at a potential decision (hypothesis) which needs validating by research. But imagine yourself now as the researcher. What flavour? There is no value whatever in sending the researcher off just to find a flavour; the result of that could be lemonade! He or she must have a definite starting point and once more there are only two real choices.

1 Find out what is right and wrong with the original drink, or
2 Test a number of new flavours, or both.

Now the researcher has something definite to look for and in due course the marketing executive will have the answer on which to base a decision. The hypothesis will have been validated or invalidated.

10.7 By Whom?

Somebody has to do the finding out and this leads to another decision.

Only the big organizations are really able to support the cost of maintaining their own marketing research department and keeping it fully employed. Even then they are probably the most prolific buyers of research services from outside. Medium sized companies will often employ a manager responsible for the research function usually as a coordinator of all information services. All too often the job falls to a sales manager, probably the least likely person to be successful at it!

The trouble with using company personnel is lack of total objectivity (see Section 10.2 above). There is a very human desire to produce results favourable to the employing organization; dependence is not the best environment in which to conduct research.

The market research industry has expanded rapidly since the Second World War and operates, similarly to advertising, on an agency basis. A company will contract an agency to carry out a specific task or investigation. But because of the increasing sophistication and development of new techniques more and more agencies are moving towards specialization in particular kinds of research. This offers both advantages and disadvantages.

A reputable specialist is by definition an expert. We have discussed specialists and generalists in the context of selling. The same argument applies here. Many of the best known agencies are automatically associated with certain kinds of research. Amongst these are those conducting what is known as 'syndicated' research. This means that the agency carries out the research anyway, prepares the results and sets out to sell them. It becomes a straightforward commercial service operation.

A potential disadvantage of agencies tending to specialize is the technique they employ. Here let me make a mundane comparison. You can buy an expensive tailor-made suit or have a cheaper one 'off-the-peg'. For good business reasons, to keep costs as low as is reasonable, research agencies will often develop a particular technique which has been extensively used successfully in the past. The temptation is always to continue to try and use that technique in the future. Potential clients are sometimes prodded into adjusting their research project to fit the techniques – which is of course back to front!

Fortunately the marketing research industry not only regards itself as highly professional but is also governed in its behaviour by Codes of Practice. This is naturally a considerable safeguard for the research buyer. Nevertheless any professional buyer should have a greater than average knowledge of what is being purchased. A research manager in a client company is no exception.

10.8 Kinds of Data

A major part of any marketing research will consist of the collection of 'data'. In due course this will be processed into 'information'. These two words need some clarification. 'Data' is the raw material of 'information'. For example let us say that the average number of people visiting a supermarket on Tuesday afternoons is 200 per hour. The 'data' is collected by observation over a number of Tuesdays, averaged to arrive at the figure which then becomes 'information', something can be done with it. The supermarket manager would ensure that sufficient checkouts were in operation to cater for the flow.

In marketing research there are two main kinds of data, each of which is given a special name and is clearly defined.

'Secondary' data is obtainable from any source, internal or external to the firm, which is relevant to the hypothetical solution of the problem and is available but was not originally collected for the specific research task.

'Primary' data is specifically collected with direct reference to the hypothetical solution of the problem being researched.

These two terms, with their numerical connotations, always used to seem to me to be the wrong way round; primary is surely first, and secondary second. However, the actual logic is based on cost. I always think of 'secondary' data as being 'second hand', therefore inexpensive, or cheap. 'Primary' data on the other hand is new, at first hand, and expensive. This is why it is always important in any research project to exhaust the secondary data sources first; they can save the cost of the primary data research.

One way of looking at these two kinds of data within a research context is to think of a series of steps leading to a funnel (Figure 10.3).

Objectives:

1 To reduce the decision risk for the executive concerned.
2 To keep research costs down.
3 To narrow down the scope of the research problem.
4 To minimize the area for primary research.

10.9 Kinds of 'Primary' Research

There are two more main divisions to primary marketing research before we begin to look at applications to the marketing mix
'Quantitative research' and 'Qualitative research'.

Quantitative research Indicative in the title, quantitative research is about collecting data which can then be processed mathematically, or statistically. This means that such data can be counted, or measured, by numerate techniques. The results provide both researcher and executive manager the means of interpreting 'facts'. This last word is important and is frequently a cause of concern, particularly to the beginner in marketing research. What I am implying here is that advanced techniques of modelling, drawing inferences and so on, are not as rigid as I intend to make out!

'Facts' about people and the things they do are answers to five questions:

Who;   (bought)
What;   (product/service)
Where;   (outlet)
When;   (weekly/monthly)
How.   (cash/credit/cheque)

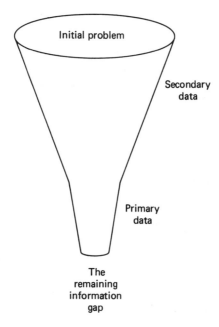

Initial problem

Secondary
data

Primary
data

The
remaining
information
gap

Fig 10.3 *The research funnel*

All of the 'answers' (data) should strictly speaking be about the past and within sufficient recency to be easily remembered. This kind of quantitative marketing research is not about hypothetical questions or future behaviour. The rigidity of my explanation here becomes significant when compared with that most common phenomenon – the public opinion poll. Take political polling – 'What party (candidate) would you vote for if there were a general election tomorrow?' This is a hypothetical question! It is concerned with an event that is not in fact going to take place and even during elections, when it is, many changes of mind can still occur. These polls undoubtedly help sell newspapers; they act as a barometer for the politicians about public opinion. Are they, however, converted to 'information' which is then used by the government or opposition to tailor policies? Most political decisions are far too long term in their effects to be dramatically influenced by poll results.

The most common form of collecting primary data is by sampling. A 'sample' is a proportion containing all the (relevant) characteristics of the 'population' to be researched. It is based on the statistical principle of 'randomness' and should follow those rules. 'Population' here is used as a technical term to mean the body of people, organizations, locations (whatever is relevant) to be researched. It could therefore be the teenage population, service stations with workshop facilities attached, factories located in the town of Slough, Boeing 747 'Jumbo' jets flying out of Gatwick airport or shops selling bootlaces! When a complete population is counted, not just a proportion of it, then that is a 'census' and usually constitutes an important source of secondary data.

Census of population;
Census of distribution;
Census of production, and so on.

Qualitative research There is a variety of names given to this type of research:
Qualitative – Attitudinal – Motivational
For our purpose they all mean the same thing. Such research is concerned with asking the question – '*Why?*'

Any answers to why call for an explanation of some kind, which, if really examined closely, will amount to an expression of belief, opinion, prejudice or bias! It will certainly not be fact in the sense of answers to the first five questions. 'Why' reveals behavioural attributes and for interpretation is the realm of the psychologist and sociologist. The methods used to elicit answers do not lend themselves to quantitative, numerate, analysis but to (qualitative) judgement, hence the importance of skilled interpretation.

10.10 Review

So far in this chapter marketing research has been examined theoretically and all too briefly. Books dealing with the subject should be referred to by serious students. However, a number of key components have been introduced in the first part of this chapter.

You will appreciate how much Figure 10.4 oversimplifies the ramifications of marketing research which we have introduced. However, it is intended as a useful starting point for organizing thoughts about a potential project. The D-I-C-E axis should serve to remind us of the difference between the interests of the marketing and research managers. The top and bottom horizontal axes lead us to examine research methodology alternatives.

The remaining part of this chapter gives a number of illustrations of the use of techniques in relation to the marketing mix. They relate to points already raised in the text of previous chapters. Finally I hope that some at least of the methods explained may be tried out by those students conducting investigative projects.

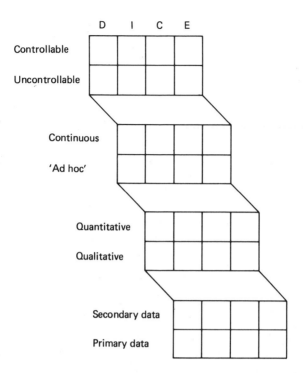

Fig 10.4   *A research planning 'cascade'*

10.11 'Investigation'

For purpose of illustration let us begin by looking for some new market target or segment. (If you need any reminder refer to Section 4.1 for the *Concise Oxford Dictionary* definition of the word 'segment'.)

The objective is to anticipate the removal of all trade barriers within the European Community in 1992. Therefore market segment(s) will be sought in continental Europe; perhaps this reminds you of the Smith Kendon problem (see Section 4.6). Using successive focusing the start would probably be made on locations.

A company marketing agricultural machinery would tend to divide Europe into regions by examining secondary data sources of the distribution of farming activity. Naturally these cross over political frontiers.

Northern plains – Denmark, Belgium, Holland, Germany, France.
Uplands   – Southern Germany, middle and southern France, Spain.
Mountains   – France, Italy, parts of Spain, Greece.

Each region would have its own economic wealth often reflected in the size of farms. The larger, wealthier farms are those most likely to purchase advanced expensive equipment.

Documentary information about such activities are easily obtained from secondary data sources: governments, the European Commission at Brussels which runs the Common Agricultural Policy and has all the relevant records, farmers' associations, trade unions would all be able to provide data.

From such data particular areas of interest could be isolated for further investigation, probably in the first instance still with secondary data. Supposing the interest was in the wine regions. From general knowledge alone parts of France, Germany and Italy and Spain would warrant attention. As grapes can be grown on both flat and mountainous land, further sub-divisions could be important for different types of machinery.

10.12 Techniques for Marketing Mix

The example just given in the previous section about identifying a market segment is of course only one possible application for 'investigation' and an oversimplified one at that. However, it illustrates adequately, I hope, the significance of using secondary data sources first. Naturally investigation can be used on any aspect of the marketing mix that warrants it. So too can 'experiment'.

Experimentation in marketing research arises when a company wishes to change some part of its marketing mix in order to get information about the effect of that change before being committed on a large scale. It is not investigating something that exists but creating a new situation, the result of which is still unknown (see Section 10.3 – 3). This is also part of the insurance mentioned at the end of Section 10.4.

This is neither the place, nor the correct kind of book, to go into any detail of actual marketing research techniques. The mention made of some of the major ones is intended to give little more than an indication of what they are and how they are used in marketing. By doing this it is my hope that the reader may attempt, given an appropriate incentive like a student project, to delve further from other sources and even try out some of the methods illustrated.

10.13 Surveys

A great many people have been introduced to surveys either in their homes or on the street. They are usually associated with questionnaires because this is the kind of marketing research which is most visible to the public. A questionnaire is a list of questions designed to elicit certain types of answer from the respondent (the person answering). Sufficient numbers of these questions have to be answered for subsequent processing and interpretation; the number is determined by the size of the sample. Although based on the statistical theory of 'randomness' (refer to Section 10.9) most surveys are carried out by a method known as 'quota' sampling. There is an assumption that the characteristics of the population are known by the researcher; the sample is then apportioned to ensure that each characteristic is covered in the same proportions as the population.

Suppose that you are surveying doctors; there is a variety of kinds of doctor, from the GP to the heart surgeon; they could be further subdivided by age and experience, and so on. The quota must reflect these divisions. The great administrative advantage of quota sampling is that the divisions are known, the interviewers can deliberately seek out the correct proportions and save a great deal of time and money. Random sampling on the other hand, on which the whole theory is based, requires a list of the population from which respondents must be drawn (like raffle tickets out of a drum) and who must then be interviewed. The assumption is that the sample size will automatically contain the appropriate characteristics of the population. You will by now appreciate that the whole system is highly complex.

There are several very common mistakes made by amateur researchers using questionnaires.

1 Because of lack of knowledge about the 'funnel' approach, secondary sources are neglected (refer to Figure 10.3, Section 10.8).
2 Other 'primary' techniques of obtaining data are unknown.
3 The disadvantages of structured questions and answers are not appreciated.
4 Attempts are made to loosen the structure of question and answer to the detriment of subsequent analysis by so-called 'open-ended' questions.
5 Too many hypothetical questions and 'why' questions are included.
6 The analysis format is not designed in advance.

This is a short-list of some of the snags. What they amount to, as do many others not included (such as the wording of the questions), is bias, or a distortion of results to the clarity and precision required by the 'scientific' approach! But it is not my intention to put the amateur off. Given the chance try as many techniques as you can, because without the attempt you will never overcome the snags nor fully appreciate the expertise that is needed – an expertise incidentally that you may develop within yourself!

10.14 **Product Techniques**

To further encourage the amateur to experiment my approach to
researches into specific parts of the marketing mix is to point the way
quite distinctly to methods that the individual can use with limited
resources. Obviously these will differ somewhat from the professional
approach but in principle remain the same.

If I mention 'common mistakes' again have patience; these are drawn
from some years of watching students make them and there is no point in
your reinventing a (bent) wheel! So my starting point for researching into
products is to start with a negative.

Negatives
The best example that comes to my mind to explain this approach was
the attempt to found a society of students. A self-selected committee met
to try and arrange a programme. They canvassed ex-students and current
ones asking what events they would like. Vague and unimaginative
suggestions were received. A programme was put together and collapsed
in due course for lack of support! What a pity. The approach was
hypothetical – 'What would you like?' Not – 'What are your interests?'
(fact); not – 'What activities do you take part in in your free time?'
(fact); not – 'Do you go to the theatre? play snooker? play table tennis?
attend professional association meetings?' (facts); 'how often? where?'
(facts). Admittedly this was an attempt to set up something from scratch;
but the approach was neither positive nor negative, it was hypothetical!

Ask yourself, or a friend, what is wrong with something – a product or
a service. You will find no difficulty in getting answers. We are very good
at saying what is wrong! Read a *Which?* report; the whole approach is
based on what their laboratory tests, or readers' assessments, consider to
be wrong. These negatives can be the creative starting point for
product/service improvement or correction. They can identify the hypothetical solution. Why is it that Japanese cars always seem to be one
jump ahead of their British equivalents? They have asked the question:
'What's wrong?' or 'What's missing?' and then incorporated the answer
into the production line. This last point so often seems to be the
stumbling-block. The negative reappears as 'it can't be done' instead of
'Ok, now how can we do it?' This kind of approach is just what is meant
by the marketing concept, the balancing scales of 'profit' and 'satisfaction' illustrated in Figure 3.3, Section 3.4.

Comparison or attribute tests
Increasing our level of sophistication when two or more products are put
together straightforward negatives are insufficient. We are entering into
comparisons. If I may again refer to *Which?* reports, you will find there

typical examples of comparative results according to what has been tested for that particular issue of the magazine. You will note that the comparatives are shown to apply to all the products concerned with the test and are usually scaled in some way. Symbols are used to convey to readers that various attributes are

Below average
Average
Above average
Excellent

An attribute in a product is related to what we called the 'functional' in Chapter 5, 'What is a product?', Section 5.3. The method shown above is known as scaling and is fairly easily applied to functional attributes, although the correct statistical procedure needs to be properly carried out. The 'symbolic' (Section 5.4) cannot be approached in this way.

Independent sources of product assessment, like *Which?* provide an invaluable service to many consumers in evaluating potential purchases; if they did not they would hardly remain in business! But they cannot measure the intangible symbolic meanings which marketing applies to its products and successfully segmented consumers adopt.

10.15 Distribution Techniques

The products you buy today were certainly manufactured some time ago; depending on the product of course that time gap will vary. But it means that the marketing decisions made now will not affect the consumption of people like you and me for some time into the future. This time gap can be dangerous. The marketing manager is, therefore, out of synchronization with the marketplace but ahead of it. We can use Figure 10.2 (repeated below) once more to elaborate.

Suppose each of the steps shown takes an average of two weeks (some will take less, some more) there is a total of just over two months. Now Figure 10.2 applies to only one set of decisions, in its original context those of a manufacturer; in addition there are similar decisions being taken by the intermediaries, the wholesalers and retailers. This could double or treble the time cycle until you and I take the product off a shelf and eventually consume or use it.

A company's own records do not help to close this time gap. They should help, when properly processed, to describe how products move through different types of outlet. Given sufficient time, trends will show up. I know of a case in which one kind of outlet took 30–35 per cent of a manufacturer's sales in the early 1950s and only 5 per cent thirty years later. In that period management had taken no marketing action.

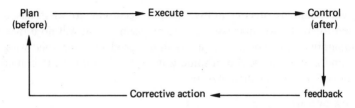

Fig 10.2   *Planning cycle*

---

1 *Retail audit* Closing this dangerous time gap can be carried out by regular retail audits. There is a number of agencies who specialize in this field, the most famous of which is Nielsen with its 'food and drug' index from grocery and chemist outlets. This kind of research is syndicated (refer to Section 10.7) and sold to clients per product audited. As a result competitor's products can be monitored as well; one only has to pay the bill.

The kernel of the reporting system is one of stock movement. If you are familiar with the standard format of a business manufacturing account, you will know that it has a section reading

Opening stock	100
add Purchases	1000
	1100
less Closing stock	90
equals Sales	1010

Stocktaking in this fashion takes place every two months over a representative sample of outlets and reports are submitted in detail to the client companies. Being computerized it is highly detailed, taking into account monetary values, units, shops types, pack sizes, price variations, special promotions taking place in the period and so on.

2 *Consumer panels* The retail audit may explain a great deal about the movement of products into and out of shops but it tells you very little about the end consumer. For this we need a research technique which gathers the data from the people who buy. The most widespread method is by a consumer panel. A number of households are recruited to the appropriate sample size to maintain records of their purchases over a period of time. Their segmentation data (location, classification, lifestyle) is cross-referenced with their purchasing behaviour, including the kinds of shops where they buy. The data is either collected by, or posted to, the research agency weekly for processing and subsequent reporting.

These operations are also syndicated and the information sold to any company interested enough to pay the price.

It does not take a lot to appreciate that syndicated research has distinct economic advantages. Either retail audits or consumer panels are collecting the data anyway. The collated and processed information is a commodity available to any customer and therefore enables companies to monitor not only their own products but also their own products in relation to competitors'. Because there are many customers for this service the costs of data collection can be spread much more widely and the whole operation becomes an economic proposition. It is inconceivable that an individual manufacturer could afford to set up a nationwide, or even international, research procedure on such a scale.

Both retail audits and consumer panels are essentially control techniques and, to be useful to the decision maker, must operate on a continuous basis.

10.16 Promotion Techniques

The purpose of promotion in marketing is to communicate and by being successful lead to purchasing behaviour. In Chapter 7 we described the promotion mix as moving the consumer through the three 'A's' of awareness, attitude, and action (see Figure 7.2, Section 7.17). Marketing research in this area must, therefore, be linked to the communication objectives, not, as is often argued, directly to sales results. You may legitimately enquire about 'action' in the three 'A's'; is this not the sales result? You are right, it is. But you will also recall that we discussed only one promotion technique which was directly linked to sales – that was sales promotion (Section 7.12).

There are four main ingredients which research needs to examine.

Message – media – timing – frequency

all of which have been the subject of a great deal of practical and academic investigation. Let us then look at each one in turn.

1 *Message* The real importance of any message is that it must be understood and acceptable by those who receive it. How often have

you had to listen to something, a lecture, a radio or TV programme, in which the speaker was incomprehensible to *you*? I am not saying that any of these was actually incomprehensible, especially to those who were interested and understood what was being conveyed. Think for a moment about segmentation! This was described in Chapter 4 as being one of the most important aspects of marketing. So also with promotion. Messages are beamed at the people we want to communicate with, not generally to the world at large.

Many messages we receive, from commercial and other sources, we reject. For whatever reason we do not find them acceptable. Now this result would not further the objectives of the promotion mix. So it is important for the message 'sender' to ensure that it will be both understood and accepted by the message 'receiver'.

The most commonly used research method to identify messages understandable and acceptable to the chosen audience is the *group discussion*. Although the amateur would not be able to carry out professional psychological analysis and interpretation, it is a technique which can be employed provided the 'results' are recognized as being superficial.

A small group of people (6–10) is selected on the grounds that its members 'fit' the profile of the market segment, they have the appropriate characteristics. For example, I was once 'qualified' by a research agency by telephone questioning on a residential basis (house owner-occupier), number of children (2), current possession of 'mixer' drinks (squashes, bitter lemon, tonic, soda water, etc.) and so on. All the other members of that group had been similarly 'qualified'. This process establishes what is called a 'homogeneous' group. When all the selected members come together they have common interests and will be likely to mix without any disharmony.

The meeting place will usually be in a private house, occasionally in research agency premises. In any event the locale is designed to provide ease, comfort and relaxation so that those present may mix and talk easily. Sometimes the participants are rewarded with a small gift afterwards but not always. The host/hostess will certainly gain something.

The research agency will provide the discussion leader and the preliminary groundwork of the points to be discussed. Usually there are about eight or ten key points which have been loosely arranged into a discussion programme. The participants do not, of course, know in advance what these will be. The amateur researcher (or a student) can really play the part of the discussion leader provided that a few rules are observed. The discussion must be led, not dominated; all members present are encouraged to contribute; given the right atmosphere members must be encouraged to spark ideas off each other; the whole process lasts about one-and-a-half hours, sometimes less but seldom more.

In professional research these discussions are tape recorded, sometimes also on closed circuit television, and everybody knows this is happening. There is nothing underhand about it. Subsequently the proceedings are also scripted and then analysed by a trained psychologist. The words used, opinions expressed and the personal interactions of those taking part will all contribute to understanding the 'verdict' of the group.

A great many advertising messages are tested out on such groups before being used. Some are investigated afterwards when things have gone wrong.

'The bank that likes to say "Yes" ' used by the TSB was identified by this kind of research. Dunlop used it to discover why one of its advertising campaigns was not the success anticipated. Oxo located Katie and her family in the United States, rather than France, because group discussions found that culinary improvement through the cube was more believable in that setting.

Depth interviews In many ways these follow the procedure used for group discussions except that they are carried out on a one-to-one basis, interviewer and interviewee. The rules for 'qualifying' the respondent are the same, a pre-prepared agenda is necessary, but the interviewer has both greater expertise in the subject matter and greater freedom to explore 'in depth'. Analysis and interpretation are again highly skilled, but this is not to say that any amateur (and many students do this for projects) cannot gain valuable insights into the subject being investigated.

2 *Media* Throughout all of marketing the target market or segment must never be forgotten. This is particularly true of the media. The United Kingdom differs from most other countries in its media distribution; we have national radio, BBC TV, newspapers, magazines, poster sites, transport systems and so on as well as having regional or local ones. With the exceptions of radio, TV and some magazines, very few other countries do. With the 'home' market changing in 1992 to the 10 countries of the European Community national differences will need to be studied.

With segments in mind the advertiser has to select the media most appropriate to those targets. Most publications will provide a profile of their readership, not merely the numbers illustrated in Figure 7.1, Section 7.9. The aim is of course to help the fit of media to target audience.

If it is possible the chosen media should ideally be the one in which the advertiser can dominate with the product or service on offer. Some years ago in a campaign I was involved in, Sunday colour supplements were chosen for national distribution because we could not find any comparable advertisements in them for the previous six months. Although the advertisements were quite small, but placed next to text, their impact was all that we desired. This sort of thing is of course not always possible; but thought should be given to the attempt.

There are a number of organizations which deal specifically with media research or aspects of it. For example television audiences are measured by consumer panels described in Section 10.15 or by instruments attached to the set. It is a very specialist field and I would recommend the student to turn to its literature for detailed information.

3 *Timing* All too often there is a belief that promotional messages act quickly. There is no doubt that sometimes they do – if they click! My wife and I recently wanted a high pressure nozzle for our garden hose, one advertised in the press. On its eventual receipt by mail order we found that the connection to the hose had to be bought separately; all the details were given on an enclosed leaflet. Could we get one? Every ironmonger, garden centre or DIY outlet that would normally stock them had been sold out!

On the other hand the process of moving people through awareness, attitude and action takes time. On another occasion I came across some totally erroneous conceptions about the time when students were looking for early information about courses in further and higher education. It was thought that they did not really start considering what they were going to apply for until about the April before the 'A' level exams. In fact this was nonsense. Any student reading this will know that UCCA forms for university applications have to be completed in the autumn; students have to be thinking about their future education six months earlier than had been thought!

Part of the misconception had been fostered by the start of the financial year in April. Instead of retaining funds for the second half of the academic year the promotional expenditure was incurred when money became available! This example shows up the wrong priorities and constraints! The correct timing had been 'discovered' from the results of a questionnaire among a sample of students.

The result of the revised timing which followed is shown in Figure 10.5. That part of research which revealed this 'information' had been based on the hypothesis that the old timing was wrong. With hindsight this seems so obvious but at the time it was not.

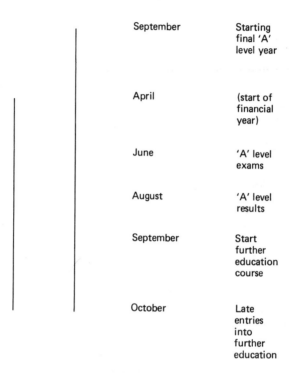

Result: 25 per cent increase in application
from 'new' campaign on similar budget.

Fig 10.5   *Campaign timing*

---

4 *Frequency* Research into this problem is more often than not experimental, that of trial and error carefully recorded and monitored. What may be relevant at one time is not necessarily so at another.

However, studies were undertaken in 1959 by Hubert Zielske in the United States, which showed that, of 13 successive advertisements, the ones spread at four-weekly intervals over 12 months, as opposed to 12 weeks, produced cumulative retention of the message. The concentrated series of advertisements over the 12 weeks were very quickly forgotten.

It would be very foolish to assume that this result would be reproduced in every case. However, it is perhaps worth speculating (even for the casual observer) how durable those messages are which we see several times in one evening on our television screens!

In the context of the effect of frequency on remembering messages two techniques remain to be mentioned – recognition and recall. Personal contact with respondents is required to carry out these methods. If you were shown some advertisements to which you had had the opportunity of being exposed, it is quite likely that you would 'recognize' them! This is what recognition testing does. Recall goes deeper. In this case you would be asked to explain, or describe, the content of an advertisement with, or without, some prompting.

10.17 Sales Force Techniques

Marketing research into the sales force must be confined to those activities which can be controlled. In other words any sales manager, after receiving research results, would be able to initiate new, or confirm existing methods of working. We are back to the requirements of D-I-C-E. Some of the 'controls' necessary were mentioned in Sections 8.4 to 8.6 such as call cycles, costs per call, frequency of call, and prospecting for new accounts.

Investigation would commonly include help for the sales representative in identifying new sources of business, possibly linked to new products. Experiments may also be conducted.

Some years ago ICI carried out an experiment involving their paint sales force. A small group was chosen and given greater than normal authority over price negotiations. In the early stages 'carving up the price' became the practice of this group until it was found that it did not really work. There is a point beyond which customers get suspicious of cut prices. Once this lesson had been learned the group really began selling – communicating persuasively – on benefits not price. A check had been kept on another group for comparison; this was a 'control' group still operating under the previous system. The experimental group was found to outperform the control group.

Marketing research by the sales force is something else again. Because of the nature of the job sales people must have a strong sense of optimism and commitment to what they are doing. This is seldom the best base for research. Nevertheless the close contact which they enjoy in the marketplace puts them into a position where information gathering should be a normal part of their function. They should be an unrivalled source of data about competitive activity, such as the introduction of new products, customer support material, changes in prices. Also (an apparently unpleasant part of their job) they should welcome and report on any complaints from their custamers as well as any (more polite) suggestions.

If it is necessary periodic training in these activities should be carried out. Any information specialist, from a detective to a spy, will tell you how small pieces of data can accumulate into valuable information by trained interpreters. There should be one such person in every business!

10.18 Pricing Techniques

Relatively little published material is available on the subject of marketing research into pricing. The reason is really not hard to find. In spite of general belief to the contrary few customers have absolute values about a price for any commodity in either the FMCG or durable categories. What they do have is a price band with an upper and lower limit; their values fall within this range and can be identified by research interviewing.

In recent years price changes, usually upwards, have become commonplace because of high, or creeping, inflation. Seasonality is also a common cause of price fluctuation especially for fresh foods.

There is another aspect of this potentially controversial discussion, because a great many people consider themselves to be highly price conscious. Retail stores, especially the big chains, conduct many pricing experiments in order to see the effect. Sainsbury's 'multibuy' approach is a good example: purchase a specific number of the same item, say cat food, and there is a price reduction. In Chapter 7 this would have been called 'sales promotion' – an inducement linked to a purchase. It becomes a source of information when the results have been measured and then used for marketing decision making. However, it is by no means everybody who is motivated by price reductions. Think of the occasions when you have gone into a store and spent considerably more than you intended; you found 'value'. What is aimed at in the sales promotion/research mix is illustrated in Figure 10.6 on page 172. The measurement part of the operation is essential.

If the sales level at the end of the promotion period is not, at a minimum, at least as high as formerly, preferably higher, there has been an unnecessary loss of revenue. The drop which follows immediately after the promotion is caused by accelerated purchasing by existing users; the increase at the end either by greater levels of consumption by the existing users (not very likely but possible) or by new purchasers switching their allegiance away from other products.

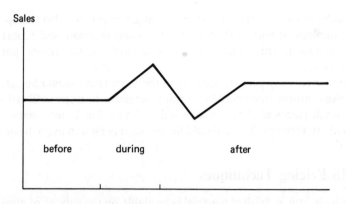

Fig 10.6   *The aim of a sales promotion*

In addition to these very human considerations there are also the economic models related to price which have a significant effect when applied to large numbers of people. For example when the Chancellor of the Exchequer puts up interest rates in his quest for control of the economy and the balance of payments, consumer spending power is reduced. A reduction in demand should have the effect of reducing prices, or in an inflationary economy, of delaying increases. These models are rarely applicable to the individual business.

From the research point of view these movements are of importance to all firms and should be constantly monitored for their effect on trade. Most especially is it important for the industrial sectors. A reduction in demand at the consumer end of the chain 'accelerates' and 'multiplies' through the supply system. Replacement orders for finished goods are deferred; supplies of raw materials in manufacturing are no longer required and labour is put on short-time working. The converse is also true. You will frequently have heard too the argument that by encouraging consumer spending imports are sucked into the country and the balance of trade is adversely affected.

10.19 Test Marketing

In fast moving consumer marketing the final stage of a research programme may be by test marketing. 'May be' because it is by no means always necessary. The purpose of a test market is to simulate as nearly as possible the conditions of a prepared marketing plan on a greatly reduced scale. It is the last stage of insurance.

All the principles of the scientific approach apply. A small area(s) is selected which reflects accurately the characteristics of the whole population. In order to avoid influence from neighbouring areas it needs to be as self-contained as possible and also have a matching neighbourhood to act as a control. The test area tries out some change in a marketing plan, whereas the control one is unchanged. In this means measurement and comparison can take place.

If TV advertising is part of the plan, commonly used test areas are Tyne Tees, Border TV, and Harlech. Any of the south-east regions are much too mixed up and have large commuting populations overlapping into other TV districts. This destroys the isolation of a test. Towns commonly used are Swindon, Southampton, Dartford, York, all of which are relatively self-contained. Within reason all these places are regions that reflect national population characteristics.

Consumer durable and industrial products are seldom test marketed; there are better ways of researching them – particularly by placement tests in which a number of people, or firms, are given them to try out. Another reason is that repeat purchasing of durable and capital goods is spread so far apart that no test could adequately last sufficiently long to be relevant to any decision maker. Repeat purchasing is an important aspect of FMCG marketing and a test can easily last long enough to cover several buying periods, say once a week. With industrial raw materials there is always sufficient close and personal contact with some customers both willing and able to try out new products or modifications.

10.20 Summary

This chapter has been divided into two main parts. The first part, leading up to the Review in Section 10.10, dealt primarily with the main theories. From then on applications were briefly described as they related to Chapters 4 through 9. Some hints were also given about research tools which could be used by the student, albeit with some doubts about the real accuracy and precision required by the scientific approach. The whole chapter was linked by the abbreviation D-I-C-E (Decision, investigation, control and experiment).

Exercises

1 What does the abbreviation 'D-I-C-E' stand for? Briefly describe any context in which the I-C-E would be used in marketing research and how that context would link to the D.

2 There are two major types of data collected in marketing research; what are they? A diagram illustrated the order in which they should be used; reproduce that diagram.

3 What do you understand by the term 'syndicated' research? Give an example and explain how it differs from 'commissioned' research.

4 Why is it that test marketing is seldom used for industrial products?

5 Sampling is widely applied to all kinds of marketing research; what is a 'sample' and what should it accurately reflect?

6 Marketing research costs money. In the text a word was applied to the value of research; what was this word and what part does it play in information for marketing planning?

7 A clear distinction was made between the kind of answers sought by quantitative data collection methods and qualitative ones. What was this distinction?

Part III

Marketing Strategy and Business Policy

11 The Product Life Cycle

11.1 Introduction

Although it has received most attention in studies of marketing, product life cycle theory concerns every part of a business; rather like a well-known lager 'it reaches the parts other theories cannot reach'. In this chapter I hope to be able to illustrate sufficient examples for you to see how much marketing is a member of a team and how this theory reinforces that view. We are, in this book, now at the stage of climbing another rung on the decision-making ladder; Part II dealt for example, with the marketing mix, those tactical specialist areas dealing continuously with a variety of functions that collectively we know as 'marketing'. Part III which we are now embarking on, takes us higher up the decision-making tree, where a decision taken in one part of a business has effects on others.

This particular chapter is divided up into three sections. The first one is mainly descriptive, explaining what product life cycle theory is and the model on which it is based. This will give us an understanding of the principles that underlie it. The subsequent sections will show how the model can be used for decision-making purposes and there will be plenty of opportunities for you to practise that art. By the end of this chapter we will be ready to proceed to the next major stage, namely the strategic management of a product or service mix for the long-term health of a business.

11.2 What is a Model?

Before we proceed any further let us be quite clear what I mean by using the term 'model'. Firstly it is a representation of a commonly recurring pattern; it is not a reproduction, and therefore not intended to be either exact nor able to take account of inevitable individual variations. Let me give you a parallel from sport. It is possible to model the perfect golf swing; the arms should follow a certain path, the club head describe a pattern of movement both before and after meeting the ball; feet, legs, body and head should be controlled in a certain way. Watch any professional competition and we see all the players with their different little foibles and idiosyncrasies. Therefore our model should be regarded as a 'generalization' to which every particular instance may not rigidly adhere. This enhances rather than diminishes our potential expertise. You and I know what trees are – we have a 'model' of them; but a forester would know each kind individually and be able to account for their differences.

11.3 The Theory and the Model

The absolute necessity of explanation cannot be avoided in this section. Therefore it will be mainly descriptive with the onus being firmly on me to do the explaining. After that, in the exercises, you will be using the product life cycle model in decision-making problems and must fully appreciate what this section covers in order to do so. My approach is going to be by the use of successive diagrams, each one elaborating on its predecessor. I must ask you to be sure that you understand each step before going on to the next one.

11.4 The Basic Model

The PLC (short for product life cycle) model is based on a graph and has two dimensions, or axes, x being the horizontal, y the vertical. The terms x and y are merely a shorthand substitute for the title of any data which may be represented on either scale. This sometimes enables us to use formulae for calculations using these symbols, for that is all they are. In our basic model outline, x equals time and y equals sales; the point at which the two axes meet equals 0, e.g. no sales and the starting point of time. See Figure 11.1.

Now a point to grasp quickly is that these two dimensions of sales and time are not scaled precisely; they are abstract. This is because the model is a generalization. For example, salt is a product which has lasted for millions of years, and is likely to last for millions more; the 'time' axis would be in millions of years! How many of you remember the Hoola-Hoop? It lasted (whatever it was) only as a craze for a few months. However, the model is applicable to both.

The sales curve, shown in Figure 11.2 is also intended to be illustrative rather than factual – a representation to repeat the word I used earlier. However, when this model is being applied in a specific instance the appropriate scales could well be shown. We will be doing this in a later section.

Apart from the general shape of this curve, the first important points for us to appreciate is that the curve is smooth, or more literally 'has been smoothed'; short-term fluctuations, in other words, have been ironed out

Fig 11.1 *Dimensions of PLC model*

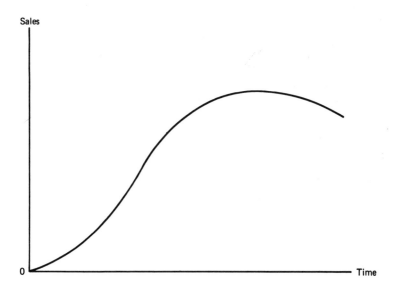

Fig 11.2 *Sales curve of PLC model*

of it. Once again this is because it is a model applicable to a wide variety of products and situations. What we now have is a graph showing a 'smoothed' shape representing sales volume over a time period.

A word here about 'sales volume'. Because we all experience these days constantly changing prices, e.g. through inflation, or interest rates, there is always a difficulty in using money values as a stable measure over any reasonable period of time, at least one extending potentially over several years. As a result of this the term 'sales volume' does not necessarily mean money. Once more we are confronted with an abstract. I would ask you to think of 'sales volume' as a term meaning a 'measure with a constant value'. This is by no means an uncommon method of expressing something when distortions are likely to be introduced by, say, inflation. Similarly I am not going to suggest that a 'product unit' would be an acceptable substitute. Products are constantly being updated, modified, even radically changed over a period of years; so the product unit being used at the beginning of the time scale might well be a very different thing from that being used at its end. You see the problem.

11.5 The Time Dimension

Although no pretence is made to put an accurate time scale on a life-cycle model, there are four discernible stages as shown in Figure 11.3.

Although they appear to be nearly equally proportioned, this too is part of the modelling process and must not be taken literally. I hope I am not stretching your ability to approach this subject matter as a concept, or as an idea, too far. You will recall that a 'representation' and an 'abstract' are intended to be conceptual.

Fig 11.3   *Stages of the PLC model*

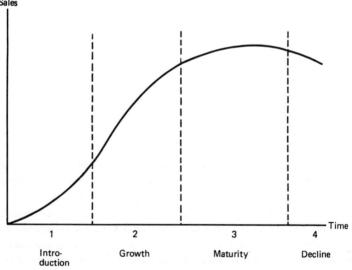

Common practice generally gives four main stages of a life cycle starting from time = 0. I mention this now because in later sections I will be going back behind this time point and developing a further stage; but not yet.

At time = 0 our 'product' first sees the commercial light of day; it appears in the marketplace for sale. From this inception it travels through the four stages of introduction, growth, maturity and decline. To put a human parallel on it – childhood, adolescence, middle age and old age. In brief, then, what this model is saying is that a product (any product or all products) has birth, life and death. It suggests an inevitability which cannot be escaped – at least in the long run (remember salt?). Now if this is so, businessmen cannot afford to ignore the implications.

11.6 **The Four Stages**

1 Appropriately entitled the 'introduction' stage, the product first makes its appearance, sales start slowly with acceleration towards the end of this period.

2 During the 'growth' stage the product really begins to 'take off'; it is in strong demand by those who want it and sales rise rapidly; the product is becoming increasingly well known.

3 As sales rate of growth begins to slow down, because most of those who will have entered the market and bought, the 'maturity' stage begins. Demand stabilizes; the peak is probably not far away.

4 In due course, and for whatever reason, demand for a product begins to diminish; possibly because it has been superseded by something better, e.g. the slide rule by the electronic calculator. It ceases to be profitable to maintain that product and it is, as a result, discontinued.

11.7 **Summary**

In conclusion let me remind you that the model outlined is not intended to be a replica of reality in any individual case: I referred to it as a 'representation' and also as being 'conceptual'. Models are used in this way to give us overall insights into frequently recurring phenomena and thereby enable us to anticipate similar phenomena occurring in the future. In its turn this enables us to predict likely events or patterns and make better business decisions to meet them. Even so, because a model cannot reflect every individual variation, there can be no certainty that a decision outcome will always be perfect.

11.8 Key Decisions

Having established what the product life cycle model is, we are ready to move on towards using it. We will be locating four major decision points on the life cycle curve, why they occur and how they can affect not only the use of the marketing mix but also other essential parts of a business. At the end of this discussion we should be prepared to make the next step, in the following section, of designing various marketing mixes to meet conditions suggested by the model.

11.9 The Adoption Process

You must be finding it easy to visualize the PLC model as showing how a product behaves over a period of time. Now both you and I know, if we pause for a moment, that no product 'behaves'; people behave. The product is the 'tennis ball' between the players called 'buyer' and 'seller'. So the curve that we have been discussing is really an effect resulting from the interactions of people. Let us think of each of the stages more precisely in this way.

These four stages describe what is happening to the product as a result of behaviour in the market – marketing activities by the sellers and responses by buyers. Supposing we take as an example the telephone, we can trace its progress along the curve in relation to its markets.

The telephone was invented in the last century so we have to go back over a hundred years to reach 'time $= 0$' on the model; even then it was only some time later that it became a commercial product. To whom was it available? A very small number of initial private and business customers with a whole lot of other developing industries behind it. Land lines had to be made available, either overhead or underground, exchanges provided, a power source, maintenance facilities, production plants, money, more research and so on. The 'introduction' stage lasted a long time as these resources were slowly made available.

Now today, where would you put the telephone? Still in the 'growth' stage or in early 'maturity', or where? Certainly not yet in 'decline'. Yet as more and more people have telephones, the consequence is less opportunity for further sales in the future.

The 'adoption' process has gone just about as far as it can. We can illustrate this in Figure 11.4.

With the exception of items essential to life (e.g. salt) few products reach 100 per cent adoption rates in any market. Figure 11.4 suggests market penetration reaching a peak of about 75 per cent; in other words there will always be some people who do not want a phone, cannot afford one or have some satisfactory (to them) alternative (such as a radio in the Australian outback).

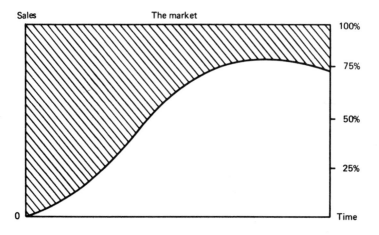

Fig 11.4 *Adoption and the PLC*

Bearing in mind that the PLC model is a 'representation', we are now in a position to begin discovering the four key decision points, and I am going to ask you to take an active part in this exploration. Firstly would you consider the model as an outline of the future; by so doing we can use it in order to avoid being caught by surprise in the marketplace. I am also going to ask you to change 'hats' (or roles) between the originator of a product, who launches at time = 0, and a competitor.

Decision point 1
Let us put ourselves in the position of the Xerox Corporation in the USA in 1960. Thirteen years previously the company had acquired licensing rights for a copying process patented by the Battelle Institute. In 1960 the first fully automatic dry copier was introduced, the 914, after $70 million had been expended on research and development. At $4 to the £, and before inflation had eroded monetary values, this amount was a high level of risk investment: *risk* is one of three *R*s, and investment, a *resource*, another one. That leaves us with the third – *results*. If you had been in Xerox in 1960 how would you 'model' the future? That $70 million investment would never have been made except in anticipation of more than recouping it in the future. How far into the four stages of the PLC would you expect to go, bearing in mind that you would be seeking information from every possible source to make a more precise prediction than that of our model? Draw in your curve in the blank below (Figure 11.5).

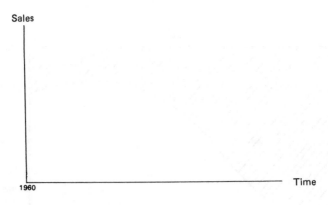

Fig 11.5   *The Xerox projection*

If you have thought this through in the way that I think you will have, the first decision point must take place before the product is ever launched, while it is still in the process of the development before time = 0. This is often what is referred to as a 'go or no go' decision. We all know that Xerox 'went'. And I think it would be reasonable for all of us to assume that Xerox before 1960 estimated that they would capture a major share of the copier market well into the 'growth' stage, partly because of patent protection.

Decision point 2
To illustrate this decision point I am going to change the example. As we proceed you will appreciate how the patent rights which Xerox enjoyed will not apply here. Our product this time will be a 'plant nutrient dispenser'. As I saw it in use only for the first time yesterday evening, and as it may be a total mystery to you, I must describe it:

Plant nutrient dispenser The dispenser is shaped exactly like a funnel through which a liquid might be poured. However, the wide top has a lid on it, and the small opposite end is blocked; there is no hole there. The interior therefore acts as a container for the nutrients, which are tablets like pills. By pushing the thin end of the dispenser into the earth by the root of a plant, a hole is made. A nutrient tablet is dropped into the hole, covered with earth and the job is completed. A tool and container in one – made of plastic.

Let us suppose that this relatively simple but nevertheless ingenious idea catches on amongst gardeners and shows every indication of rocketing up the 'growth' stage of its life cycle. See Figure 11.6 below.

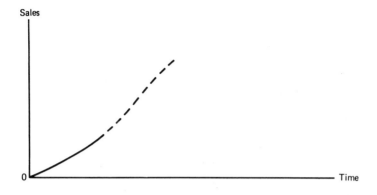

Fig 11.6 *The plant nutrient dispenser projection*

Whereas in *decision point 1* we imagined that we were Xerox, this time would you imagine that I am the originator of the dispenser and that you are one of my competitors. You make plastic products too; you also make things for the gardening market. There are no patent problems, no technology problems, no marketing problems. But you are now watching me beginning to harvest profits in what is apparently a rapidly expanding market!

You are yourself; what would you do?

What would you do if you were me?

By far the easier decision, although it is not without its risks, is the first one. Surely you would get on to the bandwagon. The problem arises when a large number of competitors see the same opportunity simultaneously and all jump upon it. In the short run, if growth is sustained, this may not be too damaging although everybody will have smaller pieces of the cake; in the long run it will lead to productive overcapacity: the resources will not be producing the results! In this context the difficulties will increase or diminish with the type of product; the factory being used to make our 'plant nutrient dispenser' could quite quickly be diverted to something else; no great harm would be likely. However, there is just this situation at the moment facing the video equipment manufacturers in the 'growth' stage of their market.

The general conclusion that we can draw so far is that the 'growth' stage of a product's life cycle will attract competition.

But what of my position as the originator of the new product? Unless I am very careful I could easily be forced on to the defensive; if you have entered with a distinctly improved version, rather than just a copy of the original, I could be forced out. But if the PLC model allows me to anticipate events I can make my plans accordingly. There are really three main options, and an infinite variety of ways of achieving each one:

• Option 1 Welcome additional competition as a means of expanding the whole market.
• Option 2 Take measures to make competitive entry difficult or very risky, e.g. by heavy promotion coupled with price reductions.
• Option 3 Anticipate events well and stay one jump ahead of the competition.

Decision point 3
For the last decade the oil companies have been having a rough time. With too much oil available pump prices have had to be subsidized in a desperate attempt to get us (you and me) to use more petrol. Now the OPEC nations have decided to cut back on production in an attempt to maintain, or increase, the $ cost per barrel.

This situation is by no means untypical of the 'maturity' stage. The question is, what to do about it? The oil producers and the oil companies offer one example – price competition. But if they are anything to go by it appears to be somewhat self-defeating. They all end up making losses, and that means less exploration and research for the future.

By far the majority of products we are all familiar with are in the 'maturity' stage of their life cycles. This being so it is the stage in which marketing is most active, when competition is at its fiercest and profits are under most pressure.

I would like to pursue this example by continuing with petrol, because one major option is closed, at the moment, to the oil companies.

Figure 11.7 is a magnification of the 'maturity' stage – the continuous line; the dotted line beneath it indicates the level of costs, total costs as we used the term in an earlier section in relation to profit volume analysis. In this figure I am making the assumption that operations are being conducted efficiently and that cost savings (always a way of influencing profit) can only be marginal and have little effect.

The option closed to the oil companies is the one on the right of Figure 11.7 'increased marketing'. At a time when conservation looms so large in the public mind, any blatant attempt to increase consumption by obvious marketing activities of persuasion and inducement would surely be counterproductive. Those of us who remember Esso's 'Put a tiger in your tank' campaign will quickly realize how inappropriate that would be today!

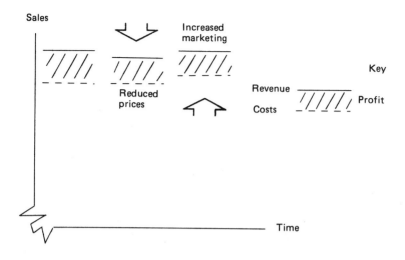

Fig 11.7 *'Maturity' and competition*

So far I have excluded you from participating in decision point 3. Let me make up for that now. In your opinion how many new products enter the market at the 'maturity' stage rather than at 'growth'? You are probably hard pressed to put either a figure or a percentage on any answer to that question. One of the reasons being, how do we define the word 'new' in relation to products? A Yorkie bar from Rowntree was a 'new' product in a very mature milk chocolate bar market. It is quite surprising how new names keep cropping up in well-established product areas and how old names disappear. In the list of brand or company names in the right-hand column below can you identify some of the 'new' entrants? And some disappearing?

Industry	Product type	Brand
Food	Soup	Heinz Tomato
		Campbell's Condensed Cream of Celery
Chemicals	Detergents	Daz
		Ariel
Metal	Saucepans	Prestige
		Swan
		Tower
Metal	Razor blades	Rolls
		Gillette
		Wilkinson

Electrical	Vacuum	Hoover
	cleaners	Goblin
		Hitachi
		Hotpoint
Vehicles	Cars	Standard
		Rover
		Honda
		Citroën

Now any business which decides to enter a mature market must believe that it has a sufficient edge over the established companies to take up a sufficient share to be worth while. The detergent Ariel has a 'biological action'; Tower saucepans were among the first to adapt space technology to non-stick surfaces. Rolls razors and blades have all but disappeared; Hitachi from Japan have apparently no fear of entering into the vacuum cleaner market in Europe; and the Honda deal with Austin Rover has brought this firm into the UK with joint development projects; the Standard Motor Company has long since disappeared.

Decision point 4
You are in the management of a business; at what point, and using what criteria, would you decide to discontinue a product?

This is the decision to be made at the decline stage. There are really only two sets of judgements that can be used:

• Externally: there is no prospect of any (further) rejuvenation of the market.
• Internally: sales revenue, costs and profits are no longer giving the performance required of them. For example the 'capital' being used to support a product could be better employed in some other projects.

The former is by far the more difficult; it is easy to hang on too long, it is easy to come out too early.

11.10 Summary

The most valuable function of the product life cycle model is its capability of focusing attention on likely patterns of product sales over distinct periods of time, what we have called the stages of introduction, growth, maturity and decline. If we include the development stage, which precedes the other four, the model also provides us with a yardstick against which investment may be judged. Given the opportunity to use foresight, better decisions should be possible by managers to avoid the most obvious pitfalls and seek the opportunities.

11.11 Change and Maintenance

The theory of the product life cycle has come under attack on occasion because it has been used, both theoretically and in practice, as a guide to undertaking standard marketing responses. If, for example, your product is in the 'growth' stage and a competitor enters, your response should be. . . . There is no such predestiny in marketing! My approach to using the life cycle model in this section will be in the broadest terms, leaving the details of tactics open to maximum ingenuity; so much so that the idea is to 'beat the system'. We are masters of the life cycle, not the other way round! However, there are limits to that mastery based on that essential interaction between buyer and seller; we can only control so much. What we control we have called the marketing mix, in Part II.

In the pages that follow the PLC model will be used to define those periods when the main aim of marketing will be either to generate change in behaviour or to maintain behaviour as it is. As these two alternatives are discussed we will see how they affect the curve and work to the long-term profitable advantage of a business. But before that I would like to remove what I consider to be a misconception about the PLC and the individual firm.

11.12 A Misconception

That an individual product will be born, will grow, mature and eventually die is hardly controversial. What may be very controversial is the reason for its death! No business can do anything about that product which has quite unmistakably outlived its usefulness in the marketplace, for example a 'chastity belt'. But many products disappear because the organization behind them is, in one respect or another, inefficient, incompetent or inadequate. For such organizations the product life cycle theory provides a convenient scapegoat. This is why I related the model to market penetration in Figure 11.4 and listed 'industry', 'product' and 'brand' (or company) name in the lists below Figure 11.7. To judge the performance of an individual product, it should be compared with its product type and the latter related to the life cycle.

11.13 Change

Now that the Post Office has lost its monopoly for the supply of telephones, British Telecom (which took over from it) has to compete

with its erstwhile suppliers, such as Plessey, GEC and others from
Europe or the US.

Self-check

Is it really true to suggest that the telephone has reached its peak at the top of
the 'maturity' stage, as I did earlier? How would you see the prospects from,
say, Plessey's point of view?

There are in fact four ways in which change can be brought about:

- Introduce a genuinely 'new' product. This will usually be based on
  some totally new technology, e.g. electronics, and is not intended to
  include modifications.
- Discover a new use for an existing product. This is quite common for
  raw materials such as plastics, synthetic fibres and so on.
- Enter a new market, such as exporting.
- Increase the level of consumption; drink more milk or have an
  extension telephone installed.

The last point is pertinent to the Self-check above, and also to the whole
subject of penetration. It may well be more cost effective for the
marketer to go for additional consumption in existing markets than for
greater penetration. In addition to the telephone there are examples of
'the second car', the portable TV' for the kitchen or bedroom and many
others. I deliberately exclude from the list any replacements. In the case
of consumer durables and capital goods replacement purchases are an
integral part of the life cycle. The marketing approach will be very
different from that for the first purchase; this we will discuss in Section
11.14.

Self-check

Revising a life cycle model (see Figure 11.8 below), which stages in your view
are the ones in which marketing should be generating behavioural change?

'Behavioural change' in this context is getting customers to do, or buy,
something which they have not previously done. This usually means that
consumer spending is going to be diverted from one thing (what had
previously been done) to something else, but still generally within the
same overall limit of spending. It is after all only when standards of living

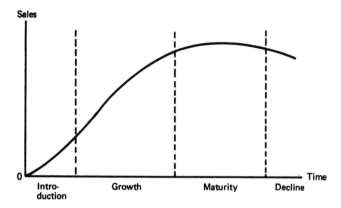

Fig 11.8 *The PLC model revisited*

rise that people are able to afford additional purchases; otherwise we substitute one thing for another.

The first point about changing behaviour must arise when a product is new; new to the market (an invention) or alternatively new to a person. Let us consider the new invention. This will start in PLC terms at time = 0 and the product will be new to everybody. Every purchase, therefore, will require a change in behaviour and marketing's task becomes clear – to make consumers aware of the product, generate a favourable attitude and induce action leading to trial. Every one of the three As just mentioned has to be changed. If the product is really so new that extensive explanation, or indeed education, may be required, the name given to the demand being generated is known as 'primary demand'. Would you agree that this process must take place in the earlier stages of the PLC as more and more people are being brought into the market; penetration is taking place? In answer to our self-check question, then, the 'introduction' and 'growth' stages are the important ones for behavioural change.

We need to pursue this argument a little further before we go on to the next step.

Supposing that you are very successful in handling the three As during the 'introduction' and 'growth' stages and generate a lot of 'primary demand', you should be in a commanding market position when competition tries to enter – what we can call the 'point of competitive entry'. Now if we link the three Rs (risk, resources and results) to the three As, the business, if it really has the willingness to commit its resources, should be set to reap the results in a growth market with a considerable lead over potential competition. This is why it so often is of advantage to be first in the market. But let us note carefully that this successful scenario requires an early commitment of resources in a situation where the risk is still high. After all the growth projection may not in practice materialize. This is the time to go to your bank manager for a loan, and his experienced pessimism will soon deflate your optimism!

If, on the other hand, there is a real growth market there, but you either have not, or are unwilling to commit, the resources to take immediate advantage of it, then another business with the resources will read the signs correctly and take advantage of the pioneering that you have done. Let me tell you a story to illustrate this.

'The second comes first' Back around about 1960, when I was a young salesman selling paint to do-it-yourself outlets like ironmongers, wallpaper and paint shops, a competitor brought out a product called Luxol with the claim that 'it covered in one coat'. Now this claim was in no way illegitimate, but it did depend on how the paint was applied. If it was brushed out too far old colours would show through. The danger of this was that application is not under the control of the maker. Also, up until that time every other paint manufacturer had been educating the growing DIY market that two coats were better than one. So the makers of Luxol were going all out to change behaviour. They put a tremendous effort in promoting their product and we watched with trepidation as it began to appear in all the shops, taking up good display space – and reducing ours! This went on for over a year. It did not succeed and the promotion could not be sustained much longer than twelve months.

Shortly after that twelve months had expired, however, another product appeared – one which not only became enormously successful but is still available today – Magicote. This went one better than Luxol: it not only 'covered in one coat' but was 'non-drip'. One had paved the way for the other, but it was the second one that survived.

11.14 Maintenance

The story I have just outlined above is about two 'new' products in an established market, or mature life cycle; there is not much new about paint. In one form or another it has been around for thousands of years! But if products are invented which are sufficiently different from what has gone before there is some justification in claiming that a new PLC has begun. The new life cycle must be judged by its penetration into the established whole. So we can begin to think about 'mini life cycles', see Figure 11.9.

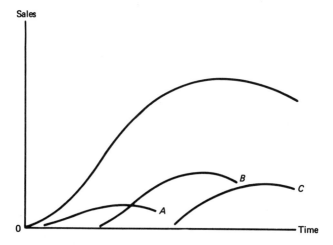

Fig 11.9 *'Mini life cycles'*

However, these mini life cycles can be dangerously misleading when applied to the activities of a single firm.

Nevertheless, I have already mentioned that many new products are launched into mature markets and for each individual case the marketing mix has to be designed accordingly. But one thing which helps us to recognize the later stages from the earlier in the PLC is the number of products available to choose from. So the marketing activity must be designed to make the products 'different'; to focus consumer attention away from the general type of product to a particular one. This process is one of creating 'secondary' demand and will tend to concentrate on the middle out of the three *A*s.

Surely in the early stages of a life cycle consumers are going to be looking for information (the need for education from marketing); so 'primary' demand situations will be calling for mainly 'functional' information. In mature markets the essential nature of the products will be widely known, so that marketers have to work hard to create 'secondary' demand through 'symbolic' differentiation. (Refer back to Section 5.5 on 'The combination' in Chapter 5 to remind yourself of the interdependence of the 'physical, functional and symbolic'.)

Most of the products we buy are well established in the market – as far as we know. If that is a logical deduction from our individual viewpoint, is it not probably the same for the makers? In which case the established products are going to be the ones that provide the bulk of the business.

Self-check

Now can you interpret the need for a very different kind of marketing approach to hold on to your existing customers, to maintain, rather than change, behaviour?

Let us trace some steps through together, and while doing so mention the effects on parts of a business other than marketing.

1 Commitment of technical and financial resources to research and development.
2 Heavy marketing input for launch of a 'new' product – demand for cash. Change behaviour.
3 The product 'takes off'; invest more in marketing and production to take advantage of the 'growth' stage. Activate more R&D in order to anticipate competitive entry and be ready to counter-attack.
4 Having successfully captured good market share, begin to reap the rewards of large scale working. Keep customers 'loyal' – maintain behaviour.
5 Ensure throughout life cycle continuous investigation of new product and market opportunities, either for expansion or for security against declining products.

11.15 Summary

The principle of 'change and maintenance' is shown in Figure 11.10.

The early stages of the PLC, namely, 'introduction' and 'growth', require a marketing mix that creates behavioural change in the consumer; he or she is being encouraged to do something different. The marketing approach is to create 'primary' demand for the product and all contributing activities will most likely be explanatory, linking with the functional performance of the product. But once market penetration has been achieved, consumers will be aware at least of the main attributes of the product type; they will know what it does. But this time, because of the likely entry of competition, there will be choice in the market; differentiation then takes place creating 'secondary' demand as makers try to create a uniqueness about their product, usually through the more symbolic appeals.

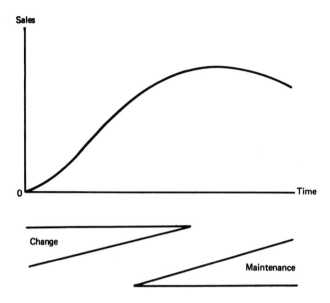

Fig 11.10 *'Change and maintenance'*

Exercises

1 What is your understanding of the use of the word 'model' as it applies to product life cycles? What are the drawbacks of models when applied to individual situations?

2 During this chapter using three diagrams to build up the model, we have described the outline of product life cycle theory. Before we go further and use this model you must be sure that you have firmly in mind its main components. Reproduce, preferably without any looking back until you have done all you can:
1 the x and y axes suitably labelled;
2 the shape of the curve;
3 the titles and divisions of the four stages.

3 Four main decision points along the PLC have been discussed. Explain each of the four, related to the relevant stages, and discuss their significance for the marketing manager to predict the future. Illustrate your answer with an appropriate diagram.

4 What do you understand by the terms 'primary' and 'secondary' demand? How do you relate them to the PLC stages? Draw a comparison between these terms and the need to change or maintain behaviour in the marketplace.

12 Most Businesses Deal in More Than One Product

12.1 Introduction

One of the difficulties I have met when discussing marketing strategies and business policy is their complexity. For example the PLC model, which we used in the last chapter and will be referring to again in this, was described by me as a 'representation'. And what is a representation but a simplified form? This makes it easier to start with by building up from a single product, but most of the people I work with are either already working in or are likely to be joining, well-established multi-product companies. In these circumstances they have to come to terms very quickly with highly complex situations which are not easy to sort out.

This chapter is going to make some attempt at sorting. First we will be looking at one method of classifying products into a 'portfolio' and then linking this grouping with life cycle theory. However, there is one aspect of particular importance in this process: our classification method will be based on 'cash flow'. Now to some readers this may be a new term. So at the appropriate time I will be giving an explanation of it and illustrating its difference from 'profit'.

The object of making up such a product 'portfolio' is to enable a business to plan what it judges to be the best combination of products for its successful future. Any planning must depend upon the best information available and have it presented in a way that enables decisions to be taken.

In addition to examining the 'cash flow' of the groups of products, we will also be taking into account the 'market growth rate' and the business's 'market share'; in other words internal as well as external factors influencing performance. You, as the decision-maker, will be looking for ways of achieving good commercial results according to the circumstances of the time; for after all times change!

12.2 Opening the Portfolio

According to definition a 'portfolio' is a 'case for keeping loose sheets of paper'. If we imagine dividers as well, they would give us a method of keeping the papers in groups according to some category or other, for example by subject matter, by size or by colour. Because the papers are loose they can easily be resorted and popped into different sections of the divided portfolio. Now instead of paper let us think of products. I have just been reading the business section of the *Sunday Times* which describes Philips, the Dutch multinational company, as making products varying from light bulbs to computerized telephone exchanges. Blue Circle Industries Ltd ranges from making cement to fish farming. And you too could think of many similar illustrations.

12.3 'The Product Portfolio'

The idea behind the 'product portfolio' was developed by the Boston Consulting Group from the USA; a consultancy organization which now has worldwide interests and influence. For strategic planning purposes they classify each item in a company's product range into one of four categories according to its cash flow performance, its relationship to market growth and its competitive position.

12.4 Cash Flow

Let us first of all clarify, if it is necessary for those who may not be familiar with the term, what is meant by cash flow, and more precisely 'net cash flow'.

When a product is sold for a given price and that price is paid immediately in cash, there is a cash inflow to the business. If the product concerned has to be manufactured by the selling company it incurs cash outflows, such as materials, wages and so on, in other words all those expenses necessary to make it – so long as they are paid out in cash. If you, as an individual, buy on credit, there is a delay in the transfer of money from you to the seller, until such time as he receives the money, the seller has a net cash outflow. Now all this so far relates to normal trading revenue and expenses and should be fairly straightforward. It is, after all, not very dissimilar to the way that profit is calculated – income less expenses.

The previous paragraph covered receipts and payments of cash which we may call 'revenue' for both inflows and outflows; but we also have to take into account 'capital' movements of cash which, if you are familiar with accounting procedures, you know are not included in calculations of profit. Capital expenditures are incurred for items such as buildings, plant and equipment, fixtures and fittings, vehicles; they consume cash resources. Therefore to be fully economic a product has to generate sufficient cash to cover both 'revenue' and 'capital' expenditure and still have a surplus.

You are the proprietor of five garages and petrol service stations, and you are in the process of modernizing their forecourts one at a time. Using the following information of inflows and outflows of cash which you expect to incur at one of the stations during the next year, calculate the 'cash profit' and the 'net cash balance' at the end of the period. You probably do this sort of thing quite regularly on your own bank statement.

Right now you have a balance in your bank account of £18 000; and during the next twelve months you expect to sell 198 000 gallons of petrol at £1.80 per gallon. From your previous experience and records, you estimate that your variable costs will be about half of the selling price: therefore 90p per gallon, which you round off to a total of £180 000. Your fixed costs are budgeted at £75 000.

1 At this point, what would your 'cash profit' be ('revenue' inflows less 'revenue' outflows)?

2 Also, what would your cash balance be at this point?

But your modernization is going to cost you a lot of money; the lowest estimate you have received from contractors to re-do the forecourt and install new self-service pumps is for £100 000.

3 After the 'capital' expenditure has been paid out, what will your cash balance be?

If you are in surplus, fine. If you are in deficit, then you will have to find the difference from some other source, such as borrowing from your bank manager.

	Outflows	Inflows
Opening cash balance		18 000
Revenue from petrol sales 198 000 gallons at £1.80		356 400
Subtotal		374 400
Less variable cash costs	180 000	
Less fixed cash costs	75 000	
Subtotal		255 000
Inflows less outflows (Cash balance)		119 400

('Cash profit' = revenue
less variable + fixed costs: £101 400)
Less capital expenditure (modernization)   129 400
_____
Net cash flow (cash balance) – positive   -10 000
or negative
_____

As you see from the calculations above, we end up with a negative
balance of £10 000. But you will also note that there is quite a difference
between 'cash profit' and the cash balance. One is £101 400 and the other
£119 400.

This little problem should clarify the difference between profit and
cash flow. Furthermore what this example also illustrates is the possibility of a product being totally self-supporting in cash terms for both
'revenue' and 'capital' expenditure. Is this reasonable over the whole life
of a product?

12.5 Cash Flow and PLC Stages

One thing we can all be sure about: any investment in a product
(outflows) must in course of time be more than recovered by inflows for
any real success to be claimed. It is in the early stages of the PLC then
that these outflows are usually made: the investment in research and
development before the product appears on the market, and then the
early marketing investment to make it known, to get it into channels of
distribution, and to get adoption going in the introduction stage.

Because the primary and secondary demand are very sweeping ways of
categorizing over the whole life cycle, it would be an oversimplification
to claim that the former gives net cash outflows and the latter net cash
inflows. But at least it is a start.

Let us now return to the Boston Consulting Group's four categories.
You would surely agree that the launch of any new product is, because of
all kinds of uncertainties, going to have a questionable future; no
guarantee of success can be assured. 'Questionable': let us therefore
symbolize such a product with a question mark – '?' But if the product
really appeals to its market, growth follows, and it will become a star
performer: a star – *. While the product is approaching, and then
remains in the 'maturity' stage it provides cash surpluses, which can be
milked to support other products: 'milk' equates with 'cow' – therefore
'cash cow'. Finally our product ceases to contribute cash surpluses, it
'misbehaves' and goes to the 'dog house' – therefore 'dog' (poor canine).

In Figure 12.1 the BCG's four categories are displayed in matrix form
and the arrows between each quadrant show the direction in which the

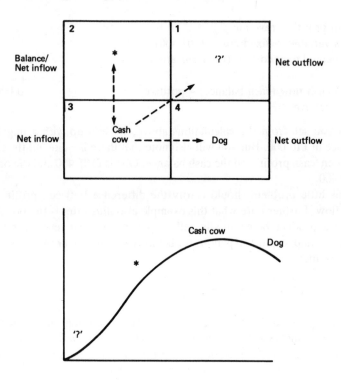

Fig 12.1   *The product portfolio quadrants*

cash moves from one to another. In this manner you will be able to visualize a number of products supporting each other as they progress round the matrix from **1** to **4**. Additionally you can view them as progressing along the PLC.

12.6 Summary

The meaning of 'cash flow' as opposed to that of 'profit' was introduced in Section 12.4 and a brief working example used to illustrate it. The terms 'revenue' and 'capital' were also related to cash movements, referred to as 'inflows' and 'outflows'. These movements of cash were then related to the now familiar idea of the product life cycle, and it was seen that there were two points at which these flows came into balance: one in the 'growth' stage, where inflows begin to overtake outflows, and one at the 'decline' stage when the reverse happens. Finally the product portfolio was identified, as named by the Boston Consulting Group, in four parts or four quadrants represented in a matrix. Movements of cash were also illustrated in the matrix, and product movement from one category to another was shown in conjunction with a life cycle curve.

12.7 Opening the Portfolio Further

The product portfolio idea of the Boston Consulting Group is sufficiently well known, especially in its older form, that further elaboration of it is necessary, and also desirable. Properly used it is a very powerful analytical tool for developing marketing strategies. We will examine its original form and then its newer one, giving the reasons for the change. In fact BCG claim that there has been no real change in their consulting practice, and I am certainly not going to argue about that. What has changed dramatically is the external environment, and it is on this aspect that we will be concentrating.

12.8 The 'Original' Product Portfolio

If products and cash moved around the four quadrants of the portfolio matrix, it did not happen in splendid isolation from events going on in the world outside! One key factor judged by the BCG to be critical was the rate of market growth, and another was market share. Both of these have been subsequently changed, but they are perfectly valid in conditions of economic expansion such as existed in the 1960s and early 1970s. Unfortunately these two key factors were constantly being paraded, not by BCG but by others including academics like myself, as paramount: capturing market share became almost a 'must' in marketing literature and lecture hall! In newspapers, textbooks and magazines articles the matrix was represented like the one in Figure 12.2.

In business you and I would be likely to express the rate of market growth as a percentage; if we thought of it as the 'growth' stage of the PLC it could be shown as a series of changing percentages.

Fig 12.2 *The 'original' product portfolio*

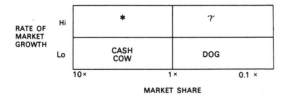

1 At the beginning of the PLC stage what sort of percentage rate of growth would you estimate? After all, it is only just beginning to really climb.
2 When things are hotting up, what would be your estimate then?
3 And finally as it comes towards the end and enters 'maturity', what would be your estimated figure?

Now obviously there is no *correct* answer! But suppose we said that the three questions I asked you were to be answered as follows: 1 7 per cent, 2 19 per cent, 3 5 per cent. Would you quarrel with the result? At present we are only estimating; in any real business situation (given sufficient information over the necessary time period) we could calculate the rate of change. But if we use, as so often we must, the PLC model as a predictor of the future, we would still have to estimate! So returning for a moment to Figure 12.2 we could say that the middle point between Hi and Lo might represent a 10 per cent rate of growth; the top of the matrix, 20 per cent and at the bottom of the vertical, of course, 0 per cent. Do not take these figures too literally because high growth in one business sector may be very different from that in another. It all depends, therefore, on what particular business you are in, and when.

12.9 Market Share

The measurement of market share along the bottom of the matrix was based on a comparison of a business with its largest competitor. If the two were exactly equal, the product would be plotted on the centre vertical line where the ratio of one to the other = 1. If the company was itself market leader, its product plot would move to the left (towards the 10); when smaller than the market leader it moves to the right.

As any business, in order to survive, must have cash surpluses, I am sure you will quickly apppreciate how the idea developed from the work of BCG that 'going for market share in growth markets' became a marketing doctrine. You can change your market share according to how you define the market. If we were in the business of making left-handed golf clubs, how would we define our market? All golfers or left-handed golfers? Do you see the problem? Similarly growth markets are few and far between. Fine if you can find one, or more accurately anticipate one, but as we have seen this does not apply to the vast majority of new entrants into markets.

Not surprisingly the difficulties that I have just outlined brought increasing criticism down on the head (or heads) of BCG, and headlines like the one in an issue of the *Financial Times*, 'Why Boston recanted its doctrine of market leadership', began to appear. In response not to the criticism but to market conditions, BCG has now refined its matrix into different components.

Because recession spread almost worldwide from the late 1970s, the rate of market growth approach ceased to be even credible as a viable strategy for marketers to pursue. On the other hand market share leadership is something that only a minority of businesses can ever enjoy; there can only be one at the top! And yet many businesses, for some reason or another have been able to succeed remarkably well, just as others have failed disastrously. Not much real consideration is required for us to come to the conclusion that there are many ways of gaining cash flow success. It is this that BCG have recognized and allowed for in their newer matrix.

12.10 The 'New' Axes

Rate of market growth and market share, as titles of the two axes in the original product portfolio (Figure 12.2), have disappeared to be replaced by 'number of approaches to achieve advantage' and 'size of advantage'. Both of these titles are far less specific than the old and recognize the much greater variety of ways in which business can react to its general economic environment and its more particular competitive one. Strategically the business should be led to examine any legitimate means by which it may obtain and hold a competitive advantage; and the greater the size of that advantage the better. There is a snag about that 'size': in many cases it can only be 'measured' by judgement. To overcome this fairly crude terms are used (see Figure 12.3).

The virtue of this 'new' matrix is that it does not isolate two variables (market growth and share) as being the ostensible cause of the cash flow effect; but it does not exclude them either. Nor does it suggest that the market is the overriding consideration. Therefore a brief word about each quadrant.

12.11 The 'New' Quadrants

1 **Fragmented** As all these titles relate to the activities of a business, this one implies a variety of activities; products, personnel skills, market segments, production technologies; research and development interests – diversity. When Imperial Tobacco took over a small potato-crisp manufacturer with a view to reducing dependence on a declining (and increasingly unpopular) activity, smoking, it was diversifying, splitting or fragmenting its portfolio into Golden Wonder. Can you think of another company with wide interests to fit into this quadrant?

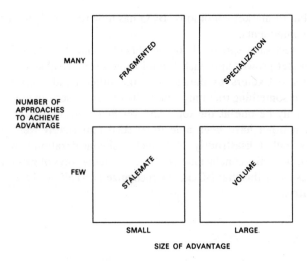

Fig 12.3   *The 'new' product portfolio*

2 **Specialization** Give me the name of the leading (the only) British company making aero engines. Think how difficult it would be for any other company to try to compete with that expertise, to overcome the enormous advantage possessed by Rolls-Royce.

3 **Stalemate** This is the least advantageous quadrant to be in. I would suggest that the airlines are in this one; Sir Freddie Laker tried to break the mould and look what happened to him. If we think of the marketing of politics, are the Social Democrats succeeding here?

4 **Volume** Name some big producers: Unilever vs Procter & Gamble; IBM; do you remember BiC? Many of the famous names, known to all of us, would fall into this category.

12.12 Summary

The product portfolio matrix was developed further in Sections 12.7 to 12.11 including the first time the influence of market growth and market share. We discussed how these two factors had received undue attention in the past to the detriment of many strategic decision options. The BCG recognized the limitations apparent in this earlier matrix and their new version based on 'advantage' was publicized.

Exercises

1 Below is a diagram of a standard life cycle model, plus the earlier 'development' stage preceding time = 0. Using your deductive powers, insert in the spaces provided below the diagram for each stage your estimate of cash flow performance for the product, using the following abbreviations:

NI = net inflow
NO = Net outflow
B   = in balance

Taking this a stage further, if you feel that there is likely to be a change as the product moves from one life cycle stage to another, insert at that change-over point a plus (+) or a minus (−) symbol.

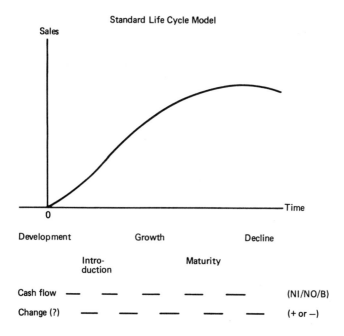

Standard Life Cycle Model

Sales

Time

0

| Development | | Growth | | Decline |
| Intro-duction | | | Maturity | |

Cash flow — — — — — (NI/NO/B)

Change (?) — — — — — (+ or −)

2 Reproduce the 'original' product portfolio and insert the titles in each of the four quadrants. Label both the vertical and horizontal axes.
3 Of the four quadrants, which two give net cash inflows, and which two net cash outflows? Explain the reasons.
4 Reproduce the 'new' product portfolio, naming all four quadrants and both axes.
5 In the light of the 'new' and 'original' matrices from the Boston Consulting Group do you believe the 'new' in any way contradicts the validity of the 'original'? Explain your reasoning.

13 What the Future Will Bring

13.1 Introduction

Whatever methods may be used, businesses are continually trying to calculate, estimate or just guess what the future will bring; they have to for making decisions, establishing priorities, assessing risk and allocating various resources.

If, therefore, the results of decisions are going to be entirely random, business cannot have any real sense of direction. Now this of course is nonsense. Every businessman has somewhere in his head a model of what will happen if he takes this or that decision. We will be looking at 'objective' methods of forecasting first by looking backwards over the past and using that to project into the future. Then we will apply 'subjective' techniques to measure the influence our own decisions have on what will happen, and any effect the environment may have on us: cause and effect, action and reaction.

13.2 'Objective' and 'Subjective' Techniques

The two words in quotes above are a bit technical and so I would like to make one or two special comments about this chapter. Because any forecast is about producing a figure (sales in £, units in production or whatever) in a period of time, numbers are involved. That can mean anything from simple arithmetic to computer simulation; we will be slightly in advance of simple arithmetic. Now some people do not find numbers easy to cope with and I have every sympathy with that feeling, but what follows is not difficult and really ought to be mastered by any student of business and marketing. I will be introducing some statistical methods mainly with the aid of graphs and diagrams. These are for illustration and some interpretation by you, with my help and explanation. They are the sort of thing that you would get a statistician to draw up for you in business (just as I have done), but you would still have to interpret their significance: this is the important thing about them. This is the 'objective' approach.

Towards the end of the chapter we get involved together in using our judgements. These can also be measured by using a simple number scale between 0 and 1, which I hope will not dismay anyone; these are 'subjective' approaches and must come from you.

So you might wish to approach this chapter with a little bit of caution; please do. It is intended to give you a taste of what can be done in this very necessary aspect of business and marketing planning – no more.

13.3 Why Forecast?

A business is part of a wider context, an economic, social, technological, financial and even political system – to mention but a few! Events are taking place in all these spheres of activity which are going to affect that business. On a smaller scale there is closer interaction with customers, suppliers, shareholders, the trade unions and others who influence the business and whom the business in its turn influences. Put briefly a firm operates in a highly complex environment. The greater the complexity, the more difficult it is to understand. So for further illustration let me try to simplify it by an analogy.

The business is a balloon! The air we blow into it (for a child's birthday party) represents the activities inside the firm: what it makes, how it manages itself, its marketing efforts, the way it controls its money and so on. Put too much strain on it by puffing too hard and it explodes – the equivalent of going bust! All the time we are blowing it up (not to be confused with exploding) we are forecasting its capacity, how big we can make it without too much risk.

All round the balloon there is environment. First there is the child for whom it was intended grabbing it between two eager hands – and immediately pushing it out of shape (customers). There is also jealous young brother, who tries to grab it (competition), against whom we immediately take protective action (parents/management). An open window, and an outside breeze spells 'loss' and ultimate disappearance. Any sharp object is dangerous to the point of destruction.

Once blown up and handed over, events have a nasty tendency of escaping our direct control; we can intervene at intervals to remove potential disasters (grab the balloon before it reaches the gas fire) but never avoid them entirely. The best we can do is anticipate. So in business. This does not mean that we are going to be right all the time, or even necessarily half the time; but it will mean that our operations have purpose and are measurable.

13.4 Resistance to Forecasting

Because every businessman has been caught by surprise at one time or another, there may be the temptation to deny the validity of forecasting:

it is, in the end, not going to be 'right' anyway. In any case the only certainty about business is 'change', so why bother? This is an appealing argument but a lazy one! The systematic study of controllable and uncontrollable variables and their interrelationships must increase our level of knowledge, and thereby reduce risk, not to its exclusion entirely, but at least in most cases to bring it within manageable proportions. You have surely heard of contingency planning. You have also heard of surveillance – keeping an eye on things.

13.5 How Objective Can We Be?

Objective methods of forecasting are those which rely on 'facts' rather than opinions and are systematic and have a laid-down procedure. Their outcomes are precise. They are mainly statistical and therefore numerate. Unfortunately numbers always give the impression of accuracy, and that can often be misleading. Nevertheless we have to use those tools readily to hand, and it is even better for us if we have a computer handy to do the donkey-work of crunching the numbers. I am not going to be asking you to get a computer (!), nor to do any but light number-crunching; the sort of thing that we have already done in other chapters.

13.6 Three Levels of Activity

In any given situation there will be at least three levels of measurable activity; in many cases there will be many more than three levels, which I am treating as a minimum. First, there will usually be an 'economic' level, second an 'industry' level and third a 'company' or 'corporate' level. Their significance is this: the 'higher' the level the greater the aggregation of data (or collective total) and the less likely any sudden or unexpected change. If this sounds a bit technical, let me try to clarify it by the example. In any short period unemployment figures covering the whole country will go up or down relatively slowly and predictably. But when a plant is closed the unemployment at local level moves dramatically.

'Aggregated data' will tend to be smoother anyway than smaller collections of data and because of that becomes easier to project using statistics. Exactly the same principle applies to the production output, or the sales of an industry in total, compared to the individual companies which make it up. After all, companies rise and fall within that total; they take shares away from each other for a time and can lose them again. As no business operates in isolation from its environment, it is often easier to measure certain significant parts of that environment first, before doing anything else.

One initial, relatively easy and certainly practical approach to forecasting is to:

1 identify an economic indicator which affects the industry of which the company is a part;
2 obtain the aggregated figures of the industry's output;
3 correlate the two (correlation is a statistical technique).

If the correlation is 'high', **1** and **2** can be 'smoothed' (as the life cycle was) and projected. An illustration of smoothing is given in Figure 13.1; the smoothed line is labelled 'trend' and is the sort of thing that commentators talk about on the news – 'the underlying trend of unemployment is going 'up' or 'down' as the case may be!

Fig 13.1   *A smoothed trend*

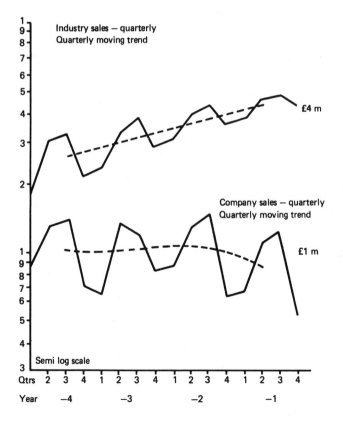

13.7 **What is Correlation?**

A brief explanation is necessary. The 'coefficient of correlation' is measured by formula and results in a figure between 1 and 0, or between 0 and −1, e.g. positive or negative correlation.

High   = 0.7 up to 1
Medium = 0.45 up to 0.7
Low   = 0 up to 0.45

We have to use our own judgement about any cause and effect relationship between two sets of data, such as the level of unemployment and the sale of cars. A high correlation does not necessarily mean that a relationship exists; it may be pure accident.

I have taken the opportunity of using real data for Figure 13.1, showing in this instance the relative movement of quarterly sales, with the trend lines running through them, of an industry and a company within it. I think I need to explain some points.

Semi-log scale (bottom left). By using a semi-log scale on the vertical axis I am able to plot 'relative' movement between the two sets of data: that is to say, as you look at the graph you can immediately interpret the differences as they appear to the eye. For instance the industry trend is rising, the company's falling. The quarterly fluctuations are diminishing at industry level, increasing if anything for the company. You would not get this 'relativity' if the data had been plotted on ordinary graph paper – on absolute scales (Semi-log paper is specially printed.)

The trend line In Figure 13.1 the trend line has been calculated by the method of moving quarterly totals for which there is a specific procedure.

Earlier I suggested correlation between an economic indicator and an industry; now I have illustrated the next level down, an industry and a company. There is greater likelihood of this latter correlation being weaker than an economic/industry one. This company is showing distinctly poor performance.

Time series All this title means is that the data being used is in some way going to be related to a time scale. Figure 13.1 is just such an example. If you look back once more you will see how the horizontal is split into years, and within each year four quarters. This kind of approach is very common indeed because it is extremely useful. But there is a snag: the trend lines do not reach the most recent 'data point', the fourth quarter of the most recent year (−1), but only as far as the second quarter. The method of moving totals, monthly, quarterly or annually according to the way you use them, has this peculiarity. Therefore in order to make a projection into the future, you have to do it by eye; draw it in as you think the trend line will continue.

There is another technique of plotting data in which the eye is used, known as 'the line of best fit'; fortunately there is a statistical method of confirming that the 'fit' is in fact the best, known as 'least squares'. For short-term projections into the future (by which I mean months rather than years) this latter technique can be useful. So let us demonstrate it.

Figure 13.2 shows what is often called a 'scatter diagram'; the dots appear to be a bit spread out but have a general sense of direction. The greater this spread the less easy it is to draw a line of best fit, and even when using the least squares method the confidence you could place in the result would be dubious. So in all these approaches we have to know what we are doing, or have someone help us.

Using your eye only, place a ruler (preferably a transparent plastic one) over the scatter diagram and try to project to April of 'next year'. I am going to calculate the projection and then give you the points to plot, from the data in the table below.

Monthly sales data £000

June	57
July	52
August	75
September	125
October	138
November	105
December	198

We are now ready, from processing the table above, to set the points on Figure 13.2 and for you to draw in the line.

Fig 13.2   *A scatter diagram*

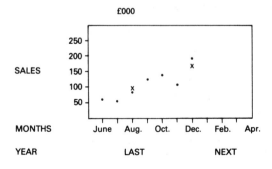

The value above August of last year* is 86; that above December is 170. Join these two points by a straight ruled line and extend that line out to the right above February and April of 'next' year. If you read off their values against the vertical scale, they should be 213 and 255 respectively. You have a forecast!

13.8 Summary

Three statistical techniques, which can be used to help us make forecasts, have been specifically mentioned. Because they are distinctly proce-dural, I called them 'objective methods' in the opening words of Section 13.5; they were correlation, moving totals and least squares. These are of course only a taste of the possibilities. Running through them was an element of time, past time, therefore history. You may well ask if history is a good enough base to predict the future.

13.9 The Certainty of Change

History is not a good enough data base to predict the future! Whether change comes gradually and smoothy or suddenly and erratically, come it most certainly will, often catching us unawares and taking on entirely unexpected directions. Yet we have to find methods of dealing with it, because in order to plan business we have to predict.

Objective methods take us so far, but seldom far enough; they are too inflexible. They are valid only on the assumption that the past will continue into the present and the future. In part this will be true; yet it is unreliable as the pace of change is constantly speeding up. In Section 13.10 we are going to make a simple model of change and also examine causes which will 'bend' projections. These causes will come from the environment, to which we must adjust, and from our own actions, which should have some effect on that environment.

13.10 'Smooth' Change

The first of the three levels, an economic indicator, is likely to be fairly smooth. For example the index of industrial production is such an indicator, and when graphed by the 'percentage rate of change from the previous period' has a wave-like appearance over several years. This is commonly referred to as 'cyclical' movement. Figure 13.3 gives an example. Imagine that you are continuing the cycle; what would it look

*The only reason I have given this value, rather than above June, is because it gets a little crowded in the corner; all we were looking for were any two points on a straight line.

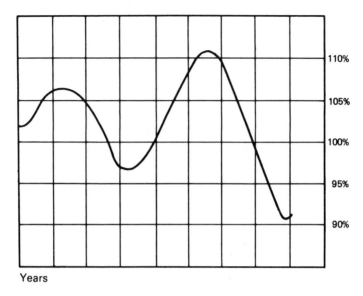

Years

Fig 13.3 *Cyclical movement – percent rate of change*

---

like? Would you admit that this is reasonably (!) predictable – particularly as I have asked you to do it with the knowledge of
hindsight? It seems as if the peaks and troughs have a time lapse of about
five years. Exactly how widely the index is going to swing is more difficult
to assess; in some cycles it seems likely to go deeper than others.

If you turn back for another look at Figure 13.1 you will notice another
type of smooth change – seasonal change. The ups and downs of the four
quarters are quite predictable; they are going to happen. To what extent
may be doubtful.

So cyclical and seasonal change is likely to be relatively predictable.
What is totally unpredictable is known as 'random fluctuation'. A
production plant is burnt down; a competitor makes a technological
breakthrough and renders your product obsolete; government imposes a
new tax which alters your price for consumers (perhaps some of these are
becoming predictable – betting, tobacco, alcohol); an overseas country
puts a trade tariff against your goods.

So far then one part of our two-dimensional model is emerging, and I
am going to show it on what is known as a 'bipolar scale' – see Figure
13.4.

The second part of the model relates to the way in which we observe
and record events. This is something which should be done systematically,

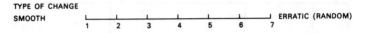

Fig 13.4   *Change – a bipolar scale*

regularly and preferably with routines set up somewhere in the organization. We can also plot this on a bipolar basis, but vertically.

Superimpose these two figures, one on top of the other, and we have a
two-dimensional map about change.

Fig 13.5   *Results of observation of change*

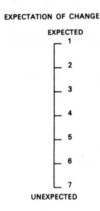

Fig 13.6   *Change – a two-dimensional map*

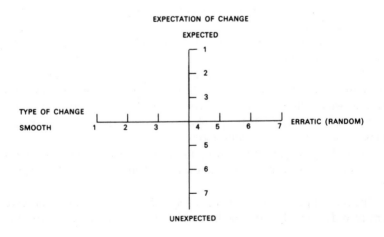

(Incidentally there is no particular magic in the number 7 for the scale; it could be 5 or 11. But it does need an odd number to get the middle point.)

Sector 4–1/1 (top left) should never really be a cause for trouble; if it is it simply means that the observation system has fallen down badly and should be rectified; you have landed in sector 4–1/7 (bottom left). When an event falls into sector 4–7/1 (top right) it is an unexpected bonus; your information system must be pretty good. The remaining sector 4–7/7 is the one that really gives trouble. Given that a firm systematically keeps events under review by some such method as that illustrated, it will quickly find the deficiencies; some will be capable of remedy, some will not, and then planning can be undertaken how to react.

Some of these events will help trade, some will hinder it, so they will have the effect of pushing any projection line up or down.

According to your particular judgement, in which I would include trade experience, your forecast would be bent; pressures are being exerted on it.

The only way that any measure can be made of the power of such pressures is through continuous observation and testing. This is the beginning of what computer simulation models consist of; instead of two-dimensional maps, such as that we constructed, multi-dimensional maps can be handled by computers.

13.11 Action, as Opposed to Reaction

Business is not passive, is it? It is not really like the balloon analogy earlier in the chapter. In marketing particularly we are setting out all the time to influence the environment; and also to allow it to influence us. These marketing activities are 'inputs' into the environment from which we hope to get 'outputs'. They bend lines too! So in forecasting we ought to be well aware of the effectiveness of our activities. One way of calculating the relationship between input and output is by regression, a

---

Fig 13.7 *Pressures on projections*

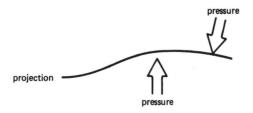

technique not dissimilar to one we have already illustrated – least squares. But instead of time being one of the axes we would use some input such as the cost of a sales force. The output would be sales volume. Just like the least squares example, a straight line can be plotted through data to arrive at a sales revenue figure for a sales force costing £375 000 or £400 000. The sales manager is asking, 'If I spend more by recruiting and using additional manpower, what is the likely sales volume that I will get in return?' Figure 13.8 shows the result graphically.

If, therefore, the sales manager increases expenditure on the sales force to £375 000, it should generate £5 million and, with an input of £400 000, make £5 400 000. Once again the computer can come to our aid in these calculations by doing much more complex permutations, using multiple regression.

13.12 Summary

We have now identified three common types of change; cyclical, seasonal and random. Using these we then went on to develop a two-dimensional model of change.

These enabled us to see how a projection line could be bent both up or down according to whether or not the situation was favourable or adverse. Finally we drew attention to those inputs which are controllable in a business and in their turn would be expected to influence an output; the projection lines therefore can be bent either by outside uncontrollable events or by business decisions.

13.13 Probable Outcomes

By calling this section 'Probable outcomes' I am guilty of using a pun! We will be approaching forecasting now from a subjective point of view, in

Fig 13.8 *Input/output using regression*

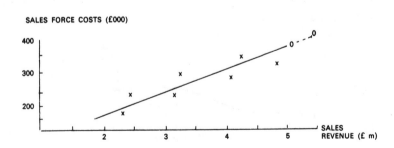

which opinions are encouraged. But how can your opinion or mine be measured in such a way that it can be taken into account in arriving at a forecast figure? Because managements, after all, are looking for something relatively precise – the sales forecast for next year will be . . . The conversion from opinion to 'precision' is done using statistical 'probability'.

We will be looking at two main sources of opinion, from outside a firm, and from inside it. Then we will be showing how this is incorporated into figures in combination with the other methods we covered in the previous sections. Finally forecasting a time will receive our attention; how far ahead can we look and what circumstances dictate the horizon?

13.14 'Expert' Opinion

Although this kind of forecasting is given the label 'expert', there are times when its literal meaning is perhaps too strong. What it is intended to imply is people who are knowledgeable, experienced, and on whose judgement we may generally rely, and who are willing to share their expertise. Now obviously, if it can be tapped, this is a rich vein of material.

As forecasts are estimates of sales surely one source of information would be the customers; if so, from which customers of the following products could you get the kind of information you want?

Product	*Customer*
Anaesthetic gas	Hospital anaesthetists
Fork-lift truck	Works managers
	Distribution managers
	Accountants
Breakfast cereal	Housewives
Jeans	Clothing shop managers
	Young people
Double glazing	Householders

I wonder if you have deduced any general conclusions from the list. I am going to suggest two:

• The more widespread the consumption, the more difficult it will be to get an authoritative estimate. For example the experience of housewives buying breakfast cereal is going to be very narrow, at most within a family or circle of friends. And as this is a fast-moving consumer product, with thousands or millions of customers, such a forecast would not be very practical.

The same would apply to the jeans and young people; but the clothing shop managers would be able to give a much wider view, at least one fairly representative of the catchment area the shop serves. That may not be good enough for your purpose; that would be for you to judge.

What verdict did you give to double glazing – consumer durable? This may be for an individual householder a 'once in a lifetime' purchase; if so he is not going to be much better for you than any old crystal ball!

- An anaesthetist is an expert in his profession. He is therefore likely to be knowledgeable in his field and should know all about the levels of gas consumption in his hospital. He will have a pretty good idea, too, whether he is getting busier or not. He could help you predict, if he is willing to.

A fork-lift truck, which is a capital good, may well be in a formal equipment replacement programme; works and distribution managers are the people under whose direct control the truck would be placed, but the accountant may be the authority to buy it. (A typical example of a decision-making unit.)

From these examples, it can be generally stated that using expert opinion is more practical in industrial contexts than in consumer ones.

There is now the problem of who gets this information. Most often it is a function of a sales force, especially if they are properly trained to do it. A salesman is, after all, closely in touch with his market; he is regularly meeting the buyers and users, and should make every opportunity to exchange information. But is this a formal or informal process? Does he in other words announce his intention of trying to build a forecast (which is sometimes done) or does he pick up a bit of information here, get tipped a wink there and put two and two together to make twenty-two?

The key to the answer of my sentence of questions is back in our purpose: we are looking for an opinion, or judgement if you prefer.

13.15 The Time Horizon

You may not be a photographer, but if I talk about 'long' or telescopic lenses for cameras you will know what I mean. The 'longer' the lens, the further it can see. But over great distances the film on which the picture is recorded loses its clarity of 'definition'. So it is with forecasting. The further into the future we try to see, the less certain we will be. Think of all the problems inherent in calculating the value of an investment of, say, £1000 million in a power station which will not come 'on stream' for twenty years! A very far cry from forecasting business turnover for next

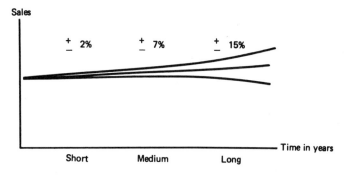

Fig 13.9 *Permissible variations*

---

month. One way of thinking of this is to open out the permissible variations. See Figure 13.9.

13.16 Using Probabilities

The best business examples of using probabilities are betting shops, gambling casinos, football pools, lotteries and others of like nature. They survive on it. In every-day language we talk of 'odds' for or against. Every time you or I say to someone, 'What will you bet?' we are backing our judgement or opinion. Turn that approach into number form and we have 'probabilities'.

There are first of all two extremes:

1 = total certainty
0 = total uncertainty

In practice we are more likely to use '1' as meaning reasonably certain, for there is no such thing as total certainty.

Supposing we are forecasting sales by using regression as we did in Figure 13.8 on page 216, we are going to have to assign probabilities to the likelihood of the two outcomes. First turn back to page 216 and estimate the width of 'scatter' that could occur around the £5 million and £5.4 million sales levels.

One way you can do this is to think in terms of plus or minus a certain percentage, say 5 per cent.

	First outcome	*Second outcome*
− 5%	£4.75 m	£5.13 m
Forecast	£5 m	£5.4 m
+ 5%	£5.25 m	£5.67 m

What we now have is a range of possible outcomes given two different levels of input, the sales force costs. But we might still feel that the variation up or down of only 5 per cent is not wide enough to give us 'certainty'; so we will enlarge it to 10 per cent each way. Now for further calculations I am going to develop the figures in the 'first outcome' only. The method can be applied in identical fashion to any other level of outcome, but I am sure one illustration will suffice. What we are now saying is that:

If I (Mr Sales Manager) increase sales force costs from a level of £325 000 to £375 000 by employing three more representatives, I am almost certain that the sales revenue in the next twelve months will fall between £4.5 and £5.5 millions. I do not think that either of the extremes is very likely, but circumstances could change unexpectedly and distort the most likely result of £5 million.

Table of probabilities

Range	Outcome	Probability	Result
− 10%	£4.5 m	0.1	0.45 m
− 5%	£4.75 m	0.2	0.95 m
Forecast	£5 m	0.4	2 m
+ 5%	£5.25 m	0.2	1.05 m
+ 10%	£5.5 m	0.1	0.55 m
		—	——
		1	5

Have a look at the 'probability' column and note the following points:

- low values are given to the extremes, higher values towards the centre of the range;
- the values are evenly distributed (in this case) around the centre so that when they are multiplied out into the 'result' column the total of that column equals the original forecast of £5 m;
- the total of the assigned probabilities equals 1 (certainty).

Now let us 'bend' the results!

Using the 'range' and 'outcome' as given in the table above, let us now reassign probability values in the light of two different contingencies:

(a) To back up the sales force we have taken on a new advertising agency and they have put to us an extremely creative and attractive campaign, which we believe will help the representatives by generating demand.

(b) There are rumours, as yet unconfirmed, that a major company is about to launch a highly competitive product into one of our markets (the one being forecast).

Using the two tables below calculate the new total 'result' after reassigning the probabilities for **(a)** and **(b)**.

Reassigned probabilities

(a) Range	Outcome (£m)	Probability	Result
− 10%	4.50	0.05	0.23
− 5%	4.75	0.15	0.71
Forecast	5.00	0.40	2.00
+ 5%	5.25	0.30	1.57
+ 10%	5.50	0.10	0.55
		1	5.06
(b)− 10%	4.50	0.10	0.45
− 5%	4.75	0.35	1.66
Forecast	5.00	0.40	2.00
+ 5%	5.25	0.10	0.53
+ 10%	5.50	0.05	0.28
		1	4.91

By increasing the probability values at the + end of the scale for **(a)** and doing the reverse for **(b)** you will increase and decrease the £5 m central figure. You are only using your judgement in the light of some other influence from that on which the original forecast was made, but backing that judgement with a number. You are still allowing for considerable variation from a precise figure; but some figure is needed for planning, for marketing activity, purchasing, manpower planning, allocating finance and so on.

13.17 Summary

Finally in this Chapter on forecasting we have brought in the human touch and developed a method of coping with imprecision. We recognized that the greater the length of any projection into the future, the more uncertain it must become.

Exercises

1 Without having to do any calculations, look again at Figure 13.1 and estimate whether the two trend lines correlate. Is there, in other words, a 'high' measure of uniformity, 'medium' or virtually none, 'low'?

2 In the chapter I mentioned 'three levels of activity'; later these led us on to correlation. What were those three levels and what was the significance of 'aggregated' data? (See Section 13.6).

3 How would you describe the difference between 'objective' and 'subjective' approaches to forecasting? If they are used together on a forecast in which order are they applied?

4 Although I know that you will not be able to plot these 'events' accurately, you should have no difficulty in placing them in the appropriate two-dimensional sectors in Figure 13.6.

1 You are a plumber: there has been a rapid thaw after a period of heavy frosts and freezing temperatures.

2 You are a tobacco manufacturer: the government legislates against all forms of tobacco advertising.

3 You are a wine importer from France: in the budget the Chancellor of the Exchequer reduces the duty to bring it in line with the rest of the EEC.

4 You are a builders' merchant: statistics published by Her Majesty's Stationery Office (HMSO) show that there is an increase in housing starts.

5 A great deal of forecasting is based on the detection of trends and their projection by statistical techniques. Like the PLC model this will normally result in some kind of 'smoothing': what is meant by this word and what are its disadvantages in the accurate short-term prediction of an outcome?

14 Putting it all Together

14.1 Introduction

The complexities of business, and in particular of marketing, should by now be more than apparent to the reader. This condition is so obvious that it leads us at once to ask the question, can these complexities be reduced to manageable proportions so that a student can handle them? There is no easy answer. The past usually can, simply because it has become fact and nothing can be done to change it. But as we saw in the last chapter the future is rather different – uncertain, to say the least.

What encouragement there is lies in providing some method for diagnosing problems, finding where we might have some apparent advantage and then using our imagination and ingenuity for the future. This chapter offers a programme.

The first part (Sections 14.2 to 14.7) deals with what has come to be widely known as *SWOT* analysis. The second (Sections 14.8 to 14.13) sets out to clarify the differences between policy, strategy and tactics. For the student in particular, the distinctions are important because they are about different aspects of the management process, marketing or otherwise.

The third and final part (Sections 14.14 to the end of the Chapter) deals with the subject of control. After these three sections management, or getting things done, will be much clearer and the reader will have to provide then his own opportunities for practising it.

14.2 Finding Out What to Do

If it were possible to provide marketers with any sort of 'map' their actions would inevitably become so predictable as to be worthless in a competitive society. One of the fascinations of marketing is the unpredictability. Much of the business of enterprise is to do the unexpected, to steal a march on the competition (at least for a time) and secure those advantages highlighted by the Boston Consulting Group. What we can do is to give students of marketing (and I am not using the word 'student' in any narrow sense) some sense of direction. This section sets out to do just that.

We are going to use a method widely known, and taught in business schools and colleges, as SWOT analysis:

S = *strengths*)
W = *weaknesses*) These two 'audit' the past.

O = *opportunities*)
T = *threats*) These two 'anticipate' the future.

The idea behind this method is to study the present and past performance of a business and all its activities (not only marketing) to find out those things it does well and those less well, or poorly. Once clearly defined this 'audit' should show up possible courses of action to be taken in the future to capitalize on opportunities and avoid threats. So in a way we can think of *SWOT* analysis as a kind of bridge, the other side of which may still be shrouded in mist!

14.3 A Word of Warning

Because there are two situations where *SWOT* analysis is carried out, I must state what they are and differentiate the approach between them. Firstly there is the student formally learning about marketing faced with a 'case study'. In the event that this term is not familiar to all readers, let me explain it by saying that a 'case study' represents the story of a firm in some detail from which students are expected to manage the business problems portrayed. Obviously these problems may be about any aspect of the business according to the intentions of the case writer. They are also commonly used for examinations. For the student this is the nearest approach to business that it is possible to simulate. The difficulty here is real and personal identification with the 'case'. How easy it is to take a lofty and superior view knowing full well that accountability is non-existent (except to the extent of pleasing the tutor!).

The businessman has the opposite problem; he is often too close to the situation to take any sort of objective view at all. To ask him, for instance, to come up with a list of corporate weaknesses (for which he is in part responsible) is like asking any male whether he drives well or not! Nevertheless there are ways in which these problems can be overcome.

14.4 The 'Audit' of Strengths and Weaknesses

I am going to make the assumption that any business reader has access to the past performance records of his firm, for it is from these that the strengths and weaknesses are found. I am going to presume further that standards of performance had been previously laid down against which

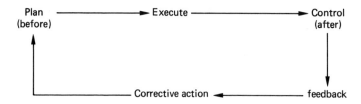

Fig 14.1 *Planning cycle*

actual execution can be measured. In outline this takes the form of Figure 14.1. This measurement is included in the word 'control'.

Self-check

Let us take this opportunity of reminding ourselves of some examples we have used in earlier chapters, which we can also use in the present context of 'control'.

1 Can you make a quick list of, say, four potential control measures of the performance of a salesman?

2 Why was it so important to keep a constant eye on 'contribution' when negotiating the price for the five executive jets to a multinational company operating in South America?

In Section 8.4 headed 'A foot in the door' about a Mr Average Salesman we were then concerned with items like cost per call, cost per hour, total turnover, turnover per call and, later in the same section, erosion rates and new business gained. Any or all of these give management an opportunity to plan and subsequently control.

Similarly in the section in Chapter 9 headed 'How to decide and subsequently verify', we 'negotiated' a sale of jets. Our control was the final level of profit, following earlier calculations of break-even points and profit volumes (Section 9.16).

From information of this kind, strengths and weaknesses can be audited. But, for the businessman, I am presupposing the existence of the word 'plan', as in Figure 14.1 above. The student has not normally got 'plans' conveniently laid out for him; he has to deduce them from whatever measurable criteria are available in a 'case study'. Such measures as are available should therefore be treated as subjectively as necessary; they can illustrate a strength or weakness, really according to preference. For example: a company has three products with a given percentage market share:

Product	% market share
A	5.6
B	0.4
C	6.1

Now unless it is stated in the case that these market shares are good, poor or indifferent, or unless there is sufficient in the story to get some clear indication, the figures alone are meaningless as performance criteria. They merely state what is. They are, however, a starting point for the next 'plan'. That is how they should be treated.

14.5 In the Absence of Numbers

Sometimes there is a danger of relying too heavily on numbers, on the quantification of performance. Suppose we try out once more some two-dimensional mapping.

If you recall we were using the two-dimensional map to plot change. In a slightly different way we are going to plot change again; first we will be taking a situation at one point in time and plotting that. Then we will be making up our minds what to do about the first situation – do we leave it or change it? If we change, then we plot the situation we wish to take up. This is where we move from the 'audit', which is historical, to the plan, which is futuristic.

14.6 Planning for Opportunities and Threats

If we can successfully locate our current position on an axis of strengths and weaknesses on the basis of past performance –

Strengths $\underset{1\quad 2\quad 3\quad 4\quad 5\quad 6\quad 7}{\rule{6cm}{0.4pt}}$ Weaknesses

– we should then be able to decide where we would wish to go to take advantage of the one, and mitigate the consequences of the other. In other words we do something.

On the basis of the following story, identify the strengths and weaknesses and locate them along the scale shown above.

Sir Clive Sinclair is probably best known today for his personal computers, the ZX range. However, first and foremost he is an innovator; he was the first to make a pocket calculator, the first Briton to make a digital watch and the designer of the C5 electric car, none of which he

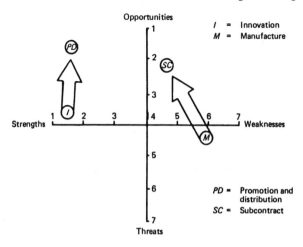

Fig 14.2 *Sinclair's decisions*

---

was able to turn to commercial success. He admits he is not a manufacturer. He is also working on a miniature flat screen black-and-white TV.

Using the single axis shown above, I would personally place Sinclair's innovation activities very high on the strength end (say between 1 and 2) and his manufacturing capability at the other end at 5, or more likely 6. Would you agree?

If Sinclair was unable to make a go of the pocket calculator and the digital watch because he could not handle or manage their manufacture properly, what did he do to turn his computer into such a success? On the one hand he had a market opportunity and on the other a production threat!

This time, instead of starting with the story, I am going to show you the two-dimensional map showing where we (and Sinclair) would probably want to go!

Story continued

Sinclair's innovative flair opens enormous market opportunities provided they can be successfully exploited; this means good promotion and distribution. What means are available to avoid the threat of failure through poor production management and control? Sinclair solved this problem by subcontracting manufacture to the watchmakers, Timex.

Would it be fair to suggest that there will always remain some weakness (that is why I have plotted SC on this side of Figure 14.2) as long as Sinclair is dependent on someone else for his production? On the other hand Sinclair retained the marketing of the ZX and Spectrum computers. He has distributed over a quarter of a million of the ZX81 alone by mail order.

14.7 Summary

SWOT analysis is a means of 'auditing' the past and present, and projecting the present into the future. Although by no means essential, it helps to plot the 'audit' of strengths and weaknesses and then show what decisions might be taken to capitalize on opportunities and avoid threats.

Because, earlier in this chapter, I directed some comments to students may I elaborate a little more? In dealing with 'case studies' most students love the 'audit' part. As far as it goes it can be based on facts elicited or deduced from information in the case; this gives an apparent sense of security. Dealing with the future poses two particular problems:

- the future must be hypothetical (both in case studies and in the real commercial world) and this leads to some feeling of insecurity and therefore reluctance to make a commitment;
- students are simply lacking in practice for decision-making.

The decision-making stage is by far the more important, and students should concentrate their attention here much more than they do. Two questions need to be asked by the student:

- What am I going to do?
- How am I going to achieve it?

14.8 The Ends and the Means

Without any hesitation, I called Part III 'Marketing strategy and business policy', but I have not yet defined adequately exactly what is meant by either strategy or policy. Nor have I explained where the term 'tactics' relates to them. This section will clarify all three, giving examples, as it does so, of practice. The transition from one level to another in the course of job promotion may give rise to personal difficulties, a reluctance to leave to others those activities which had hitherto been ours to carry out, or the inability to view the wider perspectives that a new position commands.

14.9 Definitions are Boring!

If you are to give me any argument on this title I should be surprised, but somehow I have to overcome this difficulty! How would you do it? I am going to draw the conclusions with you. In the right-hand columns I have inserted an initial to represent one of three – policy, strategy, tactics – against words in italics in the sentences below:

1 'The *means* to an *end*.'   T   S

2 'We will not *enter* any *market* unless   P
it is worth at least £2 million'

3 'Our objective is to *increase our market*   S
share from 15 per cent to $17\frac{1}{2}$ per cent
in two years without any additional
capital investment.'

4 'The purpose of our next advertising   S
campaign must be to achieve an *increase in
the level of awareness* of our leading brand
by five per cent within six months.

5 'The campaign *will be conducted* by using a   T
well-known personality.'

6 '*Short term* and *long term*.'   T   S

Taking the first and last together we can describe *tactics* and *strategy* as the 'short-term means' to achieve 'long-term ends'. We can elaborate that a little by next examining sentences 4 and 5 together.

'Increase in the level of awareness' describes an 'end' ('The purpose') whilst 'will be conducted' the 'means'. Similarly sentence 3 is also about strategy, because it describes a purpose and uses the words 'Our objective'.

The only policy statement in this section is 2. What makes it different? First it describes a form of behaviour; to be more accurate it 'proscribes'. Secondly, it limits discretion for subordinates; if you were boss and one of your staff did enter a market worth less than £2 million what would you do about it? Thirdly, it is repetitive, it goes on, it continues.

I think we can sum up so far:

- Policy sets limits.
- Strategy sets goals and allocates resources within a time limit.
- Tactics set methods and use resources within a time limit.

Using these three terms, how would you include them in a description of Clive Sinclair's marketing activities? (See Section 14.6.)

'Because the business's talent lies in developing new products, our policy will be one of continuing innovation and of subcontracting manufacture. Our marketing policy will be to capitalize on our reputation for innovation, which will support our strategy of direct marketing. Our tactics will include media advertising with mail-order and direct distribution by post, until sufficient demand has been established to allow negotiations with a national retail organization to handle our products (strategy revision).'

14.10 Strategy and Policy in Marketing

If I have taken 'policy' and 'strategy' (and 'tactics') in their widest corporate context, am I trying to imply that they do not all operate within the subordinate levels of management? No I am not, and the fact that they do play a part throughout a business, at practically every level, does sometimes make for difficulties. Let me illustrate this with some marketing mix examples, in other words straight out of Part II.

14.11 Marketing Mix Policies

1 Until further notice TV advertising will be replaced by print media and poster sites.
2 All salesmen will be at least twenty-five years old and have four GCSE's.
3 Unless special circumstances dictate, our product price position will be one of parity with competition.
4 Direct delivery will not be made for order quantities below x number of cases.

What does 'policy' set? Are the four statements 'policy' ones? Yes, they are without exception because they all set limits. I hope by now (particularly student readers) you are becoming much clearer about 'policy', what it is and how it may be used – to set a limit.

14.12 Characteristics of Strategy

We have already decided that the main things about 'strategy' are that it describes a goal, purpose or objective; secondly resources required to achieve the goals are allocated; and thirdly all to take place within a specified period of time. What is too often absent is their quantification! So what does this mean? It means:

1 What is to be done?
2 By how much or how many?
3 By whom?
4 By when (in what time period)?

And if necessary and appropriate:

5 Where is it to take place?
6 Why are we doing it?
7 At what cost?

From the following paragraph we could identify all seven.

'In view of our expansion targets we will be setting up a distributive system through agents in Germany and contract with them sales volumes of 90,000 tonnes worth DM 16.5 million over the next three years. You will do it on an annual budget of not more than DM 100,000.'

1 'contract . . . sales volumes';
2 '90,000 tonnes worth DM 16.5 million';
3 'You . . . ';
4 'over the next three years';
5 'in Germany';
6 'expansion targets';
7 ' . . . budget of not more than'.

Not that anyone would expect an answer to all seven questions every time. What should appear is what is appropriate to the strategy; and there are some occasions when quantification is not possible in such detail.

14.13 Summary

Distinctions were drawn in this section between *policy*, *strategy* and *tactics*. All three can be applicable at different levels of an organization's activities and each contributes something different. Quantification of strategy was stressed and should be used whenever possible.

14.14 The Principle of 'Closed Loop'

One of the best examples of a 'closed loop' control, and one which most of us are probably familiar with, is a thermostat on, say, a domestic central heating system. As you know it is a kind of switch. We can link it to our planning cycle quite easily (see Section 14.4).

1 we decide what temperature we would like (*plan*);
2 we set the control dial on the thermostat to that temperature (*execute*);
3 when the air temperature reaches that set by us (*in the plan*) the heating system, the boiler, has its power supply cut off automatically (*control*);
4 as a result the temperature falls (*corrective action*) until it reaches a lower level and the thermostat cuts in again by restoring the power supply (*corrective action again*).

3 and 4 in the sequence set upper and lower limits of control for the thermostat to switch power on and off. These limits are an important part of business controls as well.

14.15 **Control by Observation**

There are not many controls relevant to marketing that are as automatic as a thermostat! They are much more like the control exercised by the gas or electricity boards. Every so often somebody visits us to 'read the meter' and then we get a bill for what we have consumed; the dials on the meter are a form of control, they provide information. Unlike the thermostat they require human observation and interpretation. By knowing roughly what electricity and gas cost, and how much is likely to be used in a given period, a householder can 'plan' (or anticipate) the cost and budget for it. The householder will expect some variation between actual cost and budget; once more he will have set upper and lower limits; if not formally; at least in his mind. A period of very cold weather in a winter quarter can easily upset the best of calculations! Some people do not budget and get some nasty surprises!

In this kind of system the automatic regulation of the thermostat has to be replaced by direct and continuous human observation. If we literally went to such lengths of controlling our domestic power use, we could check our meters weekly and adjust consumption to stay within our target for a quarter. We might have some difficulty with the kids! And so the problems and difficulties of supervision raise their heads.

By going back over 'The principle of the "closed-loop"' and 'Control by observation', how many important points about controls in general can you deduce?

There are five key ones. So find them again in the following story of a business.

Minutes of the meeting.
Present: Sales manager, Production manager, Stock controller, Management accountant.

1 Sales report:	Actual for period –	15 060 units
		£9 186.60
	Target for period –	16 500 units, + or – 5%
		17 325 –
		15 675 unit range
		£11 261.25–
		£10 188.75
2 Production report	Actual for period –	16 870 units
	Target for period –	16 800 units
3 Stock report:	Opening stock at beginning of period –	9 462 units
	Add sold production –	1 810 units
	Closing stock at end of period –	11 272 units

4 Accounts report:

	Target	Actual	Variances Fav* adv*
Sales –	£10 725	£9 186.60	£1 538.40
Production – @ cost of 40p	£ 6 720	£6 748	£ 28.00 £ 576.00
Stock increase (less production variance) @ 40p	£ 120	£ 696	

Cash shortfall £2 142.40

Now it is time to confirm with you the five key points about controls.

1 There must be a measurable target set in advance.

2* 'Variances' around the target should be set and shown in 'favourable' or 'adverse'.

3 The control should convey information, e.g. by comparison.

4 The control information must be measurable, automatically or by observation.

5 The measurement must be continuous or periodic.

The 'reports' used in the story above also serve to highlight how interrelated business activities are. In the example, production, stock and accounts were all dependent on sales. There is a 'knock-on' effect. Now in practice the production manager could have introduced short-time working; but, give or take a little, he was on target, so why should he? The stock controller was very much the middle of the sandwich, between sales and production, with no opportunity of taking any remedial action to keep stock levels down. The accountant has to live with a cash shortfall of over £2000. In the next period some action has to be taken to correct the situation. However, a final point must be made here.

Because a target was not met, it does not necessarily mean that performance was poor. The target could have been wrong, or impossible of achievement in the first place; during the period internal or external conditions could have changed but the target was not. Performance could have been poor. These are all possible explanations; management must know which one is the real one.

Without looking back can you remember how we summed up what policy, strategy and tactics do? Now answer this question: to which of the three do controls relate?

If this strikes you as a bit of a puzzle let me remind you that we agreed that all three can be used at any level of management, and we worked through some statements illustrating this. Policy sets limit: so if we do not cross those limits, control seems to be unnecessary. Strategy sets goals and allocates resources within a specified time: now this seems to be much closer to control; does not control verify the achievement of the goal within the limits of the resources? Tactics set methods and use the resources; this is surely the 'execution' bit of the planning cycle, and control can only come in after the event, or at specific stages during the event – which are strategic. So strategy and control must be thought of as part and parcel of each other, two sides of the same coin (or any other cliché you might wish to use!).

14.16 Summary

Control has to be regarded as an essential part of the planning cycle. Two kinds were considered; control by closed loop and control by observation. The section concluded that control is the end part of strategy.

Exercises

1 What made 'policy' different from 'strategy' (and tactics)? One, two, three reasons?
2 Can you reproduce the 'planning cycle' diagram in the space below?

The planning cycle
3 What does the abbreviation, SWOT, stand for? Two of them apply to the past and the present performance of a business and two to the future; which are which?
4 For what purpose did we use two-dimensional mapping in this chapter?
5 You are the sales training manager for a national UK company employing 250 salesmen. Which of the following statements would you select as being suitable for your strategy?

   1 On recruitment each new salesman will have two weeks' induction training to familiarize himself with company procedures.
   2 On-the-job sales training will increase sales turnover by 5 per cent this year.
   3 The purpose of the annual sales conference will be to raise morale.
   4 Not more than ten salesmen should attend the training centre at one time.
   5 The value of sales training cannot be measured.

15 In Different Circumstances . . .

15.1 Introduction

This chapter will engage our attention in export, international and multinational marketing. There is an argument to suggest that the principles of marketing are so universally applicable that special consider -ation of this subject is not necessary. A case can be made for this point of view, but it is a lofty one, making the assumption that the principles of marketing are universally known; and, if known, can be translated to the peculiarities of other countries with that degree of understanding necessary. I do not share this view. There is more than sufficient evidence to suggest that marketing in this country often leaves much to be desired; to take bad habits abroad should be a criminal offence. The crucial differences fall into three categories: first, there is the 'foreign' environment; second, the need for new corporate skills; and third, the application of the marketing mix.

15.2 Little Local Differences

In our own home markets it is surprising how much we can, and do, take for granted. After all we have been absorbing all our lives the customs of our own nation and region. In fact because this 'education' has been so insidious and universal, we may not even realize just how different we are from other peoples. When we go abroad we take our differences with us. Go with a group of tourists to the Costa del Sol and see how anglicized is the food for the 'packaged' holidaymaker – Blackpool in the sun. It is not as if this is even conscious. The hoteliers have found, often from bitter experience, that their native fare attracts more complaint than praise and, for reasons of profit and goodwill, they are better off not serving it. I have been told by a French waiter in a Normandy hotel not to choose a certain dish – 'the British do not like it' – and I was cowardly enough to escape to more familiar ground. The first thing that strikes most of us as soon as we go abroad is the food – after all, we have to eat. But this is indeed only a small beginning.

If you have a map of the world, would you get it – that is if you can remember where you may have 'hidden' it. Never mind if you cannot lay hands on one, we see them often enough on TV at the beginning of news programmes; anyway I am sure you can visualize one sufficiently for this purpose.

1 Which are the countries of the European Community and where are their main centres of population?
2 Which European languages predominate on the continent of South America?
3 If you were trading with Saudi Arabia, which legal system would operate over the terms and conditions of trade, theirs or ours?
4 On a sea journey from Southampton to the Persian Gulf, from how many climatic variations would you have to protect your goods?
5 How do you communicate with people from other parts of the world who cannot read?

If this list even gives you a little cause for thought, be warned that it is less than the tip of any iceberg in any international scene. Nor do I intend in this instance to give the answers; if you do not know them, I want you to feel that you don't. Any acceptance of ignorance and a certain humility are two essential ingredients to international marketing; we need to find out and we need to learn from what we find.

15.3 Things to Look For – Essentials

1 **The culture, and any regional subcultures** Remember, for example, that the UK is one of the few countries in the world that has a national press and TV network (BBC) which help to reduce regional differences in the country. Not remove – reduce. There still remain very strong local loyalties. This is equally applicable in other countries: religion, social values and attitudes can all play their part in purchasing behaviour, and therefore marketing. We often stereotype too easily, and fail to investigate what really influences different peoples. Eventually, as buyers, they still come down to a collection of individuals.

Consider your own reactions to foreign goods in this country; do you have any cultural influences affecting the way you look at them?

I personally still have an aversion to buying a foreign car; a view, obviously not shared by millions in the UK. What is a 'buy British' campaign but cultural? Patriotic, if you like, it is the same. It does not have to be logical, if it is there and affects our behaviour.

2 **Politics** 'Left or right', communist or fascist, dictatorship or democracy, stable or unstable, revolution or evolution – do not these pairs of words evoke familiar situations and our judgements of them?

We judge other political systems according to our own personal standards, not necessarily those of our own country – after all, we may disagree with our own system. Would you, for instance, have any inhibitions about trading with particular countries in the world?

3 **Legal** There is not really any good excuse for falling into obvious legal pitfalls. Of course I do not intend to imply here that the law does not inevitably come into trade in order to resolve disputes; that is what the law is for. What I do find inexcusable are companies exporting abroad without legal advice and counsel – *not* from within the UK but from the country to which the goods will be going. We have personnel in our overseas embassies and legations whose function this is, and they are only too willing to help. These days they are only as far away as a letter or phone call. For instance in my list of five points in Section 15.2 Saudi Arabian law would apply (no. 3) unless you were in an extremely powerful position supplying highly specialist goods, such as defence equipment.

4 **Geography** Some goods may be affected by geography, some may not; for this is considerably greater than mere location or physical features – mountains, rivers, deserts and so on. Climate is a major influence on lifestyle; one has only to compare clothing in Norway and in Zimbabwe. Strong sunlight in, say, the Mediterranean can have disastrous effects on dyes which are not 'colour fast'. Rivers and canals, as in France, may make major contributions to transportation.

5 **Economic** 1992 has already been mentioned in previous chapters as the deadline for total economic integration of the European Community; after all it used to be called the European Economic Community (EEC)! The old title is enough to illustrate the significance. Many of us are quite prepared to accept the idea (if not always the practice) of economic integration but not yet the political one of a single European 'nation'. Even if little local differences still remain the continent of western Europe will become our 'home' market and one of the most potentially powerful economic blocs in the world.

The world at large is now often divided into three: the developed, the developing and the underdeveloped. Each of these has different economic significance: their standard of living, the population size, their rate of development, their international debt and so on. For example commentators allege that the 1988 Olympics, held in Seoul, South Korea, will do a tremendous amount to help that relatively small country of 40 million inhabitants to expand its commercial and economic interests to many nations as a result of the contacts made and, hopefully, the reputation gained. In a word so much economic progress gets rolling with 'communication' – in marketing terminology, 'promotion'.

6 Language Language has functional characteristics that go way beyond the mere demand to communicate. Our ability and method of thinking are constrained by language. For example the British sense of humour is allegedly incapable of being understood by foreigners. Would anybody but an American have answered a call to surrender with the word 'Nuts'? (At Bastogne in 1944 during the Battle of the Bulge.) It takes approximately 25 per cent more space to write an advertisement or label in French than in English. Every language has words that are untranslatable, and brand names in one language can have unfortunate connotations in another; Rolls-Royce had to change the name of the Silver Mist for the German market.

7 Technology There are two things making the world a smaller place: transportation and communications, both heavily dependent on advanced technology. Once the experimental stages are over it will not be very long before the American (and British and Russian?) shuttle flights will be carrying passengers. Research programmes in space for new products, which cannot be adequately tested on earth, are already nothing new. Work is already well under way for instant computerized translation of languages on telephone networks. How long will it be for this kind of thing to be automatically incorporated into television sets? The effect of such technological advances will have a dramatic influence on marketing practice worldwide.

15.4 Summary

The Sections so far have looked, perhaps all too superficially, considering the importance of the subject, at some of the environmental factors of international marketing. These are the obvious ones: culture, politics, legal, geography, economic, language and technology. Each area has its individuality which must be studied. Marketing principles may be universal; their translation into practice requires local, on-the-spot study of any foreign market.

15.5 How Companies Tend to Develop

There are three main stages of development by companies in international trade which all of us ought to know. This section will be dealing with these. However, I must qualify the way we will be approaching the subject by explaining that exceptions are numerous, often depending on the size of the company, sometimes because of the level of development in the country concerned or even simply because of local national pride. The 'little local differences' must be offset against the aims of international business and how it achieves them. From what follows we should be able to match conditions to intentions.

15.6 Early Days

The first stage of developing international business is exporting, which involves the least commitment. When I am using the word 'commitment', I intend to include both intention and resources. This may seem to be a very 'black and white' kind of statement; some hackles may rise a bit at it! I know only too well that many companies export with considerable commitment to it; but they have already progressed some way along the international development route.

In one company I worked for, we received an inquiry from an African country to supply so many tons of a product; it came from an import agent in Ghana, who had got our name from the (then) Board of Trade. After some debate, we filled the order, shipped it, got paid and promptly forgot it. We had no commitment! This sort of thing happens quite a lot and many companies have started their international connections in just this way – but they committed themselves.

15.7 Exporting

I am going to define 'exporting' as:

- *an organization in one country having goods or services transported to a separate organization in another, where it is not directly represented by its own employees, in exchange for other goods and services or money.*

Immediately following this definition, I would like to preempt a little what is still to come: the first distinction between export and international marketing lies in the location of employees – a resource and a commitment.

A 'buyer' (or purchasing offier) from Sears Roebuck department store in the USA visits the Boat Show exhibition at Earls Court in London with a view to finding sources of supply for sailing tackle. He does, and contracts for shipment with some British firms.

1 If the British firms have no direct representation in America are they 'exporting' or 'international marketing'?
2 If the British firms have an agent in Boston, who is not an employee but self-employed, are they 'exporting' or 'international marketing'?

3 If the British firms have an office in Toronto, Canada, which looks after all their North American business, are they 'exporting' or 'international marketing'?

The beginning of commitment are shown by a firm just as soon as some formal link is established with the other country. For example, both **2** and **3** above show commitment. **1** and **2** are exporting; **3** begins international marketing.

15.8 The Agency System

A vast quantity of international trade is carried out through agents. An agent is a form of intermediary acting on behalf of his 'principal'; he negotiates the contract, or the sale in more colloquial terms, but does not himself take over (or take 'title' to) the goods. The supplier ships direct to the customer, paying the agent a commission. This is at its simplest. You will readily recognize that there are many markets in which goods have to be supplied fast, or on demand; this means that the goods must be stored nearby. If an agent or an agency does this, he may do so on behalf of his supplier (in which case he still does not take title), or on his own behalf when he does. In the latter example, strictly speaking he ceases to be an agent, but becomes a distributor, and his reward is profit on resale, not commission. Under 'Early days' above I told you of a shipment to Ghana. The agent concerned did not at any time have legal title to the goods, indeed he probably never even saw them as we sent them direct to the customer. However, from the same company we regularly sold goods to a dealer or 'distributor' in Cyprus who, of course, took title. So an agent does not have legal ownership ('title') to goods, whereas a distributor does.

An agent, you will recall, acts on behalf of his principal; he is not actually an employee, paid a salary, but gets commission on the business he is able to generate. A distributor is really no different from one in the 'home' country; he buys from the supplier and resells, getting his 'payment' from profit.

I often find it helpful to try and put these 'systems' into some form of diagram, and so I have tried just that in Figure 15.1.

Please note carefully the way I am using the terms 'direct' and 'indirect' representation. 'Direct' = having one's own paid employees; 'indirect' = using self-employed personnel or other people's employees. There remains a distinct degree of separation between 'home' and 'other' countries, as indicated by the dotted line connections.

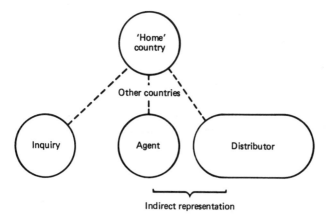

Fig 15.1 *The 'export' system*

15.9 International Marketing

In Section 15.7 I used the words 'the first distinction between export and international marketing lies in the location of employees – a resource and a commitment'. The real key here is the addition of a resource. A great many companies have strong commitments to foreign markets but do not themselves commit their own resources overseas. Without knowing their business objectives, I do not wish to imply that this is wrong, nor to have you interpret it that way. I am, however, prepared to go so far as to suggest that no company will ever achieve such a strong market position using resources over which it has no direct control compared to using those which it actually manages. There comes a point where 'second-hand' marketing is just not adequate. If your overseas markets contribute relatively little to your revenue, or take up little of your production capacity, you are presumably not after a 'strong market position'; but if you are, take a harder look at your methods.

15.10 Resources in an International Context

The use of a resource means that its commitment precludes its use elsewhere: you cannot spend the same money twice! So in business we are weighing up the benefits of alternatives. In this field there are only three:

- (continue to) devote resources to the 'home' market;
- (contine to) export;
- commit resources to foreign markets.

The first step is usually one of representation; instead of leaving everything to the agent or distributor, somebody spends time abroad. Until trade has been built up sufficiently for full-time representation, these visits may be conducted by a director, spending several weeks, or even months, visiting the various markets. Then may come an international salesman, based at home, but travelling extensively, until 100 per cent of his attention should be devoted to the foreign scene. That might be the time to ask the question about nationality! Do you send out a native of the 'home' market or employ a native of the foreign one? A careful scrutiny of the 'environmental factors' covered in the last section would help.

I think we are ready to present a sort of progression of commitment. May I remind you that very few businesses would go through each step as I have it laid out below; they would probably jump several at a time, and make one jump for one market and one completely different in another.

International progression

Marketing	Production
Visits by 'home' executives	'Home' production
Full-time 'export' executives based at 'home'	'Home' production
. . . based in foreign markets	'Home' production
Open sales offices in foreign markets	'Home' production
Open sales offices in foreign markets	Licensing agreement
Joint venture – marketing	– and production
Own subsidiary – marketing	– and production

From very simple beginnings, we can see that the progression has a greater and greater commitment of resources up to the point of having a complete marketing and production operation through a subsidiary company. By the way, not all countries will allow that. Nigeria, for example, much prefers joint ventures and will usually stipulate 51 per cent national ownership! You should also think of 'licensing agreements' as being progressive: products, in 'knocked down' form, may be shipped first and assembled locally; sometimes this develops into some local manufacture of parts, later still full-scale manufacture. In many recent cases the developing countries prefer to import whole factories and hire the expertise to manage them for a while.

We can now illustrate international markets in Figure 15.2 as being joined together, touching each other – like snooker balls!

But note that the foreign markets are not linked to each other, only to the home country.

International Markets

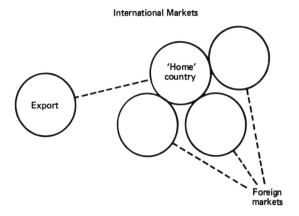

Fig 15.2 *International markets*

15.11 Towards Multinational Marketing

The distinction between *inter-* and *multinational* marketing is one of scale and of attitude. Multinational could be thought of as operating in a lot of different countries, but that is not how we use it in marketing. It starts at the bottom two items in the table headed 'International progression' in Section 15.10 above.

I would not wish to give you the impression that multinational activities must conform to having joint venture or own subsidiaries; indeed the forms of organization are almost as diverse as the organizations themselves. What happens is almost the disappearance of national identities; managerial attitudes look out at the world and see it as a whole, albeit with its local differences. They are not wedded to a 'home' market in any way at all. Their very lack of nationalism is what often brings them into conflict with governments.

What have Ferranti and La Roche in common?

Ferranti, or one part of it anyway, is heavily involved with supplying the British and foreign governments with defence and rocketry systems. It is in a very high technology industry including engineering, electronics, propulsion and so on; it has international connections. La Roche is a pharmaceutical company with its 'home' base in Switzerland and is best known for the tranquillizers Valium and Librium, two drugs which are available all over the world; on this scale La Roche sees the world as its market. They both suffered in common at the hands of the British government, which claimed money back from 'excessive' profits. Ferranti would have been bankrupted by its loss of defence contracts; La Roche

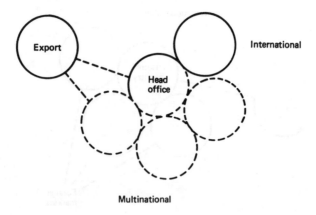

Fig 15.3   *Multinational markets*

could (almost) have shrugged off the Department of Health and Social Security.

So to graduate towards multinational status a company must not only have a wide commitment of resources outside its 'home' market, but be able to act pretty uniformly on a worldwide basis, where neither markets nor products need much differentiation.

The dotted line circles represent both fusion with each other and head office and a more 'open' perspective on to markets. They can have their own subsidiary systems of export and international still attached.

15.12 Summary

This section has built up the international marketing scene from small beginnings to a worldwide scale. The gradation is based on one of commitment and one of resource allocation. Because the character and the conditions of markets throughout the world are potentially so varied, multinational operations can most easily come into their own when they are relatively uniform – for example the market(s) for Coca Cola.

15.13 What Kind of Mix?

Sooner or later tactics must take over from policy and strategy; in this section we look at some of the tactical difficulties encountered when marketing abroad.

The central focus of any business is the product or service it offers; inevitably then this should be our starting point in considering the marketing mix. Not only that, some uniformity is the key to moving from inter- to multinational marketing.

15.14 **Is the Product the Same?**

Not as often as one might imagine. A product exists in the satisfactions that it gives, not in itself, and those satisfactions are likely to be incredibly different all over the world. Take rice. In large parts of the globe rice is a staple food, there is starvation without it; in others it becomes a form of flour; for us in Britain it may mean pudding or an accompaniment to curry. And yet rice is rice is rice. (May I take the opportunity of reminding you once more of the symbolic importance wrapped up in products.)

By contrast technological products are likely to be uniform. Imagine you are equipping a newly built airport with radar and landing instruments for the control tower. Is the product the same as at Heathrow or Gatwick? Yes, probably – unless it happens to be a more up-to-date version.

Where we have to be especially careful is to separate production uniformity and marketing uniformity. There are innumerable examples of the former: petrol, medicines, cloth, candles and so on. This may go a long way towards multinationalism; conversely there are few obvious examples of marketing on such a scale – Coca Cola being one.

15.15 **When We Don't Talk the Same Language**

Language is recognized as a universal problem in marketing and the right measures are usually taken to overcome it. Yet how many incorrect translations have you met, particularly from places like Korea or Taiwan?

How are your languages? As an example of difference of expression in two European languages, how would you translate each of them into English? You will need to find a French–English and a German–English dictionary to do it, if you have no acquaintance with them:

Nur Affen dürfen auf den Rasen.
Nous n'aimons que les singes sur l'herbe.

The German original is to be seen on the grass at Wuppertal Zoo. We would simply put 'Keep off the grass', but then we have not the same sense of humour as the Germans. Translation is not, after all so very difficult. What is difficult, because it is nothing like so obvious, is media. This raises the question of using 'home' expertise for foreign adventures, or foreign expertise on location, or yet again 'home' supervision of foreign expertise. I could easily make it more complicated.

Regardless of which country you were in, would you recognize a Shell petrol station? How?

It would be from the Shell shell; at least that is how I would do it.

Now if a company wants to achieve that sort of universal recognition, a symbol is one important way of doing it. That has to be coordinated across the world and argues for a degree of supervision for multinational marketing. When international activities are being undertaken, and individual countries not only have various languages but also different product requirements and different media, the argument for employing local talent is strong. The company itself could control those features it wishes to retain in its promotions. We can be sure of the growth of international agencies set up for just such contingencies as these.

There is another point of special importance within the whole subject of promotion applicable to particular parts of the world. Where illiteracy is the norm, rather than the exception, the printed word is useless! We take print for granted in western countries, and we marketers need to be very careful about taking it for granted elsewhere. Vision and hearing are the two ways around this: combine them in TV – if there is TV; otherwise radio becomes an important communicator, and pictures become essential on hoardings, billboards, display material and labels.

15.16 How Do Goods Get There?

As long as we use agents abroad delivery instructions are likely to be direct to the customer; that will be a normal part of shipment procedure. In any system where resale takes place unpacking and storage, in other words handling, will put extra strain on the distribution. The documentation and transportation methods for goods moving between or through countries put pressures on the seller to economize. A parcel is relatively far more expensive to send abroad than a container load. Is it less expensive to carry stocks in other countries, or supply fast by air? And what volumes will the customer settle for?

Self-check

Do you remember question **4** in Section 15.2: 'On a sea journey from Southampton to the Persian Gulf, from how many climatic variations would you have to protect your goods?'

Temperate, Mediterranean, subtropical, tropical – in each of these there are changes in air temperature and, possibly more important, humidity – especially in the Red Sea and the Gulf. Once our goods do reach their destination what kind of distribution system awaits them? Do those traders 'over there' take goods to people, or attract people to goods: the delivery, the department store or the bazaar?

15.17 Price, Value and Exchange Rate

There is no need (I hope) to repeat the discussion of price and value in Chapter 9. It does, however, need to be said that some British goods have lost their reputation for quality overseas as their manufacturers cut costs in an attempt to market on price. Enormous pressures are put on companies in international marketing by the falling value of currency such as the £ sterling. Similar and often unpredictable pressures occur through fluctuating rates of exchange: the £ buys less $ one day and more the next! Experts make a living doing little else but buying and selling currencies; international marketers need such experts near at hand, because exchange rates alone can put a company into profit or plunge it into loss.

Having made the excuses, let me return to value. The argument for offering value is just as, indeed probably more, important in other countries as in a 'home' market. Other goods suffer, or enjoy, bad and good reputations by association; we talk about Japanese or German goods almost as if all of them came from one manufacturer! If we lump them together, do we seriously imagine that other people do not? How naïve! By their rarity foreign goods attract critical attention.

15.18 On a 'Need to Know' Basis

Two questions can greatly help the marketer to identify what information is needed for activity in foreign markets (including the EC):

- What decisions have I got to make?
- What information do I need to make them?

Note the emphasis on 'decisions'. I have titled this section using the words 'need to know', not 'I would like to know'. The distinction is important because information takes up resources, money, personnel and time, and no business can afford to waste these. But possibly even more important is the requirement to use the research information for something specific – a decision. The same principle of using secondary, and then primary, data collection appplies.

About ten years ago I was surprised to read that about 50 per cent of expenditure through the marketing research industry in the UK was by foreign firms investigating British markets. (I have no idea how accurate that figure was nor what it would be today.) I mention it here simply to illustrate one possible reason for the success of so many foreign products and the decline of so many indigenous ones.

15.19 Summary

The marketing mix has been recovered, dusted down and put into a wider context, but fundamentally differs in principle not at all from Part II of this book. Product, place, promotion and price are the critical tactical weapons in the 'home' as well as the foreign market. Every marketer should approach the international scene with the greatest caution, with an acceptance of some ignorance and a certain humility.

Exercises

1 What is the main difference between an agent, or agency, and a distributor? How are they paid for their services to the exporter?

2 There were seven 'little local differences' outlined in the text; what were they and what is their significance to marketing?

3 You have sold a consignment worth £1000 at today's exchange rate to each of the following countries: France, Japan, the USA and Canada. Look up the rates for these four countries in any good daily newspaper. You will receive payment in one week: look them up again in a week's time and see how much you have lost or gained. An alternative way of doing this, which will avoid making you wait, is to get some back numbers of a paper in a public library; pretend your consignment was sent a week ago, look up those rates and today's.

4 On the left of the page there follows a list of well-known British and foreign firms. On the basis of what you know about them indicate on the right of the page under which of three headings – export, international, multinational – would you place them?

Company	Export	International	Multinational
1 Safeways (American)			
2 Fiat (Italian)			
3 Bayer (German)			
4 Sony (Japanese)			
5 Virgin Atlantic (British)			
6 Nestlés (Swiss)			
7 Hamleys Toys (British)			

5 From your own travels in the UK or abroad, from your reading or general knowledge, sort these three columns out into their correct combinations:

Country	Activity	Product
Australia	Fishing	Air conditioning
Iceland	Water spray/irrigation	Fruit growing
Israel	Office work	Refrigeration
Texas, USA	Fresh food storage	Deep sea trawlers

All of them have climatic or geographic considerations.

Answers to Exercises

Chapter 1

1 Some negative thoughts ('perceived values') on sweets and cigarettes:

Sweets	Cigarettes
They're fattening	They're a waste – just go up in smoke!
They cause tooth decay	They give me bad breath
They're also a waste of money	They make my clothes smell

2 CTN stands for 'Confectioner, Tobacconist, Newsagent'.

3 FMCG – 1, 2, 4, 5(a), 5(c) and 7.
CD   – 3, 5(b) and 6.

Both 2 and 3 are ballpoint pens but the former is cheap and disposable; the latter has a totally different perceived value, not simply because it is the more expensive. The electric toothbrush, number 5, is a mixture of both the product types.

4 Steps in the buying process: using my example of the Christmas pudding.
Step 1 My perceived need was not in this case for the product at all: I did not want the pudding (at least not this one) but wished to please a guest (the daughter) and a friend (the headmaster).

Step 2 As Christmas was not too far away the thought of presents was in the air anyway (internal search); but talking about English traditions with someone else helped with external search.

Step 3 There were all sorts of alternative presents available but not many that could be shared by a whole family and be traditionally English at the same time.

Step 4 As you know the Christmas pudding was my purchase decision. But I had also decided on the store with no considerations of possible alternatives in *step 3*.

Step 5 Step 1, you will remember, was my 'need' to please a friend. Later I heard that the family had enjoyed the pudding, and even made some brandy butter to go with it. When I think of this in future years my 'experience recall' will be good – my need had been met.

5 See Figure 1.2, Section 1.7. Steps in the buying process.

Chapter 2

1 I am sure that you will have found nothing particularly difficult in this, but what you have probably noticed is how short is the sequence that I suggested; we could easily make it much longer still using the same three words. Would the following illustration be comparable to yours?

Process: shearing the wool at the farm.
Storage: storing in sacks or bales.
Movement: shipping to manufacturer (change of ownership).
Storage: offloading into goods-inwards store.
Process: washing, and so on.

2 *Components*
Headlamp   (Lucas)
Tyres   (Dunlop)
Speedometer   (Smiths Instruments)
Brake pads   (Ferodo)
Nuts, bolts, screws (GKN)

Raw materials
Seat fabrics
Sheet metal
Wood and plastic
Floor carpet
Rubber

3 (No answer available here.)

4 From this obviously oversimplified example you should be able to identify all five roles, even though they will not be in the same sequence as the letters *SPADE*.

In the numerical sequence from numbers 1 to 6, we should have *S* (start almost by accident), *A* (negative reaction), *A* (positive reaction), *A* ('sales boys': still an unknown quantity), *E* (effect on labour), *A* (account costings cannot be ignored).

Some months later: numbers 7 to 11 are all *A*s; they are being asked to report back to the chief executive. Only number 10 has another contribution to make: 'personnel' is an *A*, but the 'unions' are representative of the 'end users', *E*.

Number 12 is *D*: the chief executive has made the decision to proceed and instructs the buyer (number 13) to place the order or purchase, *P*.

I wonder if it has struck you (at least from this example) how many *A*s there were!

Chapter 3

1 Definition – 'Marketing is the process which links producers and consumers by enabling exchange transactions to take place in conditions of competitive choice to the mutual and continuing benefit of both parties.' Section 3.3, 'Summary'.

2 The product/service which you have bought will have (should have) met a need and provided you with a level of satisfaction. The 'offering' and 'evaluation' matched sufficiently for an exchange to take place.

The one you did not buy made an 'offering' but it was not for you; your 'evaluation' did not match and no exchange took place.

3 In Section 3.4, a little after the Self-check, the 'marketing concept' was described as an 'attitude', 'frame of mind' or 'business philosophy' governing the whole behaviour of a commercial organization.

Thus the 'concept' is different from the 'function', which deals with the practicalities (see also Exercise **1** above).

4 The Trade Descriptions Act 1972 insists that a commercial organization must accurately describe its 'offering'. This should be the natural embodiment of the 'marketing concept' aiming at 'mutual and continuing benefit of both parties'. The Act was brought into being because 'caveat emptor' (let the buyer beware) actually allows a seller to deceive – at least by omission. In an age when many products are technically highly complex, it is inconceivable that the buyer is still in a position to judge, or evaluate, performance.

Chapter 4

1 *Kinds of people*

Kinds of people	Types of need
Old people	Emergency purposes and to maintain social contacts
Fire, ambulance, police	Emergency services, for maintaining contact with the community and with each other
Businesses	Communications with customers, suppliers and other interested people
Newspapers	Ability to receive communications and news from far and wide
Governments	Maintain international communications with their embassies and consulates or government to government
'Hot lines'	Enable leaders of nations to contact each other quickly in case of emergency

2 Businesses use market segmentation strategies to provide for themselves a particular market niche. Indeed small companies who specialize in particular areas to compete against their bigger rivals are often identified by 'niche marketing'. Variations of consumer behaviour are so wide that no company can cater for all people all the time. Furthermore, imaginative market segmentation can serve to avoid the worst effects of competition.

3 The four main elements of the marketing mix are: product, place, promotion and price.

4 Because of the range of possible products which you might use to illustrate the question I cannot give a definitive 'answer'. But you were probably already well aware where you could buy, either from your own observations and general knowledge or because you had been specifically told by the seller. If the latter was true in your case, this was part of the promotion message. Other parts of that message might have included the use to which the product could be put and what you could gain from that (offering and evaluation).

5 The three main methods are: location, classification and lifestyle.

The Met Office could/does first subdivide the country into areas (locations) but preferably using the same ones in the same order all the time to get people familiar with them. Within each area the seasons will be important to target certain activities, e.g. farming, sports events and so on. Finally the lifestyle considerations are likely to be those in which the weather may cause heavy financial loss or damage, e.g. harvesting, cricket or tennis, whereas golf and football (rugby and soccer) are only affected by the severest conditions.

Smith Kendon could easily have gone first for one country (language area) in the Common Market and concentrated their efforts there. In such circumstances their sweets would probably not have been called 'travel' sweets. As in the UK their outlets are usually chemists (rather than CTNs), sports clubs, e.g. aiming at selective purchase situations and hence people. Quality would remain the lifestyle parameter.

6 1 Childhood
2 Adolescent/teenage
3 Young adult
4 Young married
5 Middle age
6 Old age

The stages people go through are referred to as 'life cycle stages' and from them very clearly identifiable needs are discernible. There is the dependence of childhood; the growing independence and changing lifestyles of the adolescent teenager, young adults very commonly leave home and set up some establishment on which, for the first time, they are able to impose their individuality and personality. A dramatic change takes place after marriage, involving the setting up of a home, building a family with its needs and priorities now taking pride of place. In due course middle age and old age bring with them their own distinctive and separate requirements.

Chapter 5

1 What gives value to a product or service was discussed in Section 5.2: people bring value to products and, because people are individual and therefore different, they may bring different values to the same product. This is why it is important to 'segment' particular kinds of people.

2 The four main ingredients of the marketing mix are often abbreviated to the '4Ps': product, place, promotion and price.

3 Those which have been touched upon in the text include 'production', 'marketing', 'R & D', 'marketing research'; we could add 'administration', 'finance', 'personnel' and many others.

4 Unfortunately I cannot in this instance give you any suggestion of an outcome because the product you may choose could be anything at all. But I would love to join you when you do it. If you do, and I sincerely hope you will, reread this whole chapter first; get yourself totally familiar, indeed immersed, with the theme of the physical, functional and the symbolic. Then be prepared to shed your prejudices because (go on, confess) you know you have got them!

5 The three principles are 'newness', 'technology' and 'risk'. The applications you decide upon are going to be unique to yourself and therefore no preconceived answer notes are possible.

Chapter 6

1 Most of us know the brewing industry best by its major outlet – the public house! It is very probable that you have heard of the expression 'tied house'. This means that the pub is tied to one brewery and will sell, in the main, those products supplied by that brewery both in its range of beers offered and often in the ranges of wines and spirits. Sometimes, when a supplier creates a sufficient demand in the market for a product, even 'tied houses' have to take in that product for resale to avoid possibly upsetting their customers or clientele; the white rum Bacardi would be a case in point.

The main reason for all the various forms of integration is to extend, or to establish, control. This is another way of avoiding excessive competition and preventing new entrants. By ensuring adequate numbers of outlets the brewery groups can also maintain better control over their financial flows, both in (revenue) and out (expenses). When well managed in accordance with the marketing concept, the consumer can benefit by reasonable pricing, investment into research, and easy access to products.

2 I have not made the questions in this activity so clear cut that in every case the answer is obvious in its distinction between 'buy' and 'not buy', but I think your responses will be sufficient to indicate fairly clearly that you, the shopkeeper, will tend to go for those product types that represent the least risk to you. (Remember you too are also balancing the three *R*s – risk, resources, results.)

Let us look at each of the six situations individually:

(a) There cannot be much doubt that the answer to this one – a well-established product in good demand – would be a very safe bet indeed for any shop and is something that almost certainly you would have bought.

(b) This is a little bit more doubtful but you are protected by the source being a well-known company. There is no mention here of any advertising or other promotional support and we do know that it is a new product; there is an element of risk and you would probably add your own local knowledge and your estimate of local demand before actually buying. You may well hesitate a little before making up your mind.

(c) A new product with extensive advertising support is likely to be a more successful one from your point of view. You, after all, are not being required to do much; you would hope that the advertising would generate demand in the locality of your business and from that would make sales.

(d) This is a much more uncertain proposition – a small company, no advertising support but with a product that is distinctly superior. Depending again on your interpretation of the local market the fact that you had a superior product to offer, and demonstrably superior at that, could enhance your personal reputation, and you would probably therefore be likely to back the product. This backing, however, would be dependent upon your own support activities, such as displaying it well, drawing people's attention to it when the opportunity arises, possibly attaching some special offer to it in the introductory stages and so on. Your creative ingenuity is being tested here.

(e) Many businesses carry more than one range of a product type to offer their customers a selection. For example go into most hardware stores and you will find probably two, at least two, or even three different brands of household paints. In other circumstances you will find stores specializing in one particular brand. There is no clear-cut answer to this particular point; the decision may depend on what other support services are being offered by the supplier.

(f) Any product offered to you with exclusive rights in a particular geographical area certainly has an advantage. You would in most circumstances probably buy, always assuming, of course, that the product itself is relevant to the district you serve.

Because of your interests, those of moving goods through your shop, in from the suppliers and out to your customers, you are likely to adopt any activity which in your estimation makes this easier. You are more likely to support any supplier who helps you in this.

3 The three sub-divisions of 'convenience' were – time, money and effort.

How they would operate in a specific example of a purchasing situation will, of course, vary considerably with the values of the individual concerned and the conditions in which he/she is operating. For example, in an emergency time is of the essence and money may be much less important.

4 Example

For our purposes as customers there are two major influences brought about by the motorcar which have had a profound effect on our shopping habits: first, it enables us to seek out goods and services at greater distances from home and, second, it enables us to carry greater quantities of goods from any one shopping trip. On the distributive side of the same picture this has led to out-of-town shopping centres, large car parks, domestic bulk buying for deep freezing and far fewer shopping excursions.

Example

The cost of hiring tradesmen has resulted in a very wide spread of skills, commonly known as DIY (do-it-yourself). New products and techniques, constantly being developed for this kind of market, present us as customers not only with wider choices for, say, décor, but also with problems of learning new skills from the distributive network. Would it be fair comment to claim that all too often this advice is difficult to come by?

Example

The important thing for us having obtained a prescription from a doctor is to be able to get it as quickly as possible. There are inevitably some occasions when a special drug is prescribed and may not be available at the local chemist. If this has ever happened to you, you will know that most chemists are able to obtain these more unusual drugs very quickly indeed, usually later the same day, from their wholesaler.

5 First identify the end users (or consumers) to whom the products will be directed through the intermediaries (or distribution system):

Examples: Housewives – for the children or the family.

> Young adults.
> Armed Forces.
> Sportsmen and women.
> etc.

Most housewives would be reached through supermarkets and grocery stores.

Young adults (and for that matter older people) might be reached through public houses and off-licences.

The Armed Forces would distribute their products through the NAAFI.

Sportsmen and women would frequent appropriate grounds for training, sports clubs and other such facilities, and so on.

Chapter 7

1 If in 2 you chose to send samples and direct mail to all the doctors you have been caught by the note under, 4: these costs would be disproportionately high! The calculation of total costs is (4000 × £1) + 2(4000 × 0.25) + £5000 = £11 000/40 000 = £0.275 per prescription. At £0.20 each there would be 55 000, and at £0.30 each 37 000.

The target market share aimed at is $\dfrac{40\,000}{25\,000 \times 140} \times 100 = 1\%$

bearing in mind that this target is for the first, and launch, year only and would be expected to improve in subsequent periods.

2 *Key words*
Reputation
Newsworthy
Influence behaviour
Inducement
Visibility
Information/access
Make conspicuous

3 1 PR, 2 publicity, 3 publicity, 4 PR.

4 Changing or maintaining   AWARENESS
Changing or maintaining   ATTITUDES
Changing or maintaining   ACTION
The principle of TIME AND DISTANCE.

5 The diagram showing the 'Overlapping effect of promotional techniques' is shown in Section 7.17, Figure 7.2.

Chapter 8

1 Obviously there are many possibilities and permutations but the following suggestions will serve to illustrate the 'mix'. Your own selection will probably be different. What is important is that you have remembered the key functions of each promotional technique.

	Non-personal	*Personal*
Chief executive	Public relations	No
Marketing manager	Publicity	No
Design engineer	Direct mail	Yes
Production manager	Advertising	Yes
Personnel manager	Public relations	No
Accountant	Public relations	No
Buyer	Sales promotion	Yes

2 Representative's workload in an eight-week journey cycle:

	Number	Call rate	No calls	Cumulative
	20	2 weeks	80	80
	80	4 weeks	160	240
Existing	40	8 weeks	40	280
customers	75	12 weeks	50	330
	100	16 weeks	50	380
Prospects	20	8 weeks	20	400

3 The five main criteria were: the kind of purchase; the people involved in the purchasing decision; the types and numbers of products; the ability of the salesman; and the cost of the personal promotion task. In this exercise we are only concerned with the 'kind of purchase' (situation) and the 'types . . . of products'.

FMCG	Straight rebuy	Generalist
Consumer durable	New buy	Specialist
Consumer service	Modified rebuy	Generalist
Industrial component	Modified rebuy	Specialist
Capital good	New buy	Specialist
Raw material	Modified rebuy	Generalist
Industrial service	Straight rebuy	Generalist

See also Section 2.13, Figure 2.4.

4 The three '*I*s' were 'investigation', 'identification' and 'interaction'.

They are significant because they cannot be carried out by means other than personal ones. See Section 8.2, 'Why use people?'

5 As in previous activities, this one does not produce absolutely correct answers; there is far too much ingenuity in marketing to be that rigid. So what I am going to list is just one suggestion among many to serve as a comparison with your own. Once we have made the comparison, I would like you then to elaborate in note form what your roles would be.

3a, 5b, 9b, 11a, 11b, 13b, 15b, 17, 19 – if my list is any guide most of your activities would be on behalf of your key account customer. The reasoning is that most of your activities will be directed to help your customer 'sell out' to the public by support or joint advertising (5b); by devising and possibly financing special promotions (9b); negotiating with your own company for special pack sizes or packaging for your key account (11a, 11b); provision of signs, posters, tickets conforming to your account's policy (13b); making, where appropriate, special display units, gondolas, dump bins and so on (15b).

3a (publicity) would be information supplied by you to your own company about the relationship with your key account – provided it is newsworthy and approved by both.

Most of your selling would be linked to new, rather than existing, products. Big organizations, particularly amongst intermediaries, have computerized ordering routines. While you would obviously keep a close eye on sales and stock levels held by your key account, your main selling activity would be linked to new products (19) and negotiating continued support for the existing ones (17) by the other promotional means mentioned.

This very abbreviated resume of a promotional mix and the illustration of the role of a senior and responsible sales representative to an important account is not 'right'; I would go so far as to suggest that it is quite likely that no reader will exactly duplicate it. That does not matter. What does is your involvement in *an example* of such an exercise.

Chapter 9

1 As a market declines or shrinks a business must become more cost oriented in order to prevent potential losses as volume decreases; when the market is growing profits are much easier to make.

Stationery is quite a competitive sort of product; that is to say, a number of firms are in the market making and supplying it. If you reduce prices in a declining market just about everything is going against you – so I would suggest 'hold/reduce/reduce' for question 2. Postage stamps are a monopoly, only the government can supply them, so there is no (direct) competition. Even in a shrinking market (say more people use the phone) costs have to be covered, so we could take the following courses of action – 'increase/increase/hold'.

If your natural inclination is for fashion clothes, is price going to be a major criterion? Probably not; so there will be relatively strong demand, particularly as fashion clothes are nearly always supposed to be unique! Your taste in colour, style and material will probably dominate the decision to buy. Would you quarrel with a 'hold/hold/increase' price policy? Garden bulbs are much less important. Unless you are an expert gardener, price may be your major consideration, even for such relatively inexpensive products. But for the supplier it is doubtful that he could go too low even in a shrinking market, so I would suggest 'reduce/hold/hold' on the assumption that stocks could deteriorate and the supplier would be better off getting a reduced price than having total losses!

2 If one presents this by a formula the break-even point may be calculated (as we did in the text) as in (a) below.

(a) $BE = \dfrac{\text{Fixed costs}}{\text{Unit contribution}}$

On those occasions when unit contributions are not available the following formula may be used:

(b) $BE = \dfrac{\text{Sales Revenue} \times \text{Fixed costs}}{\text{Sales revenue} - \text{Variable costs}}$

3 BiC would be an example of the last column of the table in Exercise **3** (stationary *B*); advanced mass production techniques almost automatically incur high fixed costs which can only be covered by high volume. In the right kind of product/market low price is one way of encouraging high consumption. Your talented pianist would pay a high price for his Bechstein – a stationary *A* column tick is appropriate here.

The low-priced personal computers (Commodore, Sinclair, Tandy and others) are still not capable of meeting the total demand; supplies are still short. Prices are coming down steadily, so here we have movement from *A* to *B*. De Lorean cars are the reverse: from *B* to *A*. The intention was for these cars not to be priced as luxury vehicles; you will remember that less than half the volume was in fact sold. The price was pushed up in an attempt to cover the fixed costs with the result of being priced out of the target market. Cut-price fares on Laker's Skytrain were similar to personal computers (movement *A* to *B*) but with the major difference of shrinking demand: with the demise of Laker Airways fares will probably reverse direction back to *A*.

They did. But the demand for lower airfares continued inviting into the market the new competition like Virgin Airways.

The profit volume direction for the cinemas goes back and forth: (a) requires sufficient to cover all costs and a little profit, so will generally stay stationary at *B* – as low a price as possible to maintain at least a minimum level of demand (cost orientation); but when a really good film comes along the price can be shifted upwards – movement from *B* to *A*.

4 Obviously the potential answers to this question have an enormous variety. Consideration should be given here to 'necessities' and 'disposables' (high and low priced). Other considerations are the number of firms which provide the products/services; the more there are the greater the competition – the opposite of monopoly. It is a common economic theory (and belief by some political parties) that competition contributes towards cost efficiency. Customer power, and therefore the ability to switch from one supplier source to another, derives either from the availability of choice or from some other power, consumer groups or special supervisory bodies (users associations) either voluntary or government appointed.

Chapter 10

1 D-I-C-E standards for decision, investigation, control and experiment. The descriptions of I-C-E are given in Section 10.3 – 1 to 3. The purpose of all marketing research is to help the decision maker remove uncertainty – as far as possible before committing resources.

2 The two major types of data collected are 'secondary' and 'primary'. They are put in that order in accordance with the reasoning behind the research funnel (refer to Section 10.8, Figure 10.3).

3 'Syndicated' research is the name given to that kind of data collection carried out by a research organization and sold to clients, or customers, as a service. The main examples are retail audits and consumer panels. Their particular value lies in providing 'continuous' information; 'commissioned' research would usually be 'ad hoc' (one-off) for some special study.

4 Test marketing is seldom used in industrial marketing because supplier companies will have far greater direct contact with customers. Testing can be carried out directly by cooperation between the two. Another reason applies to the speed of repeat purchasing. Many industrial products are bought infrequently and a test market would be impractical over long time periods.

5 A sample is a proportion of a whole 'population' containing all the (key) characteristics of that population.

6 The word this question is looking for is 'insurance'. Research is a precaution using relatively small resources to reduce risk and uncertainty prevalent in the marketplace before large sums of money are committed to a marketing plan.

7 Quantitative data collection seeks answers to 'what, when, where, how and who'; qualitative data provides the answer to the question 'why'.

Chapter 11

1 A 'model' was described as a 'representation' of reality, not reality itself. That is to say it could be called an average, and is therefore not necessarily a true representation of a particular circumstance or situation. Another way of thinking of it, is a 'generalization'. The PLC model is a model in so far as it represents a pattern of events which have proved to be generally true over many years and many products. In individual cases it would not be true to form. However, because it has been proven as a general pattern it may be used as a predictor of likely events taking place in the future.

2 Your check on the answer is Figure 11.3 in Section 11.5

3 The four main decision points are discussed in Section 11.9 and a diagrammatic example (unlabelled) is given below.

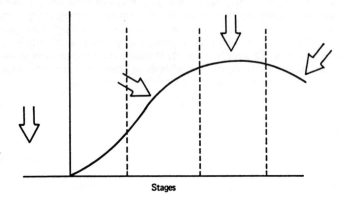

Stages

Decisions

4 'Primary' demand is that generated for a generic, or category, of product; 'secondary' demand relates to a particular type, or brand, within a category. Example: there is a generic (primary) demand for milk chocolate, but because the market has reached maturity in life-cycle terms there is now secondary demand for particular products from Cadbury's, Rowntrees, and so on.

The equivalent in PLC terms is that primary demand is generated by changing behaviour; the market is still in its early introduction and growth stages. By the time competition has entered into the picture and there are brand share battles between companies, there is strong emphasis on maintaining brand shares through secondary demand.

Chapter 12

1 Without showing the curve of the PLC the diagram below illustrates an answer to the cash flows and the changes from positive to negatives.

2 The 'original' product portfolio is illustrated in Figure 12.2, Section 12.8.

3 The 'star' and 'cash cow' give the net cash inflows (although the former may only just have come into balance; the main one is the cash cow. The '?' and 'dog' account for the net cash outflows.

The '?' is a new product/service which will need support in its initial stages. Hopefully it moves into the growth stage of the PLC and becomes a 'star', beginning to generate cash. When the marketplace has stabilized in the maturity stage, and adequate market share has been gained, the cash cow is the key factor, it generates plenty of cash. Finally as demand changes, or the

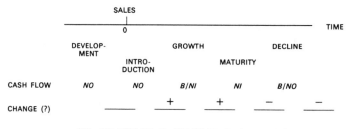

Cash flows and the PLC

product is overtaken by others, extra money would be needed to support it, absorbing higher and higher levels of cash until it becomes totally uneconomic and becomes a 'dog'.

4 The 'new' product portfolio is illustrated in Figure 12.3, Section 12.10.

5 The 'new' product portfolio is complementary to the 'original' one. BCG always claimed that both are used in consultancy practice but that the 'original' one caught the publicity. In fact the virtue of this 'new' matrix is that it does not isolate two variables (market growth and share) as being the ostensible cause of the cash flow effect; but it does not exclude them either. Nor does it suggest that the market is the overriding consideration' (end of Section 12.10).

Chapter 13

1 Now if the correlation were very 'high' the trend lines would be almost parallel; they are not. Conversely they are not vastly different, 'low'. In fact the correlation is 0.5, 'medium'.

2 The 'three levels' were first an 'economic' level, second an 'industry' level and third a 'company' or 'corporate' level. Their significance is this: the 'higher the level the greater the aggregation of data (or collective total) and the less likely any sudden or unexpected change.

3 'Objective' forecasts are based on 'facts', that is to say historical data is used (usually of a numerical kind) and projected forward by a statistical technique. The assumption is that the future will follow the pattern of the past. 'Subjective' forecasts are based on the opinion, experience or belief of individuals in an outcome some time in the future. This may be quantified by the use of 'probabilities'.

Objective projections would be used first, and subjective ones applied to the former in order to 'bend' the projection.

4 However you plot these 'events', any decisions you took as a result of them would be a reaction. The plumber would anticipate a number of burst pipes and get ready for the emergency calls (4–7/1). The tobacco manufacturer might fall into sector 4–7/1 or 4–7/7, according to how pessimistic or optimistic he was. My view of the Chancellor of the Exchequer would be 4–7/7. The builders' merchant is a lucky man because the change here is likely to be fairly smooth and he would probably get early warning – sector 4–1/1.

Note: the number given before the oblique line (/) always refers to the horizontal scale, the number after to the vertical.

5 'Smoothing' is a statistical process of manipulating and aggregating data usually for the purpose of finding, and projecting, a trend. It may be compared with an 'average' which conceals the data, particularly at the two extremes. Averaging will find a central point, or value, 'smoothing' a central trend over time. In the short term it cannot predict the individual pieces of data which would make up the time points into the future, e.g. weekly or monthly production figures.

Chapter 14

1 First it describes a form of behaviour; to be more accurate it 'proscribes'. Secondly it limits discretion for subordinates; if you were boss and one of your staff did enter a market worth less than the amount specified (£2 million in the example in Section 14.9) what would you do about it? Thirdly it is repetitive, it goes on, it continues.

2 'The planning cycle' can be seen by reference to Section 14.4.

3 S – strengths; W – Weaknesses; O – Opportunities; T – Threats.
Strengths and weaknesses represent an audit of past and present performance and opportunities and threats relate to interpreting the future.

4 In this chapter two-dimensional mapping was used to plot intended movement as a result of a plan; from the current position to a future one. The example was related to Clive Sinclair's decisions about the manufacture, marketing and distribution of his computers.

5 Statements of strategy are only valid if they can be substantiated afterwards; pious intentions are not enough, for example number 2. How can any link be established with training and turnover? Number 3 is equally dubious without knowing the level of morale beforehand and being able to measure it again after the conference! 1 and 4 are certainly practical; 5 is probably true!

Chapter 15

1 An agent, or agency, is an organization independent of its 'principal' (the exporter for whom it is operating) and does not take title to goods despatched to the customer. A distributor is also independent but does take title to goods as they are usually delivered to it and in many cases will be held in stock. An agent is paid by commission on the value of the goods; the distributor is 'paid' by obtaining a profit through reselling.

2 The seven 'little local differences' were:

culture, politics, legal, geography, economic, language and technology (see Section 15.3).

3 No answer can be given to this exercise here as the exchange rates are constantly varying.

4 Let us recap quickly. Exporting does not commit resources in a foreign market. There is only one candidate from our list and that is number 7, Hamleys certainly sends goods abroad. At the opposite end, and I wonder if you knew that Safeways was American, this company has resources here in the UK – international. 2, 4 and 6 I would place as multinational, with 3 and 5 international.

5 *Country*   *Activity*   *Product*
Australia   Fresh food storage   Refrigeration
Iceland   Fishing   Deep-sea trawlers
Israel   Water spray/irrigation   Fruit growing
Texas, USA   Office work   Air conditioning
NOTE: the 'answers' above are not absolute; you may have arrived at some
different combinations.

Index of Names

Index of Subjects

frequency of reps' calls 113–14
functions of products 52–6
  planning and 58–9, 63–5
further education 168–9

G
geography, marketing abroad
  and 237
gold bars 57
group discussion 166–7
growth stage of PLC 184–5

H
high-priced disposables 139–40
high-priced necessities 138–9
higher education 168–9
hired media 90
horizontal integration 74

I
identification, salesmen and 110
illiteracy 246
inducement 95–6
influence 89
information 45, 155
  merchandising and 98–9
integration, economic 237
intermediaries 69
  added value 75–7
  system 72–3
  view of distribution 73–6
international marketing 241–3
  see also marketing abroad
  investigation
  marketing research 159–60
  by salesmen 109, 111

J
Japan 30
joint ventures 242

L
language 43, 238, 245–6
least squares 211–12
legal advice 237
licensing agreements 242
life cycle of product *see* product
  life cycle
lifestyles 40
line of best fit 211
location, differentiation by 38–9

low-priced disposables 140–1
low-priced necessities 139

M
maintenance 192–4
  change and 194–5
management, marketing 153–4
market growth 201–2
market segments *see* segmentation
market share 201, 202–3
marketing 26
  varied meanings 33
marketing abroad 235–48
  exporting 239–41
  international marketing 241–3
  local differences 235–8
  marketing mix 244–8
  multinational marketing 243–4
marketing research 150–73
  D-I-C-E 151–2
  experimentation 160
  industry 154–5
  investigation 159–60
  kinds of data 155–6
  marketing abroad 247–8
  planning and control 152–3
  primary 156–8
  surveys 160–1
  techniques 162–72;
    distribution 163–5; pricing
    171–2; products 162–3;
    promotion 165–70; sales
    force 170–1
  test marketing 172–3
maturity stage of PLC 186–8
media
  hired 90
  research 167–8
merchandising 97–9, 100–1, 120
messages, promotional 165–7
mini life cycles 192–3
mini-monopolies 37
miniature television 128
models 177–8
  change 212–15
  product life cycle 178–81
  purchasing 7–10
  use at exhibitions 125
moving totals 210–11
multibuy approach 171
multinational marketing 243–4

product planning and 59
public relations 85–7
publicity 87–8
sales promotion 94–6
salesmen: specialized 115–16,
    119–23; travelling 112–15
    see also communication
psychology 58
public opinion polls 157
public relations 85–7
publicity 85, 87–8
purchases, types of 24
selling and 116–17, 118
purchasing 3–12
behaviour 3–4, 6–12; prices
    and 133, 134
business 20–4
process 6–8, 9; promotion
    and 82–3

Q
qualitative research 158
quantitative research 156–8
questionnaires 160–1
quota sampling 161

R
Random fluctuation 213
random sampling 161
rational consumer behaviour 133
raw materials 15, 16
recall 170
recognition 97, 170, 246
regression 215–16
repeat purchasing 24, 117, 173
representation, marketing abroad
    and 240–1, 242
representatives 112–15
frequency of call 113–14
number of customers 113
sales objectives 114–15
reputation 84, 86–7
research
and development (R&D) 60–1
marketing *see* marketing research
resources 21
Restrictive Trade Practices Act 34
retail audits 164
revenue 197–9
Rhodesia 44
risk 21, 64–5

S
Sales promotion 94–6
as marketing research 171–2
sales volume 179–80
salesmen
and expert opinion 218
marketing research: by 170–1;
    into 170; specialization
    115–23; ability 119–20;
    cost 121–3
travelling *see* representatives
sampling 157
satisfaction and profit 31–2, 33–4
saturation 71–2
scatter diagrams 211
search 8, 10–11, 83
seasonal change 213
secondary data 155–6
secondary demand 193
segmentation of markets 36–46
differentiation 38–40; and
    products 63
investigation and 159–60
matching interests 36–8
marketing mix 44–6
successive focusing 40–2
selection 71, 72
semi-log scales 209, 210
services 5, 19, 52, 56
skimming 135
smooth change 212–15
smoothed trends 209
socio–economic groups 39
sociology 58
South Korea 237
SPADE 23
specialization
in marketing research 155
of product 204
in selling 115–23
by shops 5
specification 50–1
stalemate 204
strategy 229–30, 230–1, 233–4
strengths, audit of 224–6
subjective forecasting 206–7,
    216–21
successive focusing 40–2
suppliers, distribution and 69–73
surveys 160–1
SWOT analysis 224–8

Also available in the Macmillan Professional Masters series

MARGARET ATTWOOD
Personnel Management is the ideal book for those studying for professional and business exams, especially the Institute of Personnel Management and BTEC National level courses. It will also be useful for the personnel management elements of other management, business and psychology courses and a handy reference for practising managers.

JOHN BINGHAM
Data Processing is self-contained and up to date, and is ideal for relevant business and accounting courses or anyone who wishes to improve their existing knowledge and skills.

CHRIS BREWSTER
Employee Relations is a comprehensive and readable explanation of the parties, institutions and systems which are involved in the relationships between managers and employees. It is ideal for use on Institute of Industrial Management, Institute of Personnel Management and NEBBS courses and for all practising managers who carry employee-relations responsibilities.

E.C. EYRE
Office Administration is suitable for all syllabuses in office administration and relevant parts of business administration and management courses. It is an invaluable text for students studying for the examinations of the Institute of Administrative Management, the Institute of Chartered Secretaries and Administrators, the Society of Company and Commercial Accountants, BTEC and NEBBS.

ROGER HUSSEY
Cost and Management Accounting is a clear explanatory text covering the principles and techniques of the subject. It will prove invaluable for students in further and higher education, particularly those studying on accounting foundation, A-level and BTEC courses. It will also suit practising managers who wish to improve their existing skills.

ROGER OLDCORN
Company Accounts shows how to interpret published accounts to obtain maximum information and insight about a company. It explains the full significance of the key statements set out in these accounts.

ROGER OLDCORN
Management is a clear, accessible text which will appeal as a self-contained text to students on BTEC, SCOTVEC, Diploma in Management Studies and Institute of Personnel Management courses and as introductory reading for higher-level courses. It will also prove invaluable reading for practising or aspiring managers.

KATE WILLIAMS
Study Skills offers students practical, step-by-step suggestions and strategies to use in their studies, whether these are academic, professional or vocational in nature.

All these books are available at your local bookshop or, in case of difficulty, from John Darvill, Globe Education, Houndmills, Basingstoke, Hampshire RG21 2XS (Tel. 0256 29242).